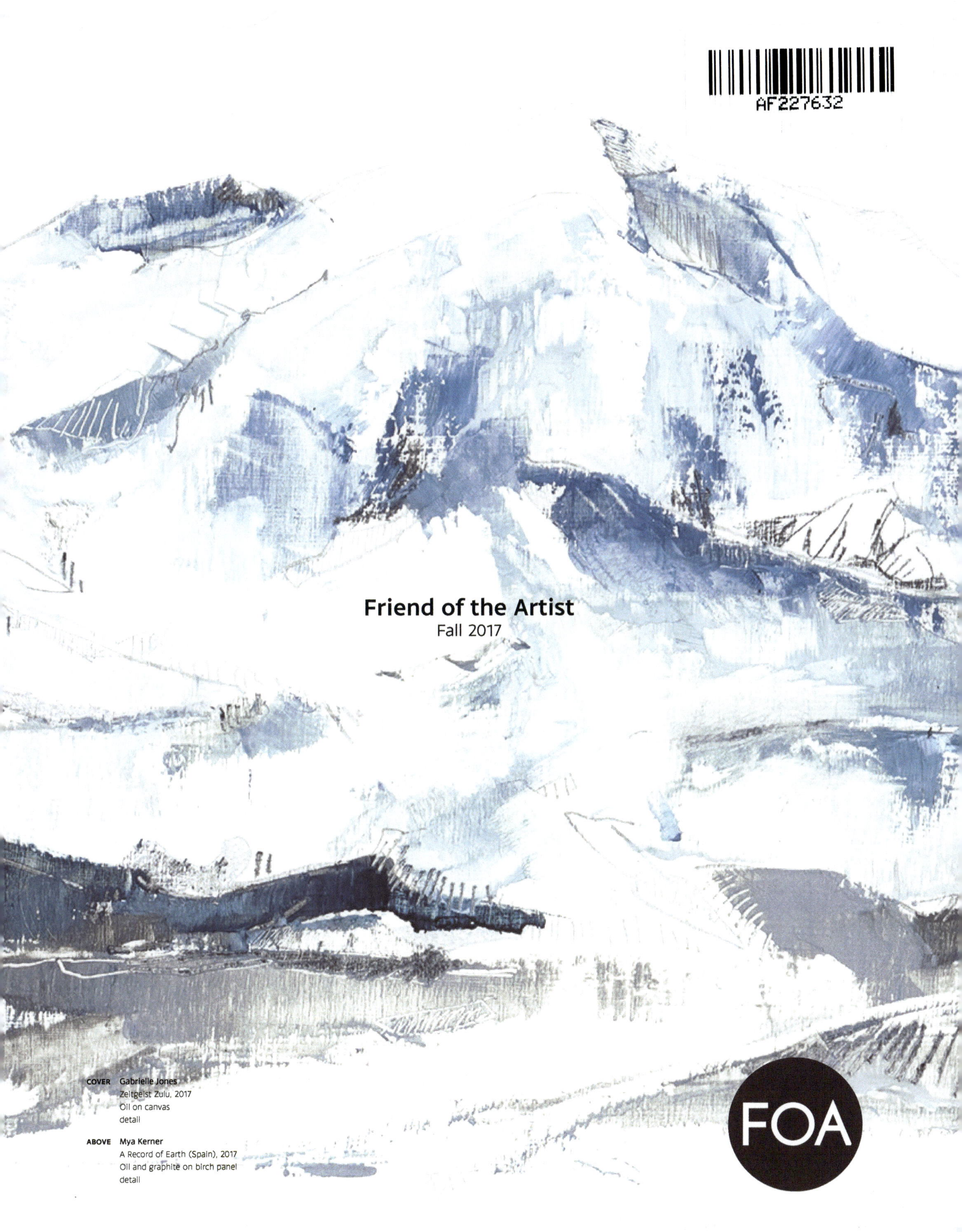

Friend of the Artist

Fall 2017

AF227632

FOA

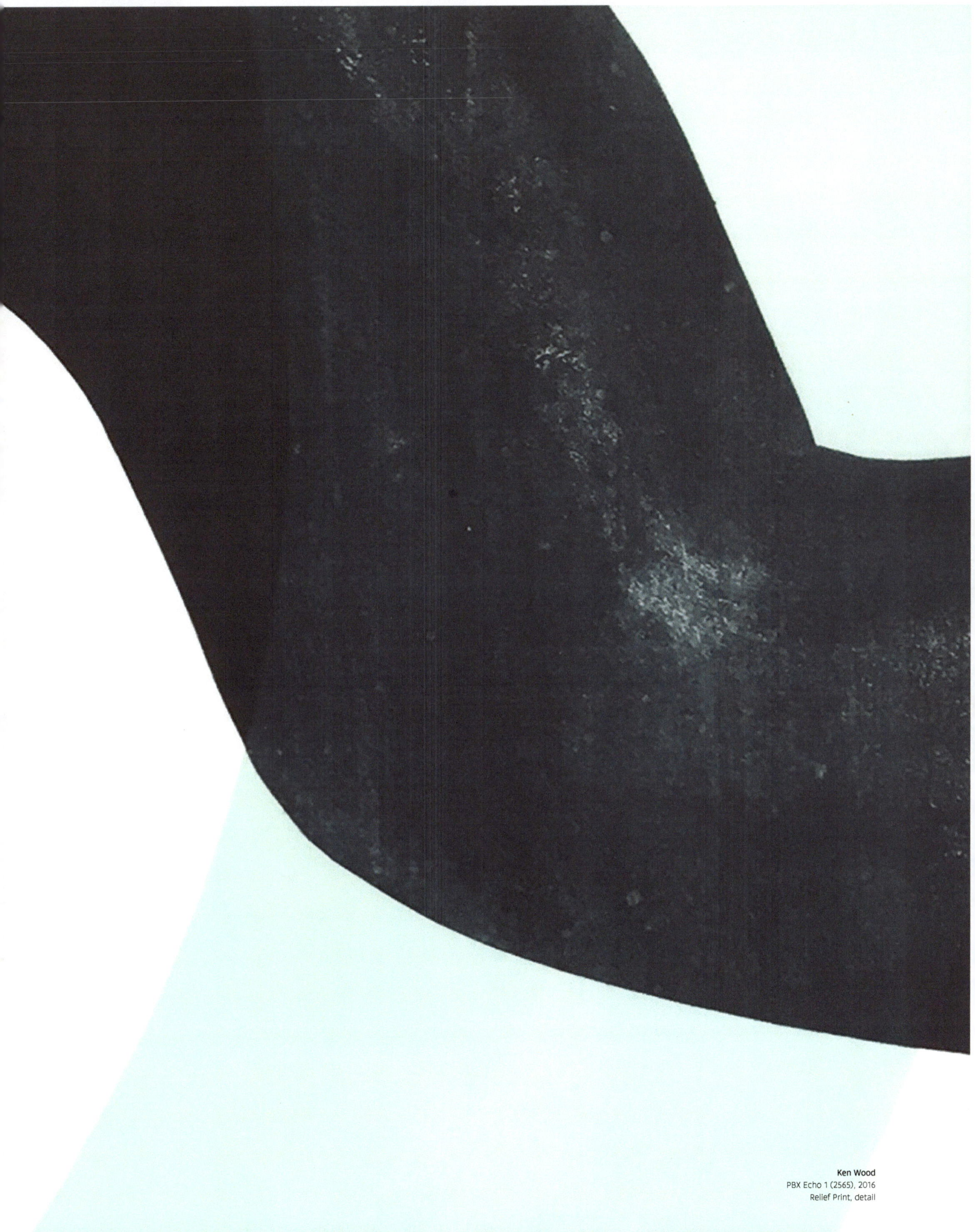

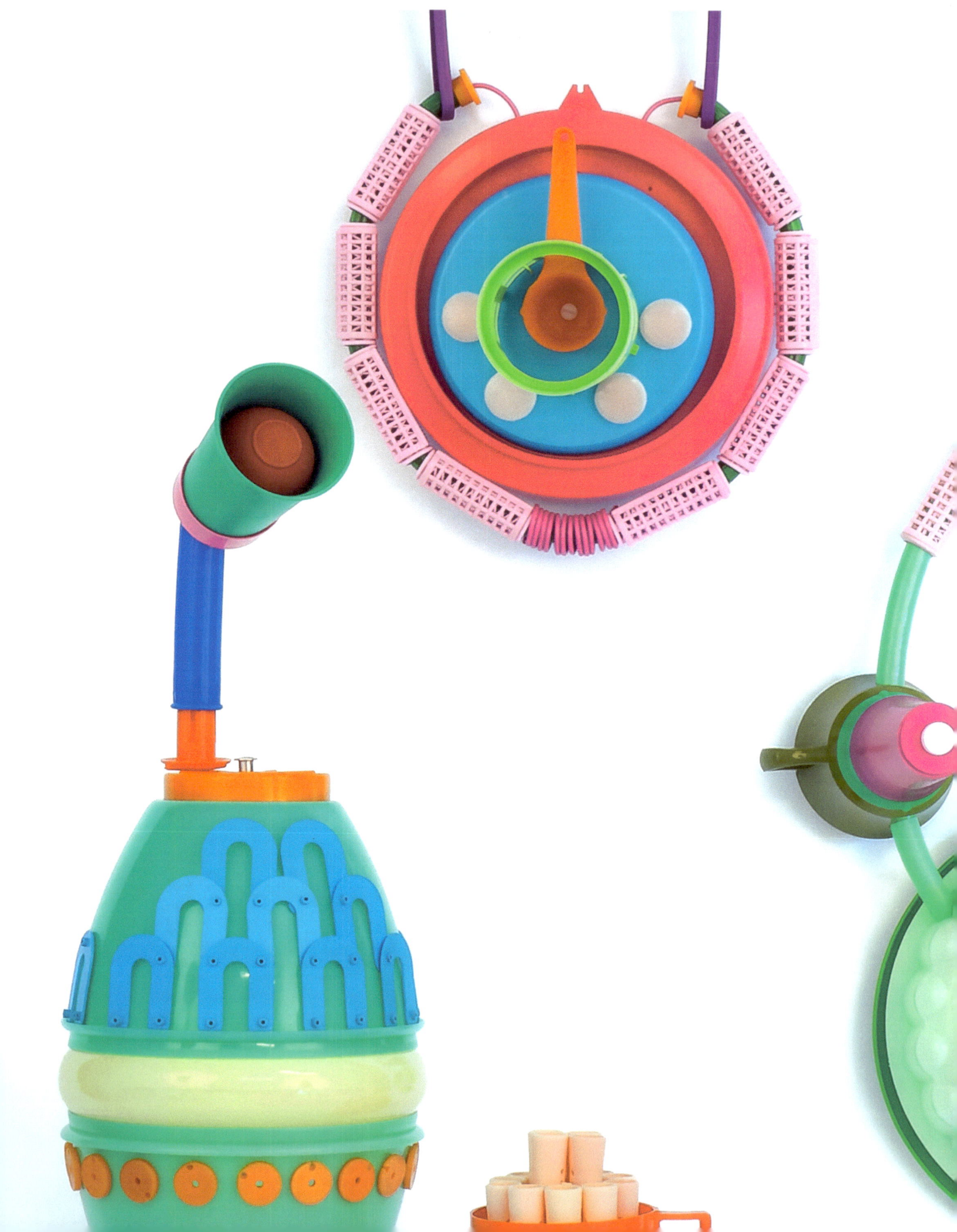

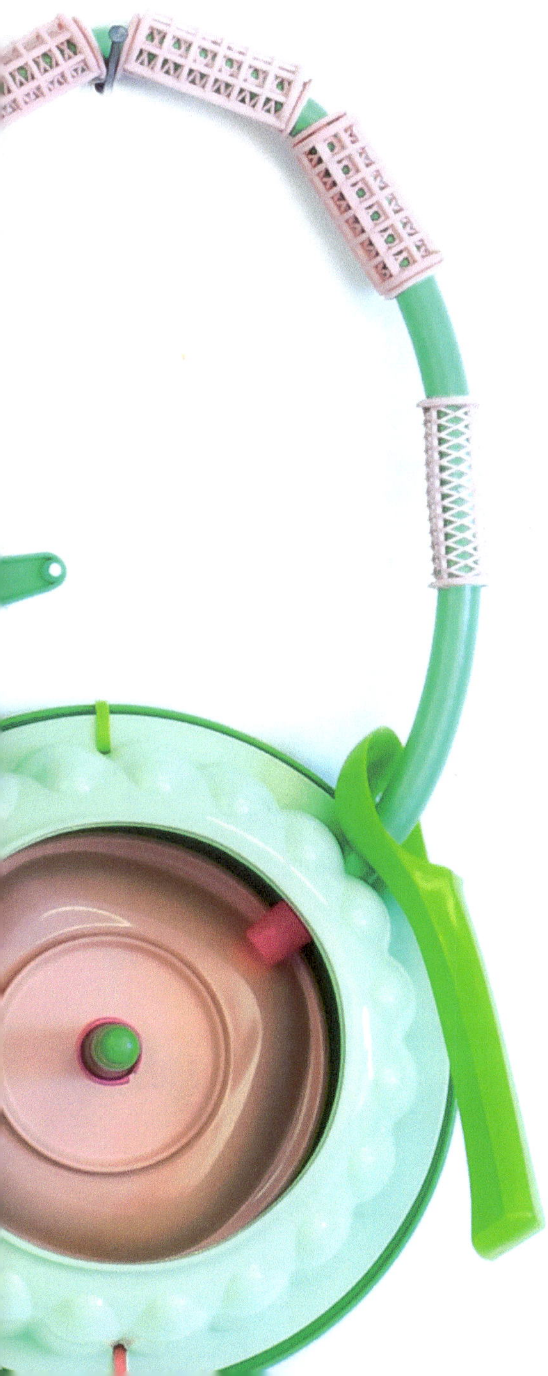

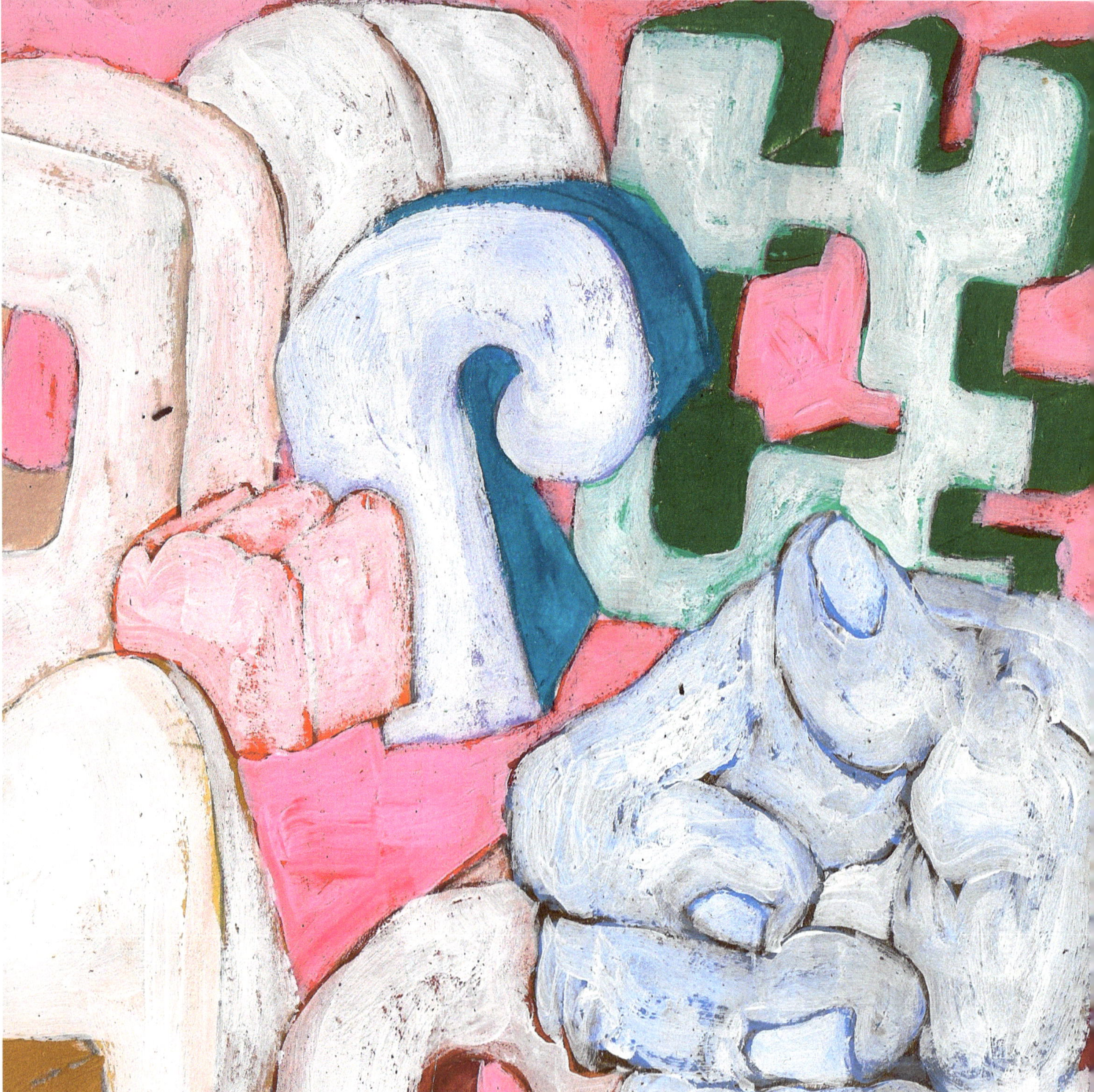

Friend of the Artist (FOA)
friendoftheartist.com
contact@friendoftheartist.com

Fall 2017 is published by Friend of the Artist

Produced and printed in the United States of America

Editing by Dannie Liebergot

ISBN: 978-1-64136-499-7

Austin Furtak-Cole
AEIOU, 2017
flashe on paper, detail

FOUND ON PAGE 34

Contents

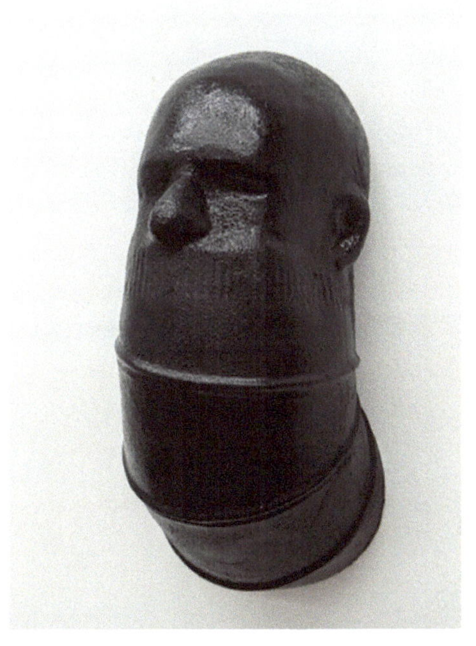

Lara Nasser
Agrippa, Is That You?, 2016
Plaster and shellac, 16.5 x 7.5 x 8in.

FOUND ON PAGE 62

Opening Remarks

Fall 2017 is a big milestone for FOA. It's our fourth issue which makes a full season worth of publications. A year later, our publication is proudly read in four continents and shows artists from many different backgrounds. With this growth, we are changing the titles of the publication from season to volume In Order to accommodate to our audience. In future releases, expect even more great content. As we celebrate this moment of success, we look to the future of all the things that FOA can be. Our number one priority will always be showcasing talented artists from across the world in a print format. We want to bring the art gallery home, and our publications are the perfect way of achieving that. Our publication is a platform for art to be experienced, engaged with through interviews and articles, and for artists to show their work. We thank all those who have helped us with FOA's accomplishments.

We were pleased to invite Taylor O. Thomas to jury this publication. Taylor is an accomplished artist based in Tampa, FL and Visual Arts Editor of the EcoTheo Review. She did a great job selecting a talented diverse group of artists in their location and medium.

We are Also really excited about partnering with Natasha Arselan, founder and CEO of AucArt. They are the worlds first online auction house dedicated to emerging artists. We love what she is doing to promote the work of emerging artists in the UK and wish them success on their first ever auction In early November. You gotta Check out her article of do's and don'ts for artists which was written after she toured the UK's top art schools. This is fantastic resource, especially for artists about to graduate from art school. Thanks for reading and supports the arts

Ty Bishop, *Publisher*

As Friend of the Artist continues to develop our staff has transitioned into articulated role. As Communications Manager, I have had the opportunity to engage with the artists represented in the Fall publication in unique ways. It is always encouraging to reach out to the artists and share in this organization with them. We had a great deal of successful work in this publication, and I am continually surprised by the amount of powerful work there is to discover. In this publication I felt particularly

DRAWN TO GEMMA LOPEZ'S IMAGES. HER MASSIVE, HAND-COLLAGED PHOTOGRAPHS EXPRESS ENVIRONMENTS WITH INCREDIBLE FRAGMENTATION IN BEAUTIFUL, ALMOST SCULPTURAL WAYS. I AM GRATEFUL FOR THE CHANCE TO SHARE HER STUDIO PRACTICE WITH YOU. IN ADDITION TO WORKING WITH THE ARTISTS, I HAVE BEEN RUNNING OUR SOCIAL MEDIA ACCOUNTS. THE FEEDBACK AND REACH OF FOA'S INSTAGRAM HAS BEEN A GREAT RESOURCE TO SHARE WORK WITH ENTIRE COMMUNITIES THAT OTHERWISE WOULDN'T ENCOUNTER YOUR WORK. I AM REALLY EXCITED TO SHARE OUR FALL 2017 PUBLICATION WITH EVERYONE, AS WELL AS ALL OF THE DEVELOPMENTS WE'VE BEEN PLANNING WITH OUR MEDIA ACCOUNTS. I WOULD LIKE TO THANK TAYLOR FOR ALL HER HARD WORK IN JURYING THIS VOLUME, THE STAFF HERE AT FOA FOR ALL THEIR DEDICATION TO MAKING AN IMPACT ON THE ARTS, AND OF COURSE, ALL OF YOU.

JUSTIN ARCHER, *Communications Manager*

AFTER ATTENDING THE NY MOMA PS1 ART BOOK FAIR IN SEPTEMBER, IT'S SAFE TO SAY THAT THERE IS QUITE AN ATTRACTION TO ART BOOKS, ZINES, INDEPENDENT PUBLISHING, AND ENAMEL PINS – YES, I BOUGHT A PINK SQUIGGLY ONE FOR MY DENIM JACKET. ARTISTS, WRITERS, DESIGNERS, MUSICIANS, LIBRARIANS, AND BOOK LOVERS OF ALL SORTS WERE THERE. THE FAIR WAS REASSURING THAT FOA IS MOVING TOWARDS THE RIGHT DIRECTION, AND WHEN IT COMES TO INDEPENDENT MAGAZINES FOR AND ABOUT ART, THERE ARE NO RULES. WHEN I SHARED MY LOOT WITH TY AND JUSTIN, WE DIVED RIGHT INTO BRAINSTORMING FOR HOW WE CAN MAKE FOA A STRONGER PUBLICATION AND INCREASE READERSHIP. WITH THIS IN MIND, WE ASK OUR READERS TO BE FLEXIBLE ALONGSIDE US AS WE GROW IN CONTENT, DESIGN, AND OVERALL FLOW OF THE PUBLICATION.

THANK YOU TAYLOR FOR A WONDERFUL SELECTION AND FOR YOUR HARD WORK, ESPECIALLY DURING THE EVACUATION FOR HURRICANE IRMA. THANK YOU ARTISTS AND READERS WHO CONTINUE TO ENCOURAGE US TO KEEP DOING WHAT WE LOVE TO DO! ALSO, SHOUT OUT TO JUSTIN AND TY FOR BEING A GREAT TEAM TO WORK WITH AS WE NAVIGATED OUR RESPONSIBILITIES AS STAFF AND FOR THEIR PATIENCE WITH ME DURING THE WEBSITE REDESIGN! I THOROUGHLY ENJOYED REVAMPING THE WEBSITE, AND WE HOPE YOU DO TOO. IF YOU HAVE ANY FEEDBACK, PLEASE LET US KNOW.

DANNIE LIEBERGOT, *Editor & Media Manager*

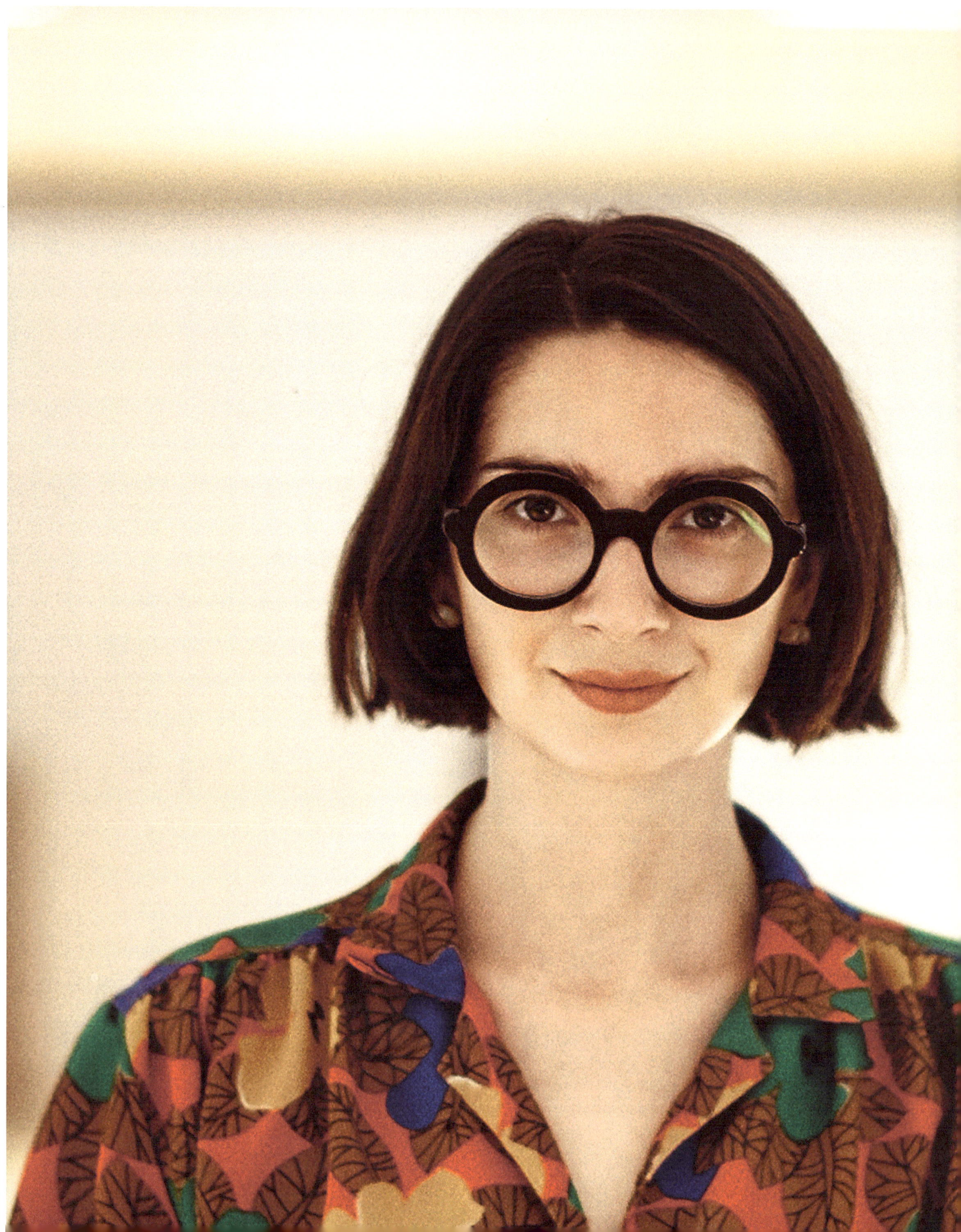

Natasha Arselan, Founder and CEO of AucArt

What About Art School?
A Few Do's and Dont's

As roles and responsibilities become blended and integrated for artists, galleries, and institutions in the art world, artists are expected to take a more proactive approach to become involved and market themselves. As an artist you are more likely to have interest by making yourself fully accessible; building networks and interacting with your audience is key. Throughout the summer at AucArt, we toured and began selecting artists from the UK's top 30 art school's BA & MA degree shows. There's nothing worse than finding a great artist at a degree show and getting back to the office to discover that the details on their business card are inaccurate or the website doesn't include an email address. It's more likely that they'll disappear forever, which is a nightmare. Based on our experience, here's our list of do's and don'ts. Remember this is just the beginning. Best of luck!

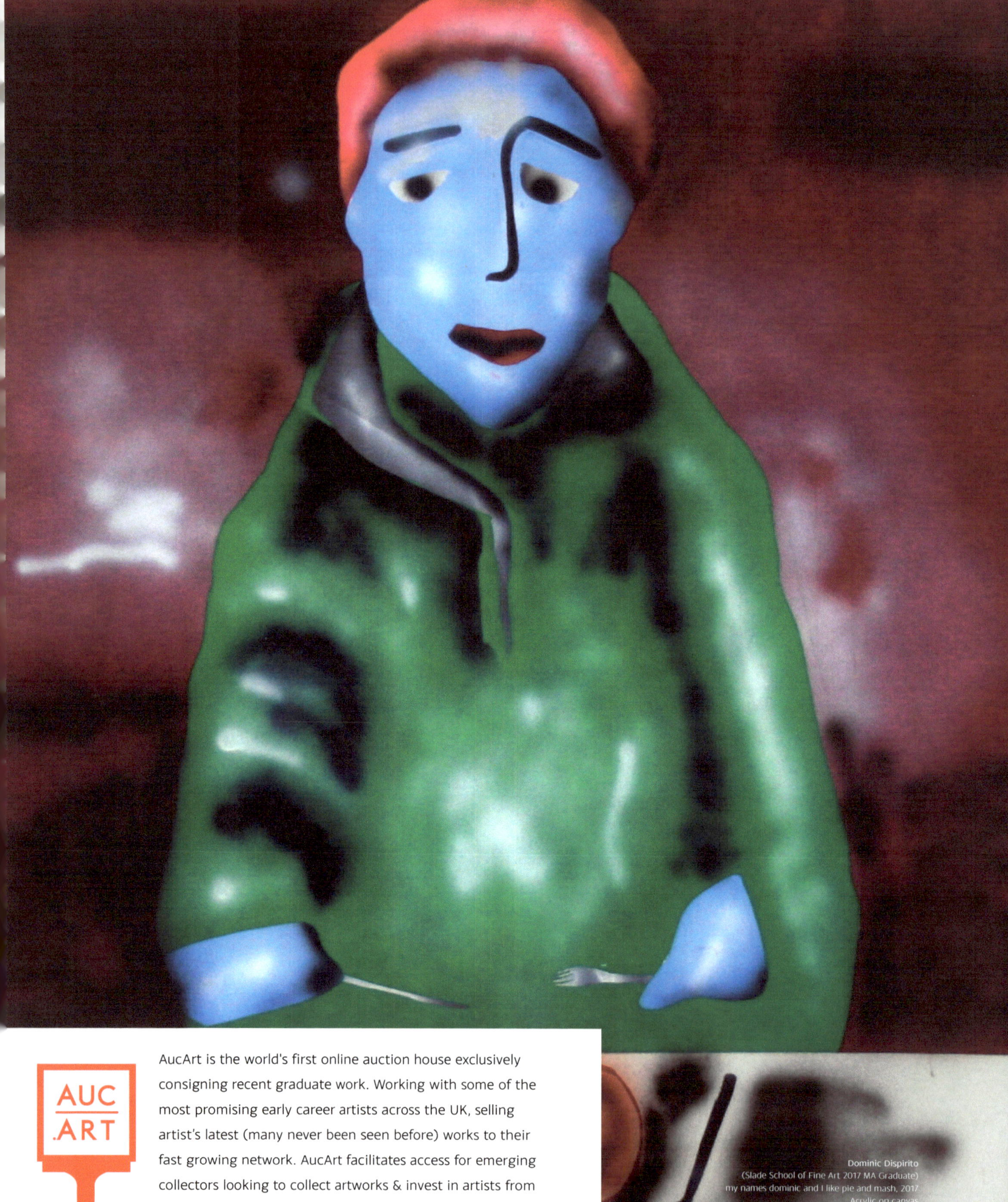

AucArt is the world's first online auction house exclusively consigning recent graduate work. Working with some of the most promising early career artists across the UK, selling artist's latest (many never been seen before) works to their fast growing network. AucArt facilitates access for emerging collectors looking to collect artworks & invest in artists from the beginning of their career.

For more info, visit aucart.com

Dominic Dispirito
(Slade School of Fine Art 2017 MA Graduate)
my names dominic and I like pie and mash, 2017
Acrylic on canvas
detail

DO

- Set up an Instagram account and post regularly - think of this as your visual diary.

- Build a simple website including images of latest work, CV, contact details. Include your email address, Instagram handle, phone number and mailing list sign up. Market yourself through social media, mailing list, any upcoming events, available work, etc.

- Set up a reasonably professional and simple email address.

- Begin engaging with your community as early as possible. This is something as simple as replying to their comments on social media and attending art openings.

- Studio Visits - Have an open studio event and be prepared to speak about your work in a concise and professional way that is engaging and not too long. Allow time for questions and answers.

- Make the most out of your degree show! Take professional photos since you'll be marketing your work for the next few months using these photos. Make the most of this opportunity.

- Always have cards next to your work and make sure your name and contact details are CORRECT and identifiable. Be at the show everyday until it closes - you never know who may turn up on the last day.

- Invite as many people to your degree show as possible.

- Do some research on pricing before the opening. If someone shows interest, you need to know the value of your work and check with the exhibition space on the percentage of their cut.

- If there are any particular curators / gallerists you are interested in working with, introduce yourself at any given opportunity, whether at their gallery or an opening elsewhere. All relationships, even in the art world, are human.

- Wrap your work properly/professionally either when taking the work to present to somebody or shipping the work to a buyer. (As seen here: http://videocenter.van.fedex.com/learn/how-to-pack-artwork)

- Read contracts carefully and ask as many questions as you feel necessary.

DON'T

- Take an opportunity that sounds too good to be true without asking as many questions as possible.

- Assume ANYTHING.

- Be sloppy with emails - keep up to date with admin and correspondence (organisation and time management are key.)

- Don't give rights to all of your work (whether it be a gallery or an agent) in the first year without building and trying out the relationship with a few consigned works at a time. You want to test the waters and gain interest from multiple sources. Do not "put all your eggs in the same basket".

- Rush into a master's degree if you don't feel ready for one.

- Print business cards without any contact details or incorrect info. It's not cool, it's annoying.

- Bad mouth members of your network for no reason; you should appreciate the people who support you and your practice. The art world is small.

- Don't take anything or anyone for granted.

- Rely on anyone to do anything for you... even your gallerist.

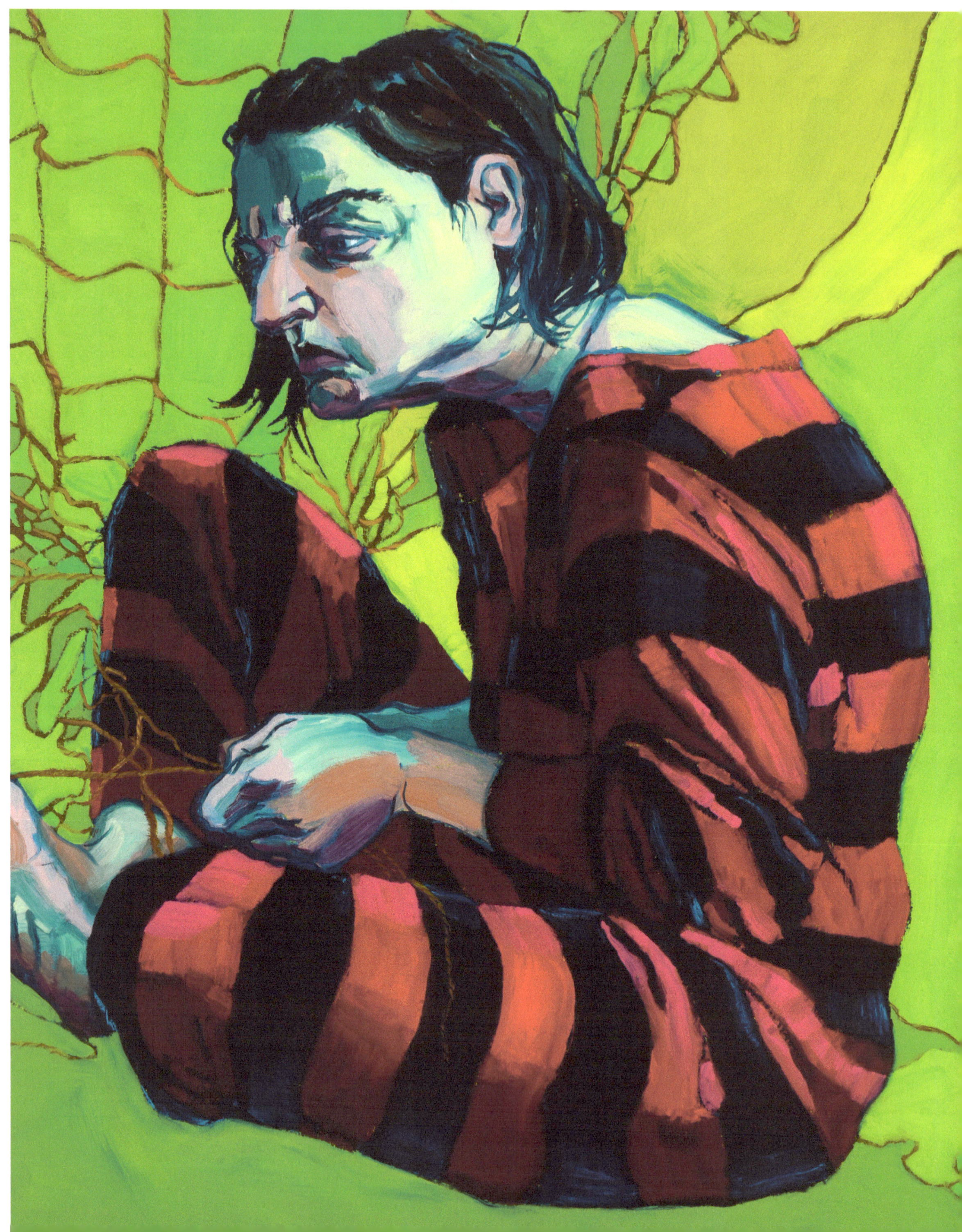

Portraits of an Alter Ego

Work by Dara Engler

Interview by Taylor O. Thomas

T: When did you begin pursuing your artistic practice? Have painting and drawing always been your go-to methods of image making?

D: When I was little I used to line up my dolls and stuffed animals in front of cardboard box desks to teach them art and math. Eventually, math lost out. Painting and drawing have been my media of choice, but recently, I have been incorporating object making into my practice. They began as props for the two-dimensional images, but are becoming as much a part of my work as the paintings themselves.

T: In your artist statement, you mention that your paintings and drawings are "portraits of an alter ego." Can you explain how your practice allows you to tap into desires, curiosities, or aspects of yourself that may not be expressed in everyday life?

D: I think most of us have a feral side; we're just too busy to explore it. Making that investigation part of my job gives me permission to dip my toe in that world. I took an animal tracking class this summer as research for my work. I have my fishing license and learned to gut and scale fish. It's a chicken or egg situation. It's hard to tell what came first: am I learning these things because she's doing them or is she doing them because I am interested in learning them? I can say that if it were not for my work, I would not have made it a priority to follow these impulses. They would have stayed on some unwritten "to-do someday list."

T: Can you tell us more about your creative process? What does it take to arrive at a finished piece?

D: Mostly, finishing a painting is a constant battle to stop working well before I intended when I began.

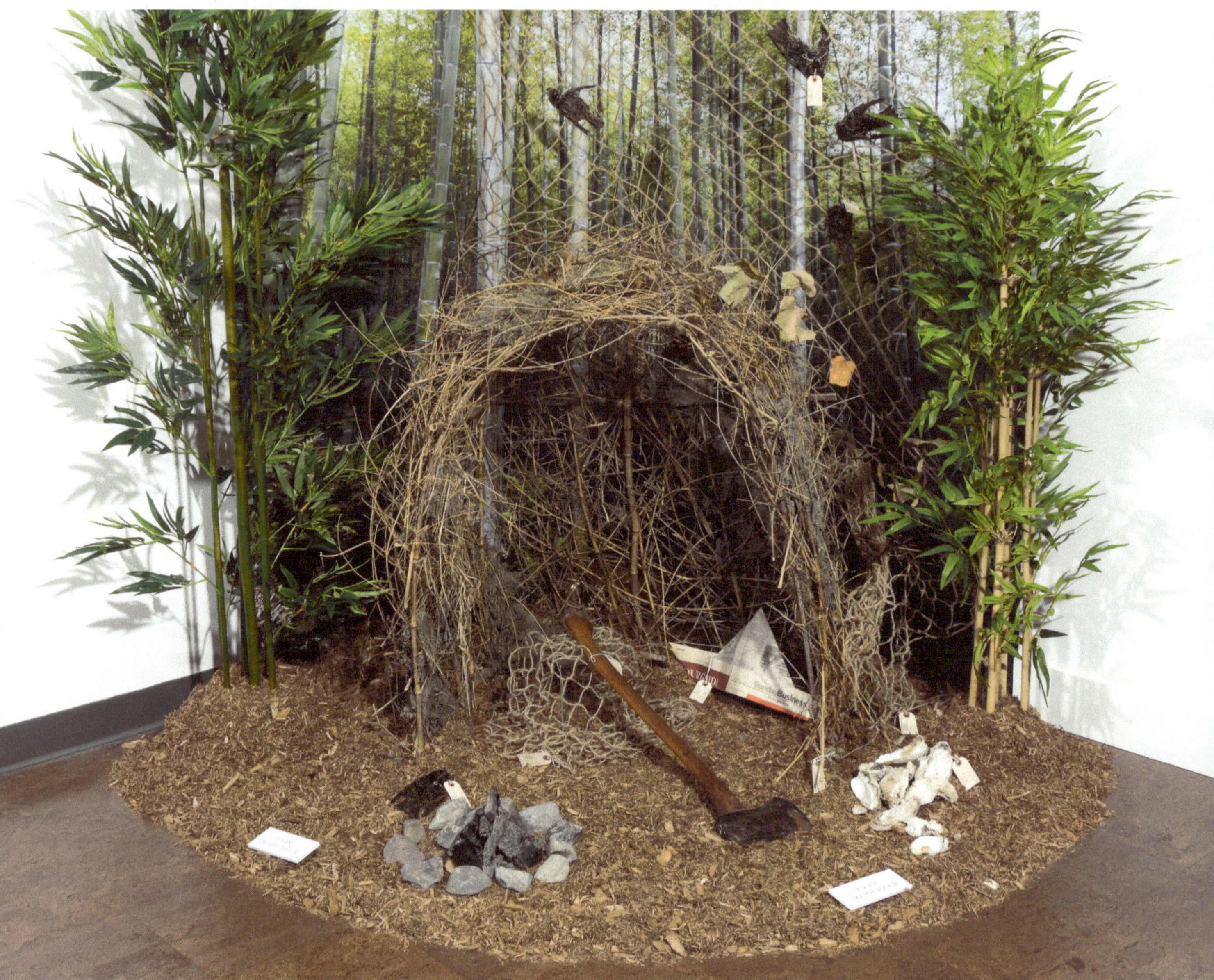

Dara Engler
Pirate Shelter Diorama, 2016
Bamboo, twine, mud, and objects,
84in. x 72in x 60in.

The process prior to that might involve research and building props. Often I spend time studying something like, how to skin a squirrel, only to realize that I can't imagine *her* doing it so efficiently. I learn how and she does the opposite. After researching topics like that, I have to watch You Tube videos of cute kittens and puppies to balance it out.

T: In reviewing your work, I was particularly struck by your seamless integration of traditionally shaped canvases alongside the canvas cutouts in Paper Doll Meat Locker, A Pirate's Guide to Heat and Meat. Have you always been experimental in choosing your materials and installation process, or does this piece mark a shift in your practice?

D: I would definitely call it a shift. I have always enjoyed tools and hands-on processes and found that lacking in my painting process. I have also begun showing the props that I make alongside the paintings as artifacts in a natural history museum-like display, including life-size dioramas of dwellings. I actually started college as a double major in art and technical theatre, so this shift in my practice is more like a return or inclusion of a past life.

T: Themes of identity, femininity, and survival seem to ooze from your works—topics that carry a lot of weight in our current political and cultural climate. How much does our world and your personal context within in it affect the works that you make?

D: Since we are intrinsically linked, my world affects that of my character entirely, but this work began years ago. Human foible, our subconscious, allegory and storytelling are always relevant. However, I have always been prone to escapism and our current cultural climate definitely compounds that problem.

T: If you could invite two contemporary artists into your studio, who would they be and what would you want to ask them?

Beth Cavener. She is a ceramic sculptor who speaks about humanity through work of anthropomorphized animals. I heard her lecture in the early 2000s. The way she spoke about the content of her work and the process and challenges of "making" was disarmingly personal and candid. It has shaped both my studio and teaching practices, giving me permission to do what feels sincere and unpretentious. I don't have a specific question for her. I just want to have her in my studio and to chat one-on-one. The second is hard to say. Caleb Weintraub? Njideka Akunyili Crosby? Amy Cutler? Hope Gangloff?

T: As an interviewer and juror, I feel a certain level of responsibility to not only consider an individual artist's contribution to this particular publication, but more importantly to consider the artist's voice within a larger contemporary context. In your opinion, do artists today have a responsibility to the world that surrounds them? What do you consider your artistic responsibility to be?

D: I think emphasizing humanity is the best thing artists can do right now. I've found that the only way I can do that is to follow whatever path feels honest and genuine. The more I worry about the value of what I'm doing in the contemporary world, the less authentic the work will be and then, ironically, the less relevant it becomes. All we can do is share what we have to offer, whatever lens that may be.

T: What is next for your work? Are you going to continue the narrative of your part- inventive, part- incapable, part-"pirate-y" alter ego?

D: I do plan to continue my character's narrative, but she tends to have a mind of her own. It's best when I admit that I'm just along for the ride. However, as the construction of artifacts becomes more important in my work, the narrative may be created by the absence of the figure, with these pieces as evidence of her life. I'd like the installation of the paintings and artifacts to become more crowded and winding, with a creepy cabinet of curiosities spin. Instead of just depicting the pirate's life, the installation would create a dusty, dark world for the audience. The viewer would be left asking, who is this character? What obsessive collector catalogued her life? The exhibition would be a double portrait: of the pirate and of the invisible curator.

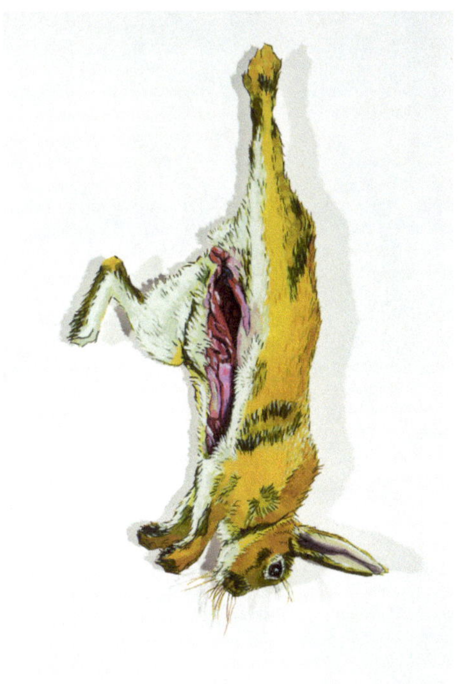

Dara Engler
Paper Doll Meat Locker, 2016
Oil on paper
(Rabbit detail)

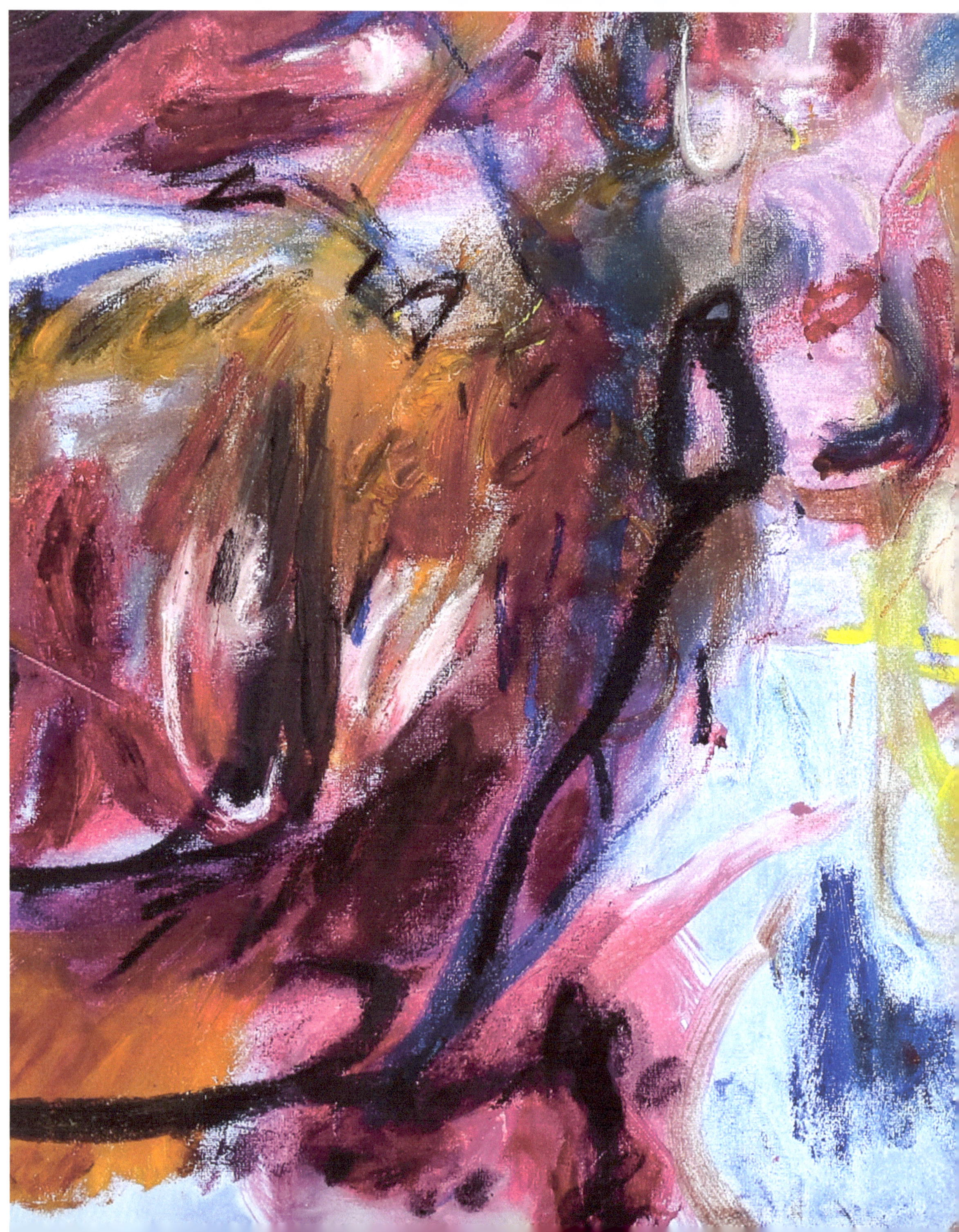

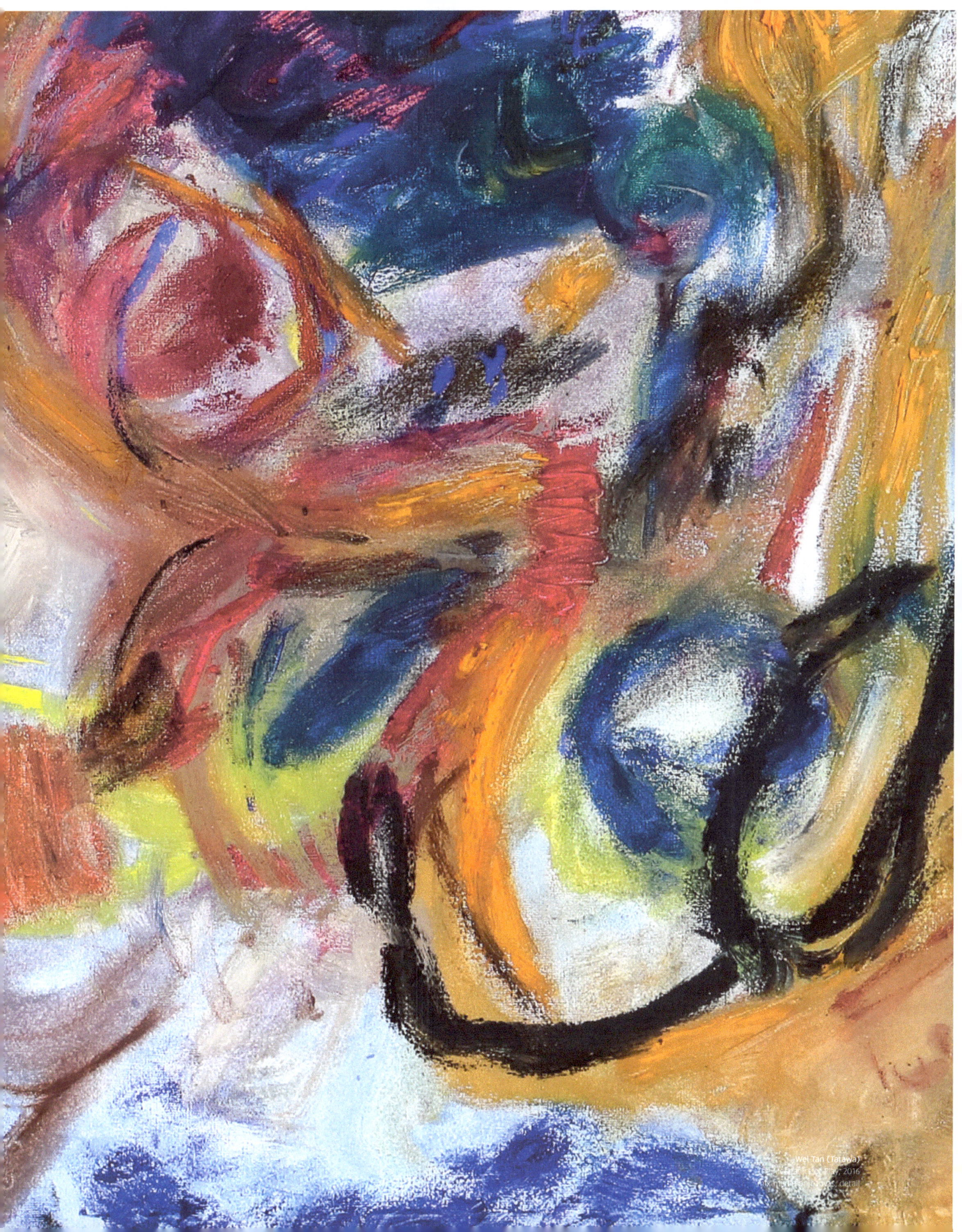

Wei Tan (Tatawa)
The Weariness of Play, 2016
mixed media on canvas, detail

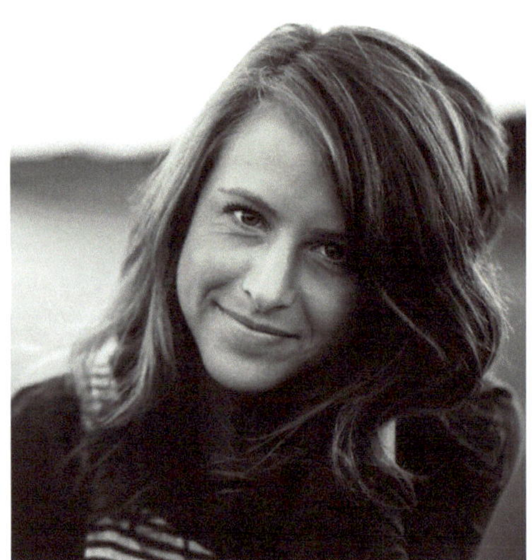

Taylor O. Thomas

Artist & Visual Art Editor of EcoTheo Review

Taylor O. Thomas was born in Birmingham, AL, and now lives and works as a visual artist in Tampa, FL. Thomas's work includes abstract paintings, drawings, and installations, which have been exhibited in galleries and private collections in the United States, Italy, and China. In 2012, Taylor graduated magna cum laude from Davidson College with a BA in Studio Art, and has since used painting as a means of investigating identity, spirituality, and human connection. She views her works as evolving stories, noting, "my layered materials are beginnings, not ends. Mark-making and manipulating media is my mental, physical, and spiritual confrontation of questions and issues—whether they are deeply personal or widely shared."

Thomas recently received the University Graduate Fellowship from the University of South Florida, where she is currently earning her MFA degree. Her works are represented by The Road Gallery (New York, NY), Rachel Nash Gallery (Dallas, TX), and Nomad Collective (Nashville, TN).

Juror Statement

What if the lens through which we viewed artworks was less based on finding connections and more focused on the significance of disconnection? What if a group of artists were united by their dissimilarities, more so than an overarching set of similarities? These are the questions I asked myself while selecting the artists for FOA's Fall 2017 publication. Through their diversity of work, process, and perspective, the makers included reflect the truth that multiplicity is a much more accurate depiction of our zeitgeist than singularity. In these pages, viewers will see that contemporary art (and life, for that matter) is drenched with and open to all forms. Some paintings harness historic traditions; others simulate the graphic nature of here and now. Some sculptures ground us in a tactile environment; others let us tarry through glitches of a virtual world. Some photographs and installations depict personal narratives; others capitalize on the power of fiction to tell tales that seem truer than false. I am honored to have gathered this particular group of artists, not simply because of the creative quality they individually present, but because of the bold diversity that their works collectively provide. This issue stands as an important demonstration of how differences in style, vision, and voice can beautifully coexist. Now, more than ever, let us learn from this example.

Kieran Riley Abbott

Johnson, Vermont   kieranrileyabbott.com

I make prints, objects, and print-objects that pursue the ambiguous space between two and three dimensions. These are works from my current series of plaster monotypes, in which I pour wet plaster or hydrocal over a water-soluble crayon drawing, transferring the image but not perfectly.

The patterns in this series reference the checkerboard floors depicted in Renaissance paintings and prints to demonstrate an artist's mastery of linear perspective. When these checkerboard floors are depicted in isolation, out of the context of an interior space, they become abstracted and placeless. The illusion of linear perspective is further disrupted when the grid begins to undulate ever so slightly, and solid shapes start to blur around the edges. Perception is malleable. The floor is lava.

Working within the context of printmaking, I am fascinated by the intermediary step in which the printmaker loses control of the final result, whether by running an inked block and paper through a press, or by pouring plaster over a drawing - in both instances, awaiting the mystery of the reveal.

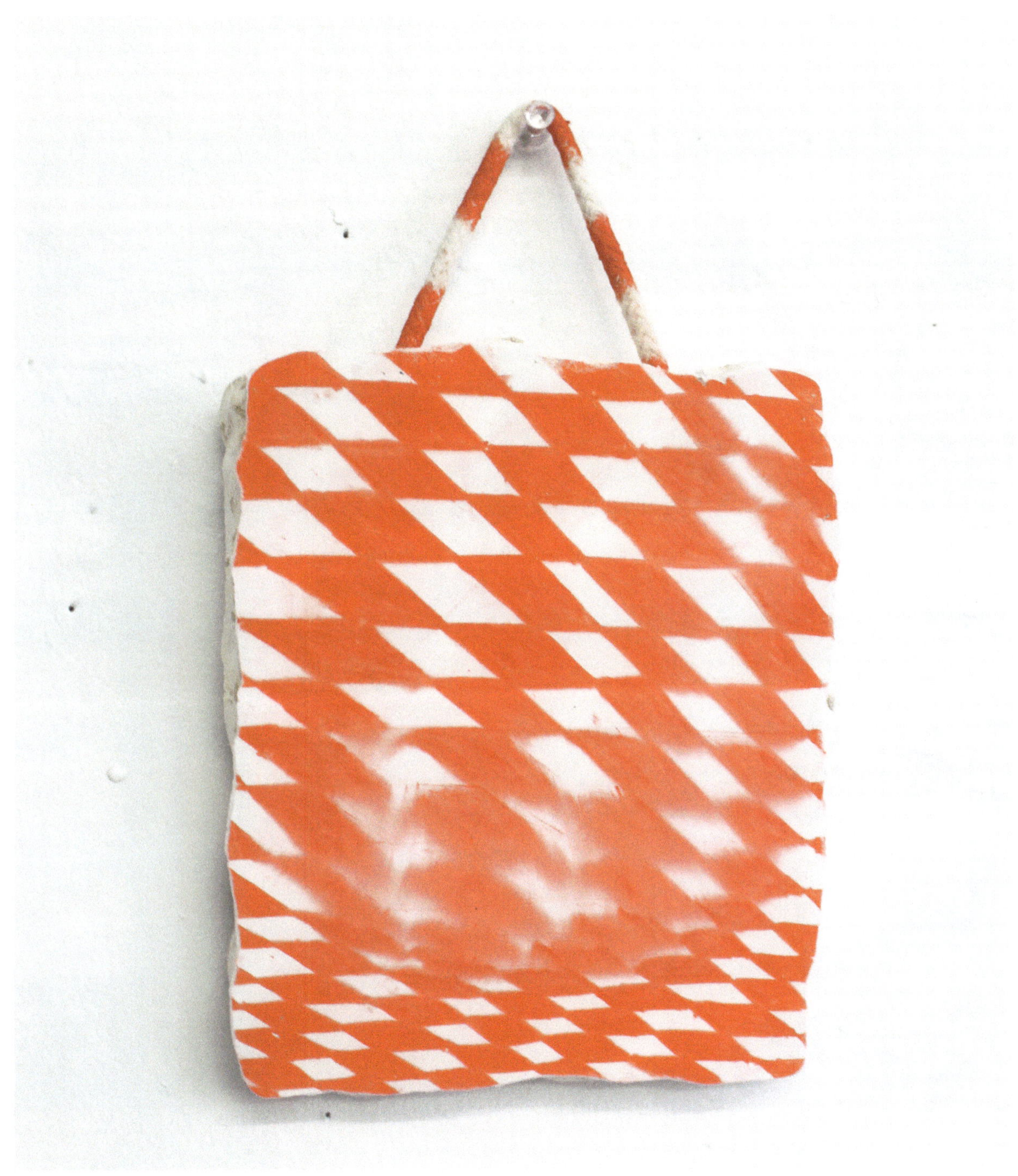

Kieran Riley Abbott
Untitled, 2017
Monotype on hydrocal and rope
5 x 7 x 0.5 in.

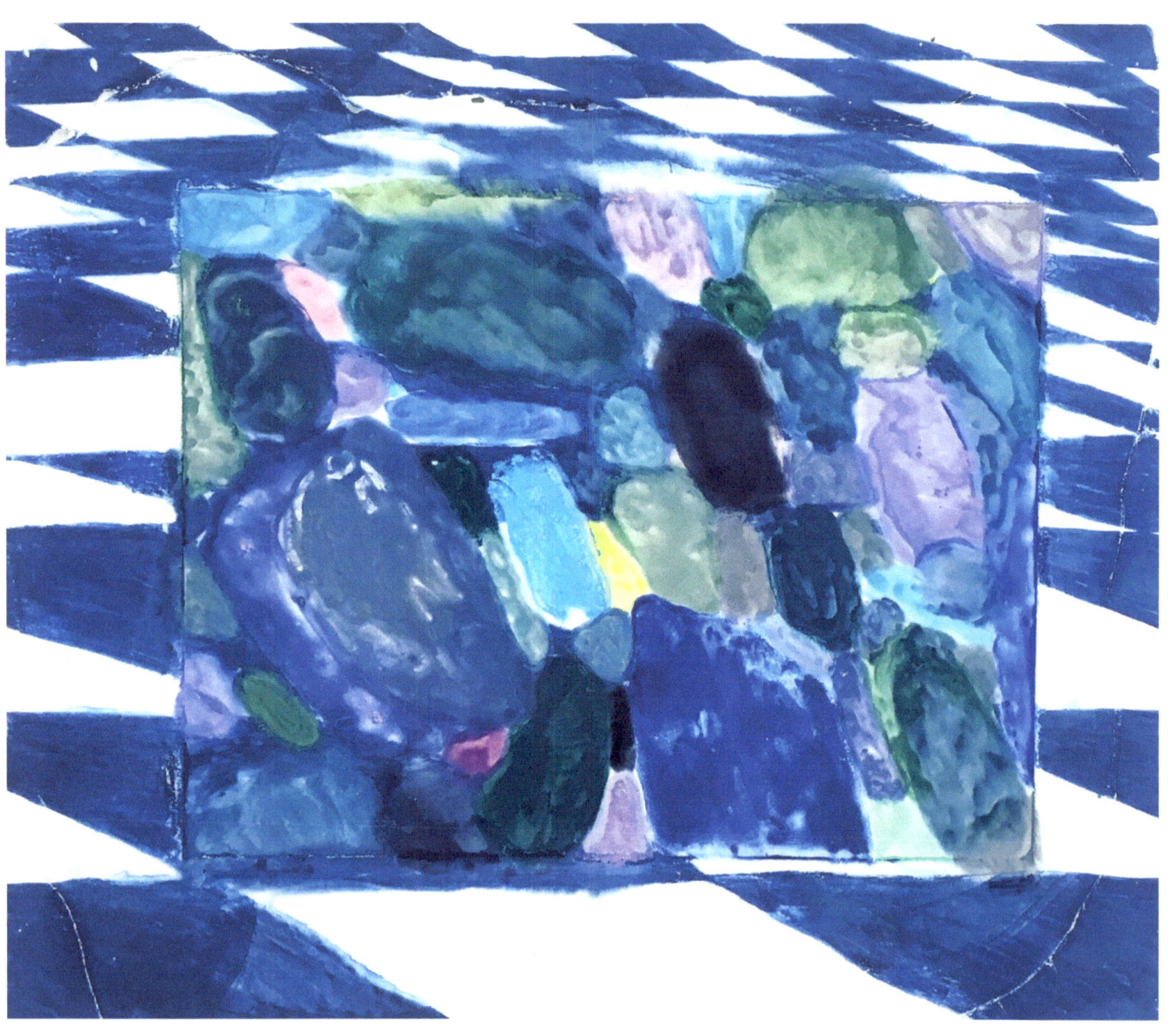

Kieran Riley Abbott
Untitled, 2017
Monotype on hydrocal
19 x 24 x 0.5 in.

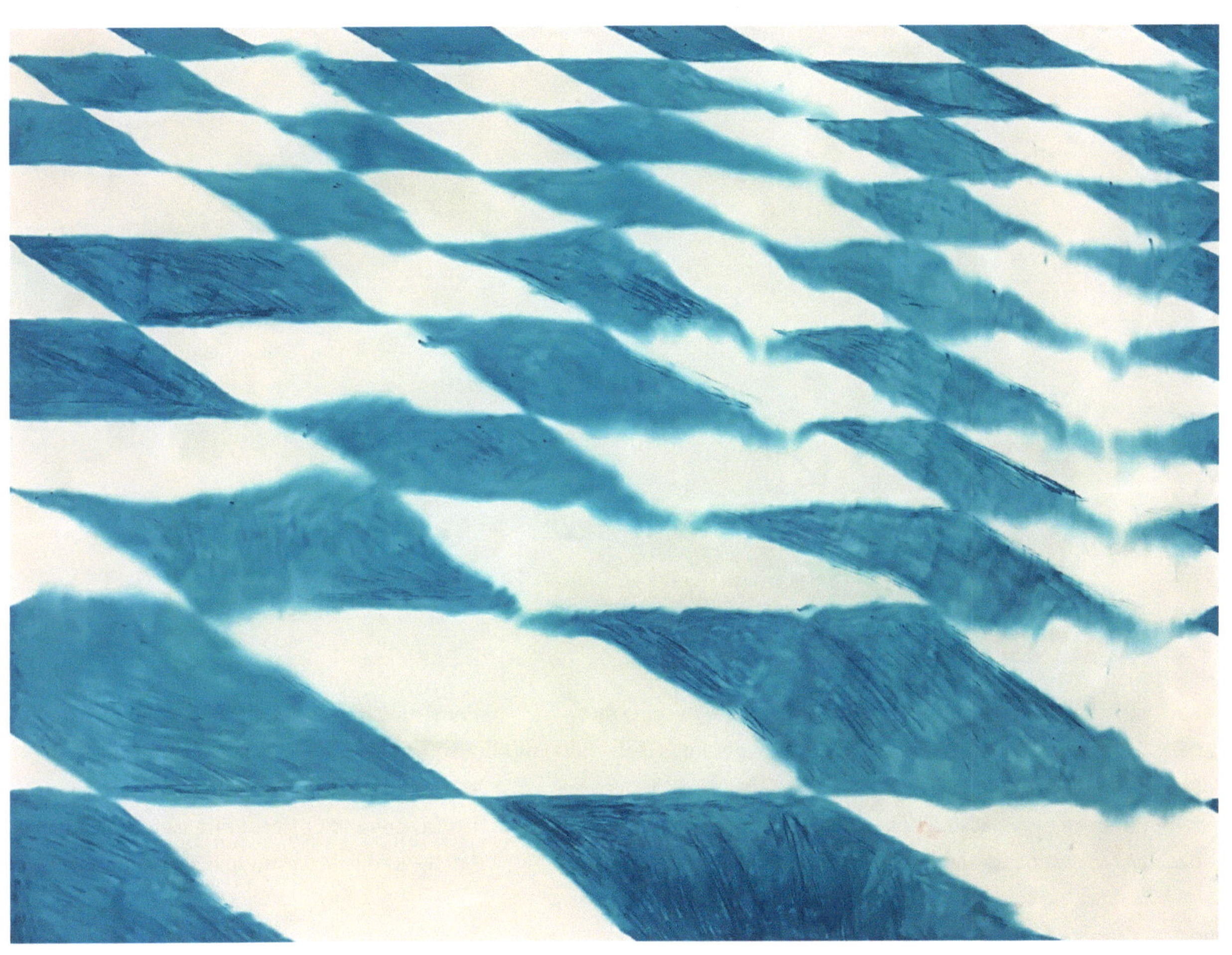

Kieran Riley Abbott
Untitled, 2017
Monotype on hydrocal
8 x 10 x 0.5 in.

Patrick Brien

Visalia, California   patrickbrien.com

As virtual reality goggles and augmented reality have become more accessible, I wonder how these open frontiers might impact our notions of the built environment. Over the past few years, my paintings have evolved from picturing abstractions of physically built environments to ones that look as if they were constructed in digital spaces. My work acknowledges the connection between the internet and the canvas as portals available to transport the viewer into other places. The paintings are the result of all of the bits of visual information I collect as I go about my day. I tend to pick up pieces of torn magazine pages that I find on the ground and take pictures of layers of painted lines on the pavement with my phone. The works are painted in many layers and display many gestural and mechanical methods of applying the paint on the canvas. They reflect my interest in the way that digital interfaces have become enmeshed into the way that we perceive the world. In this way, the paintings are abstractions that provide moments of recognizable landscapes and objects to transport the viewer, briefly, into illusionistic spatial environments.

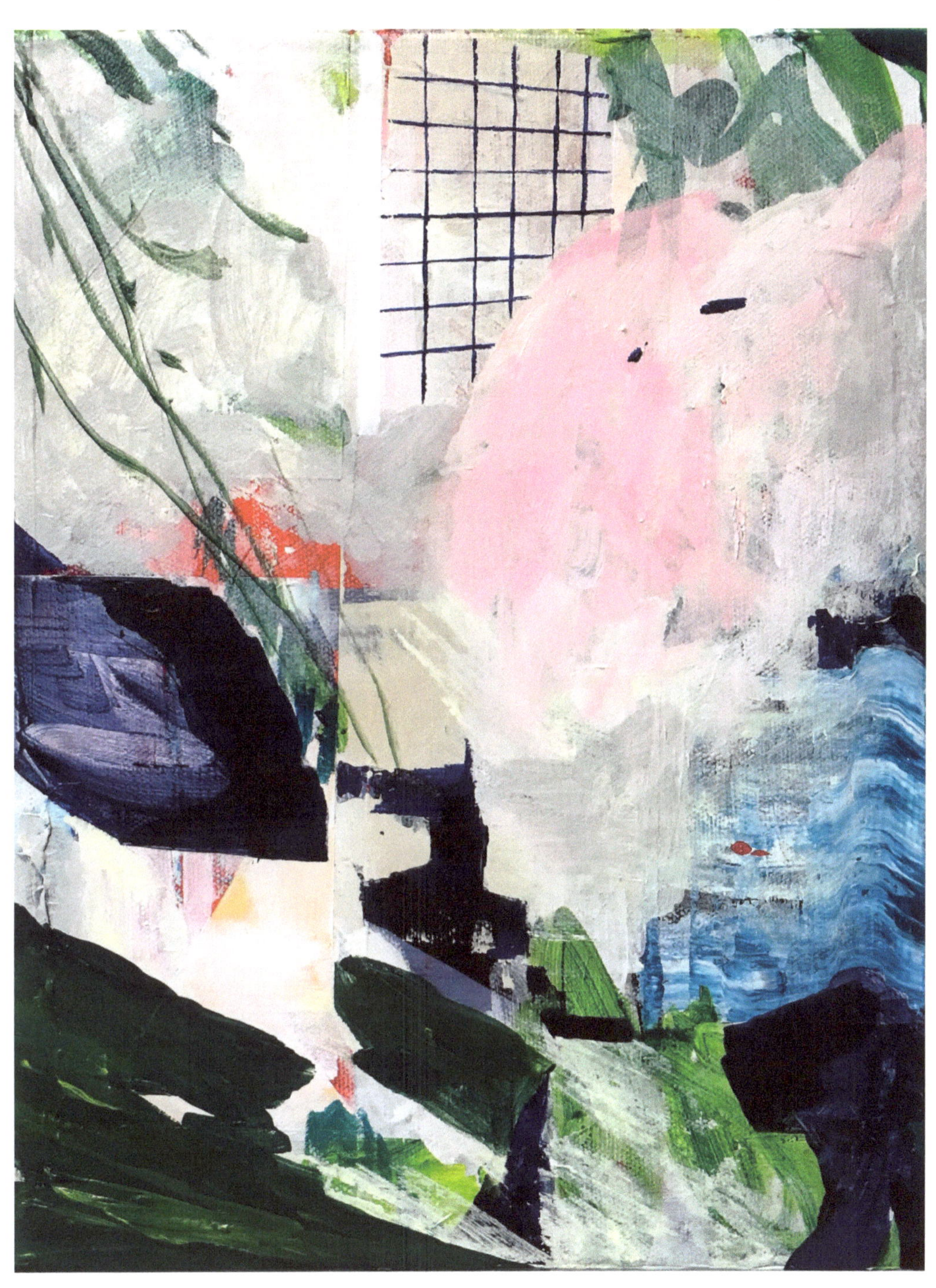

Patrick Brien
Open Window, 2016
Acrylic and oil pastel on canvas,
12 x 19 in.

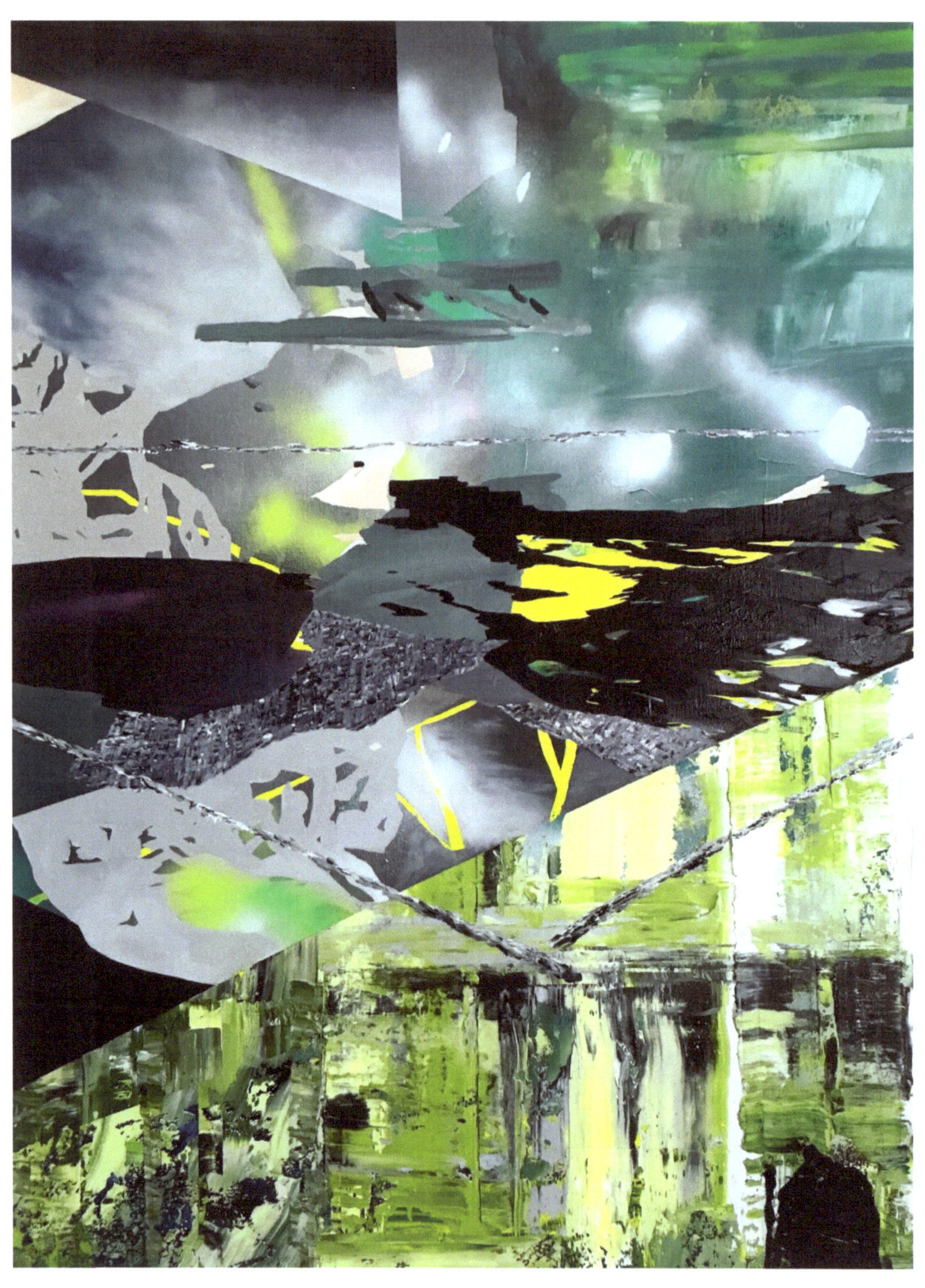

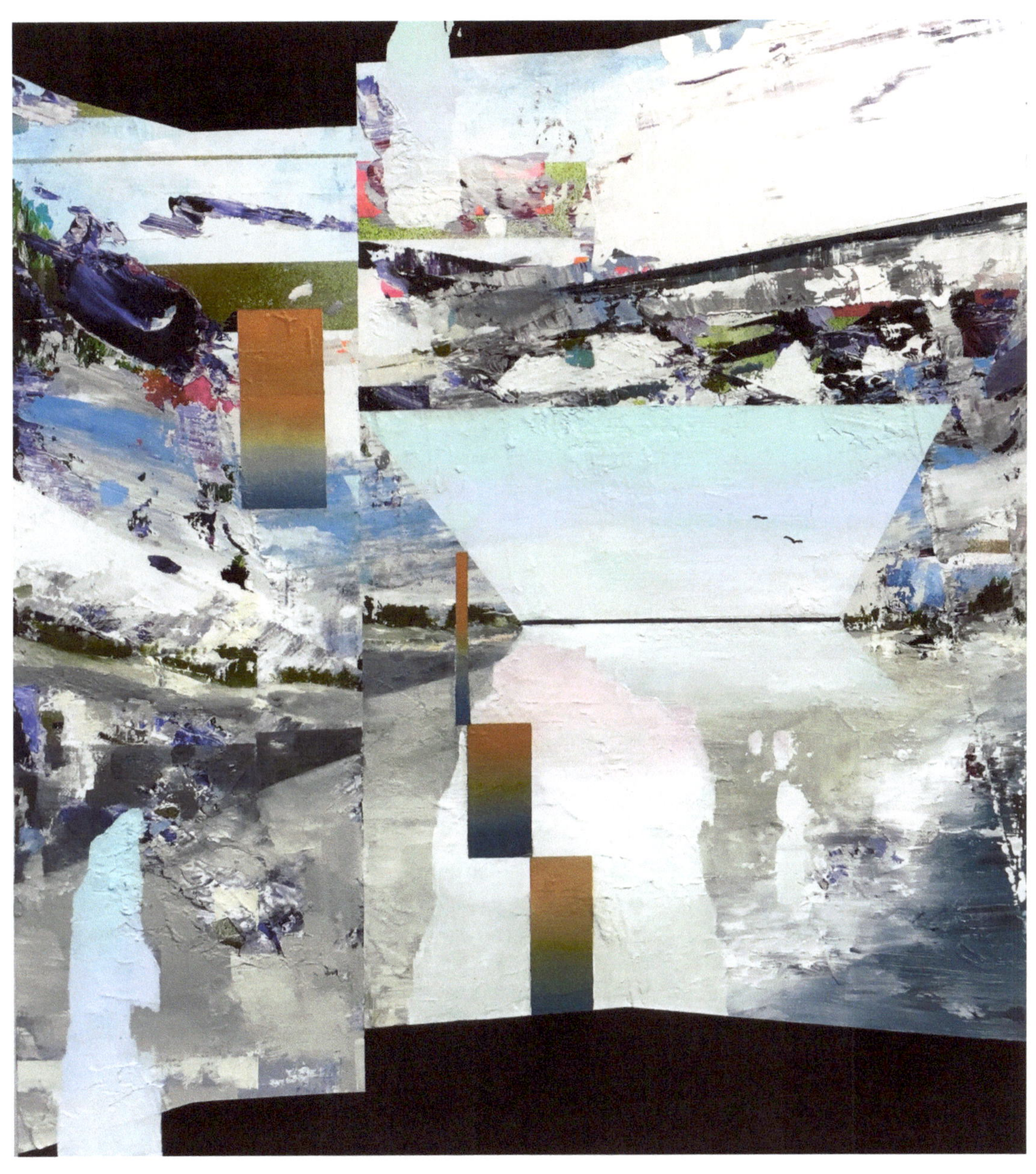

Patrick Brien
Surf, 2017
oil and acrylic on linen over panel
21 x 18.5 in.

Ani Collier

Gainsville, FL   blackcproduction.com/ani-collier

The first half of my life, I was always performing in front of an audience or a camera. Although I retired my pointe shoes more than fifteen years ago, the pull from the ballet world was too strong for me to walk away completely. The stories, the shapes, the lights, the dancers, the choreography, and the compositions were all too ingrained in my mind. Slowly, but surely, I picked up where I had left off; however, this time I returned to dance behind the lens of a camera.

There are a few themes that have emerged in my work since taking up photography and film more than eight years ago, which are evident in the pieces I am submitting. One is my fascination with cities; having grown up under Communism in Bulgaria, I never imagined that I would see the Berlin Wall fall or that I would be able to travel freely to the West. Other themes include my love of movement, architecture, and beauty. It is evidenced in the way that I capture my subjects and how I manipulate a composition's lines and shapes.

Although a photograph only records a single moment in time, the collages and films that I make tell stories – stories of love and loss, struggle, and quests for understanding. I feel that through digital photography, filming, and manipulation, I am able to choreograph again – albeit virtually. In a way, I am still dancing; only now, I dance with my images.

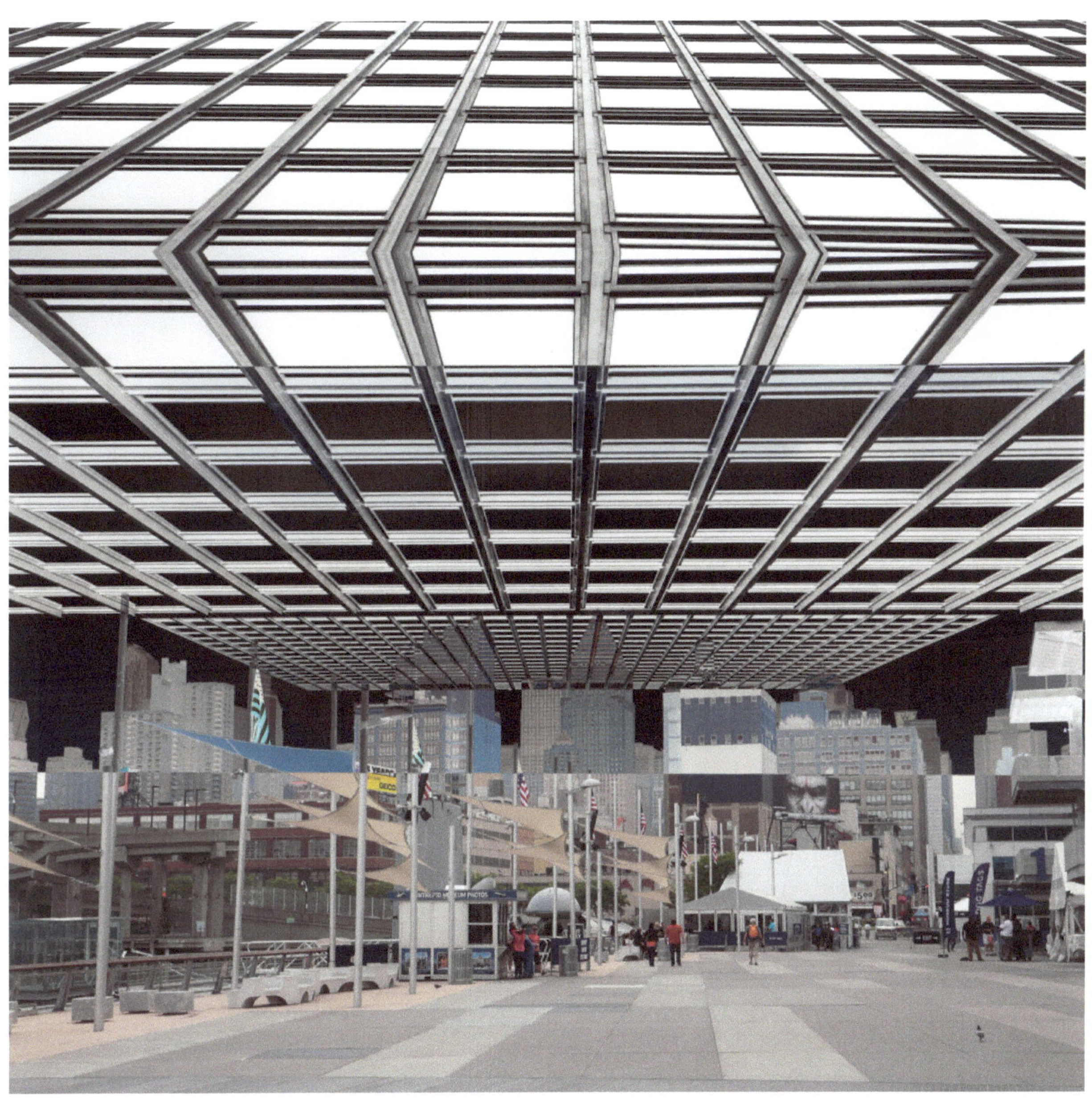

Ani Collier
NY Series: When the Ground Meets the Sky, 2017
Digital Manipulation on Sublimated Aluminum
40 x 40 in.

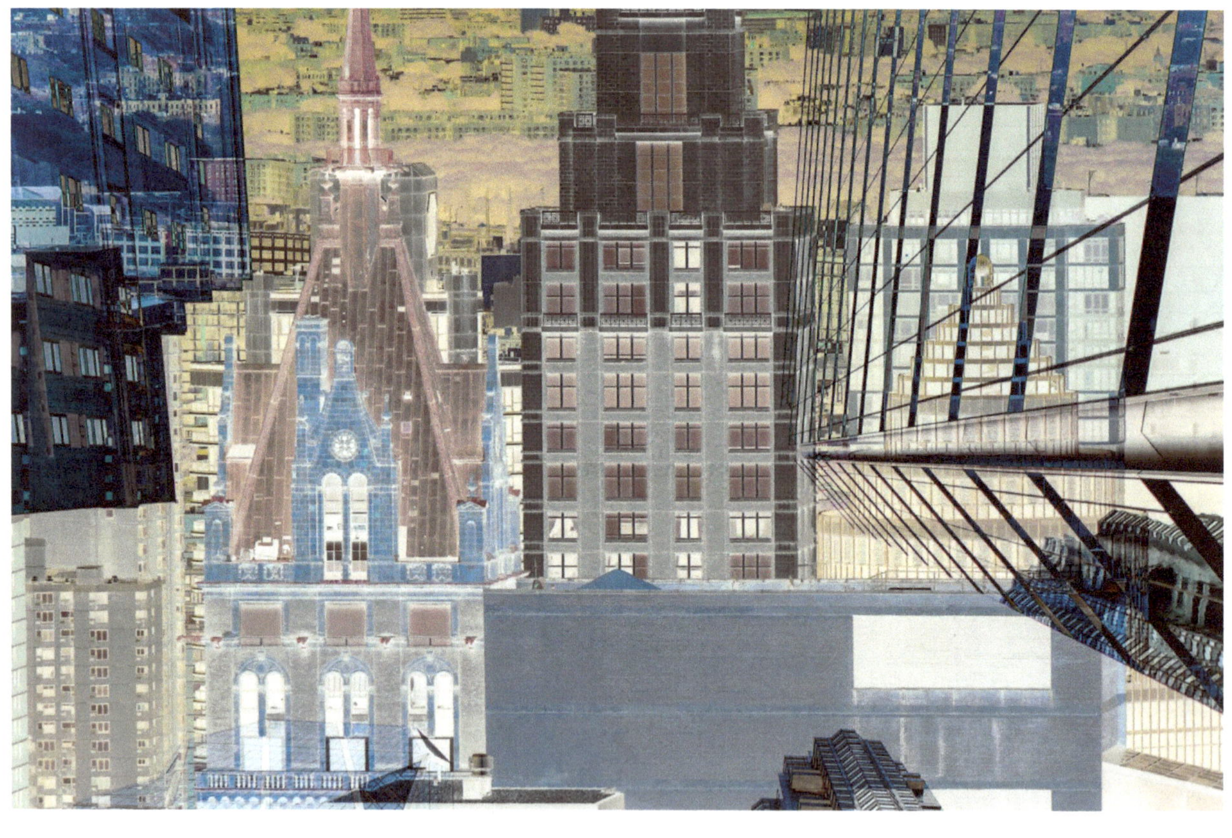

Ani Collier
NY Series: Converging Perspectives, 2017
Digital Manipulation on Sublimated Aluminum
40 x 60 in.

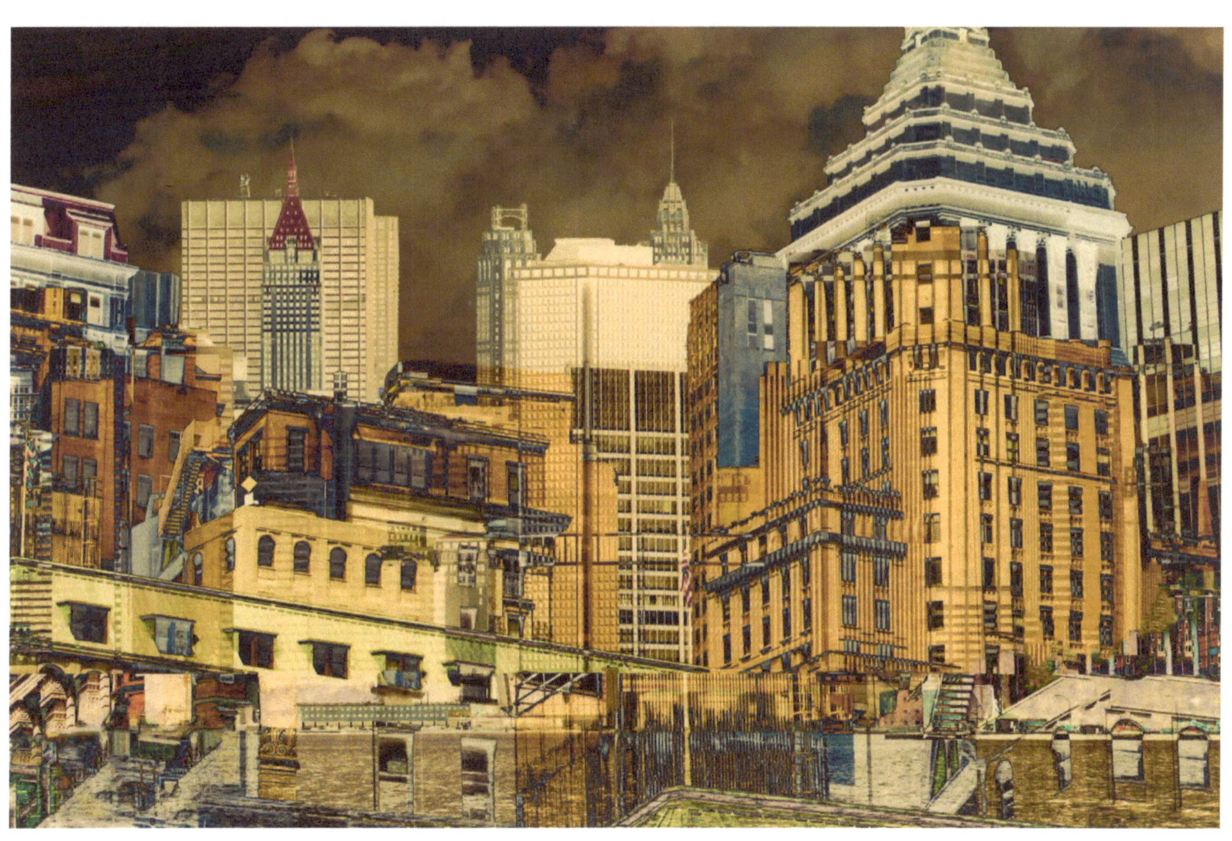

Ani Collier
NY Series: Skyscrapers in Umber, 2016
Digital Manipulation on Sublimated Aluminum
40 x 60 in.

Austin Furtak-Cole

Brooklyn, New York   austinfurtakcole.com

Painting and art have become a space for me to grapple with myself. Through a process of self-examination I try to expose my vulnerabilities and share fantastical versions of my experience. The paintings curiously reveal what I find interesting, strange and absurd by depicting saturated, amalgamated scenes of the figure and other human detritus. These figurative still lives draw from my own philosophical, visual and fanciful observations and touch on subjects of love, fear, struggle and the unknown.

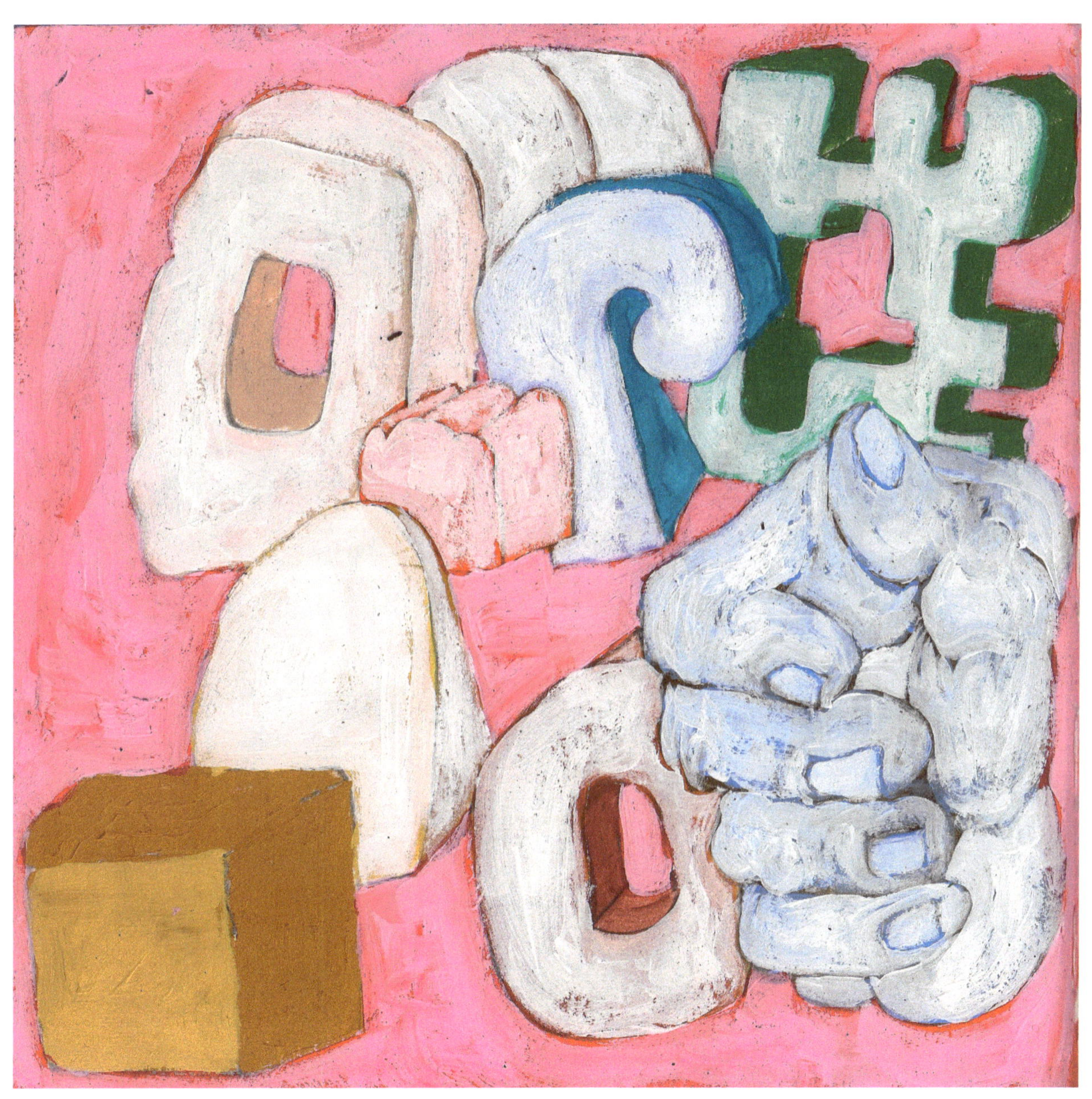

Austin Furtak-Cole
Just Won't Let It Go, 2017
Airbrush and acrylic on multi-layered duralar,
12 x 12in.

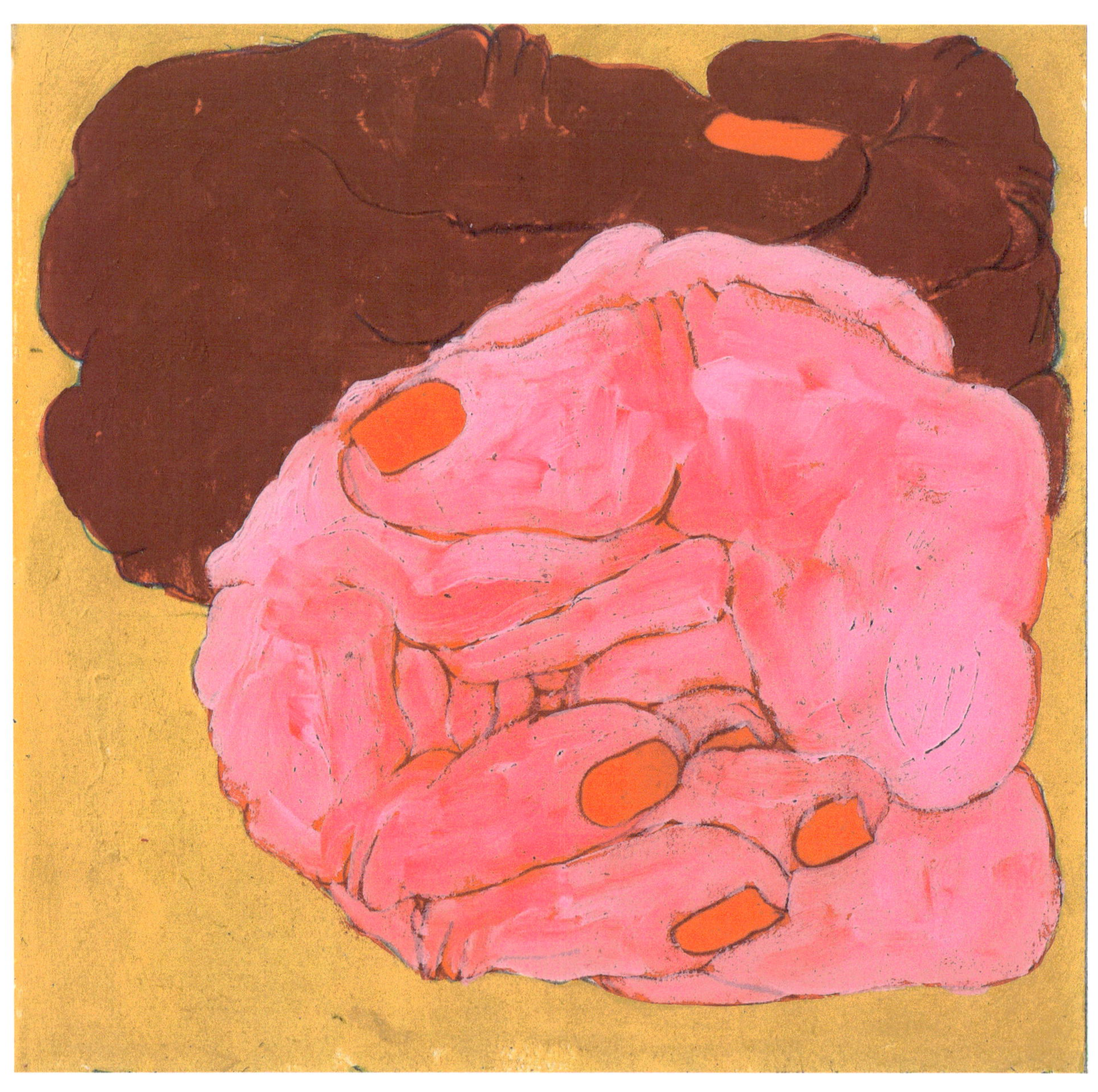

Justin Burns
Since It Closed Down, 2017
Airbrush and acrylic on matte duralar.
31 x 40 in.

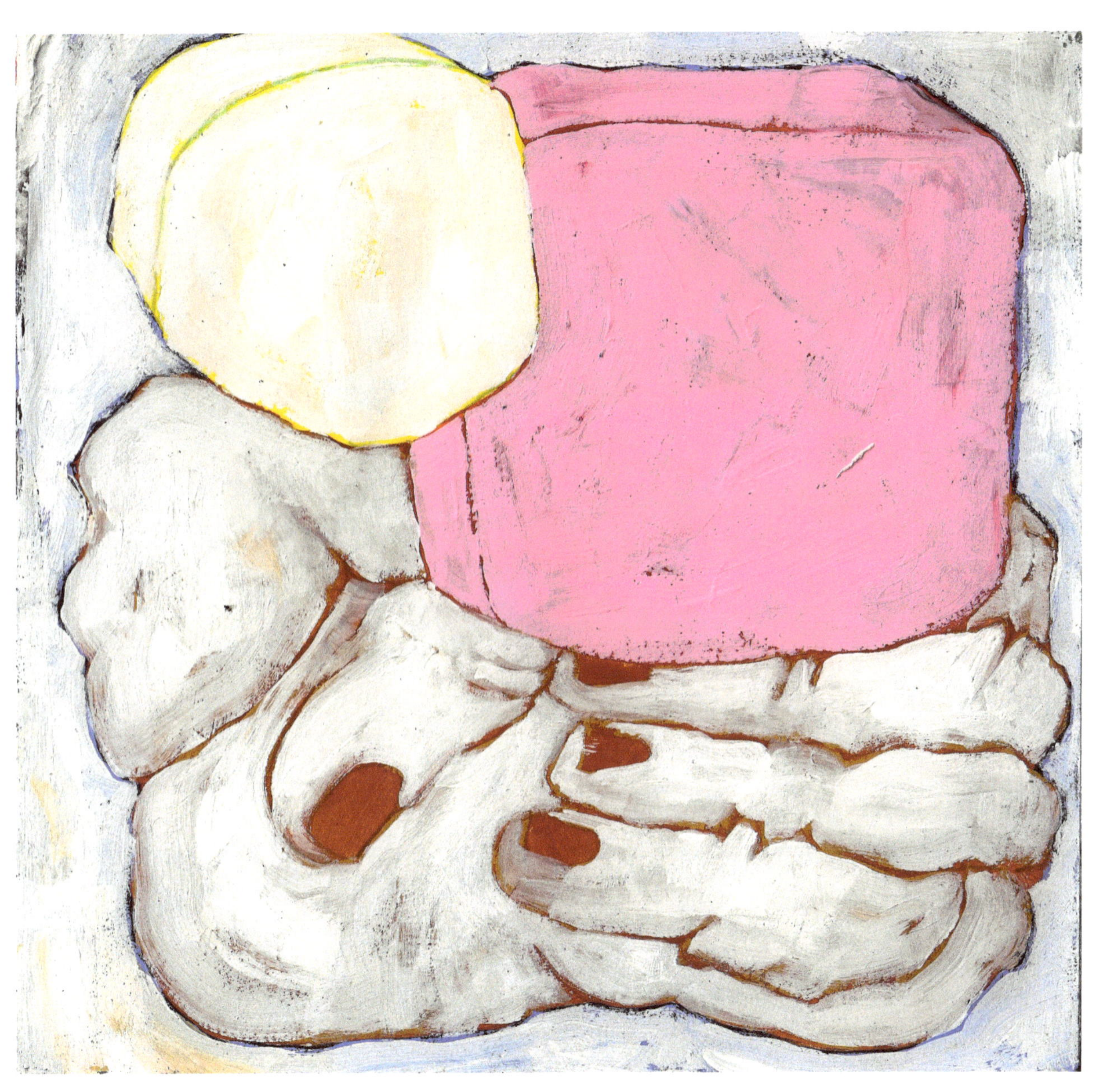

Justin Burns
Weathered, 2017
Airbrush and acrylic on matte duralar,
24 x 45 in.

Dara Engler

Ithaca, New York   daraengler.com

My paintings and drawings are portraits of an alter ego, often rooted in exaggerations of my own experiences. Their loose narratives are allegorical, embracing human foible and the humor that comes with it. My interest in the figure lies in facing these awkward obstacles.

Inspired by my four years in Louisiana and by Karen Russell's book "St. Lucy's Home for Girls Raised by Wolves," my pirate-y anti-hero adopted the curiosity of Russell's characters. I was struck by her character's combative reverence for their natural environment. My pirate is tracking animals, skinning squirrels, and learning to tie nets. Despite her adventurous nature, the pirate is subject to an awkward and fumbling learning curve. She approaches tasks in the least efficient way possible. The painting, How to Skin a Squirrel, would be more aptly titled, How NOT to Skin a Squirrel. She brandishes the knife with absolutely no technical skill. As in any allegory, her trials are emblematic of our daily struggles.

In her book, The Feminine in Fairy Tales, psychologist Marie-Louise von Franz says, "Dreams either compensate for the lopsidedness of our conscious view or complement its lacunae. Fairytales, because they are also mostly unsophisticated products of the storyteller's unconscious, do the same. Like dreams, they help to keep our conscious attitude in a healthy balance, and have therefore a healing function." (p.10) I view my work through a similar lens, as an unapologetically "unsophisticated" product of my unconscious that manifests in this humorous pirate-y alter ego. By painting

CONTINUED ON PAGE 130 →

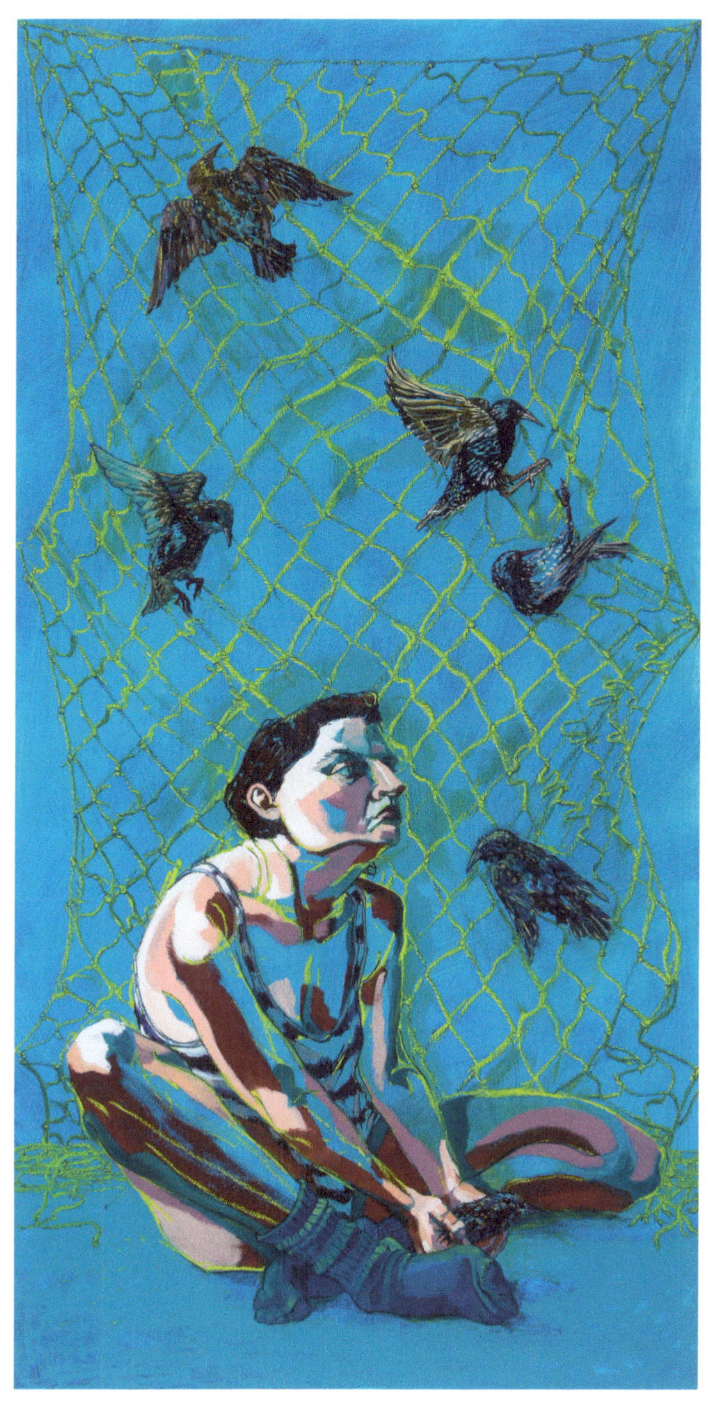

Dara Engler
How to Catch a Bird, 2016
Oil on canvas
80 x 40in.

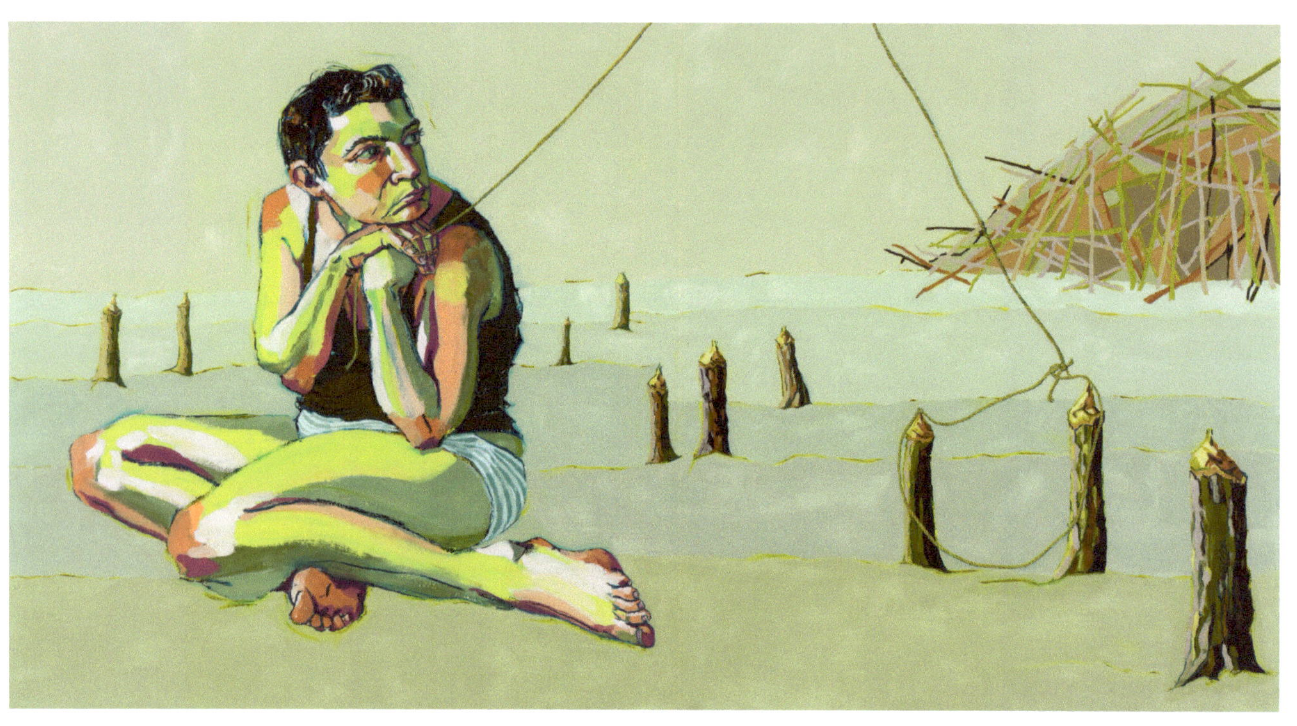

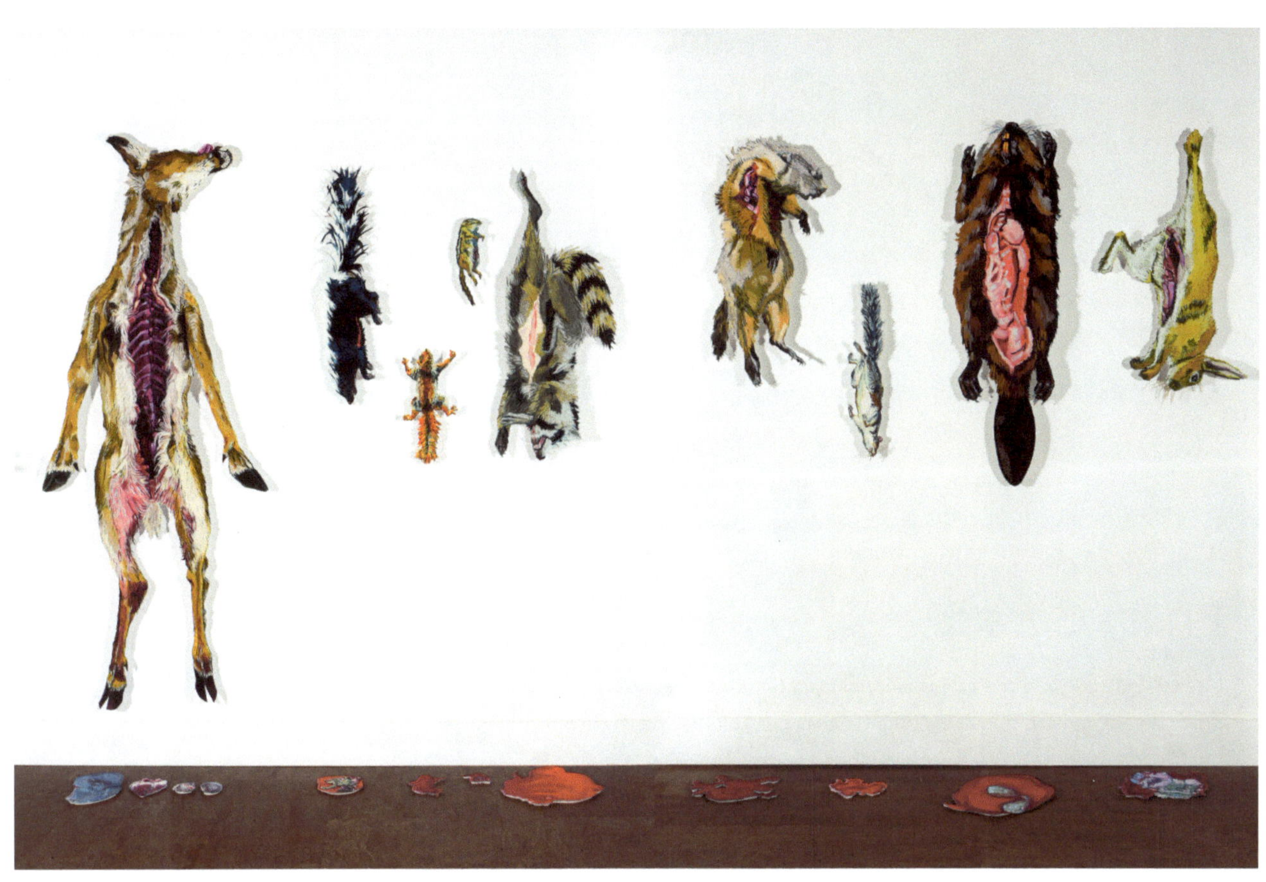

Dara Engler
Paper Doll Meat Locker, 2016
Oil on paper,
varying sizes (life-size)

Philip Gerald   *Dublin, Ireland*

Inspired by the crude and grotesque sublunary nature of medieval painting Philip Gerald's paintings employ bright, obnoxious colours and landscapes populated by cutesy-happy trees, clouds and bushes where nude genderless figures seem to blankly smile at the viewer. There is something eerily uncomfortable in the idea of an anthropomorphised world where everything is smiling, in the same way clowns are so often the subject of nightmares. These bizarre portraits, although they seem devoid of anything real, endeavour to discuss representation when the line between sincerity and insincerity is being purposefully blurred. Beyond the bright painted veil of childlike humour and rude jokes is an intense unease, they depict the awkward silence that follows a joke that fails to land, the deflecting smile.

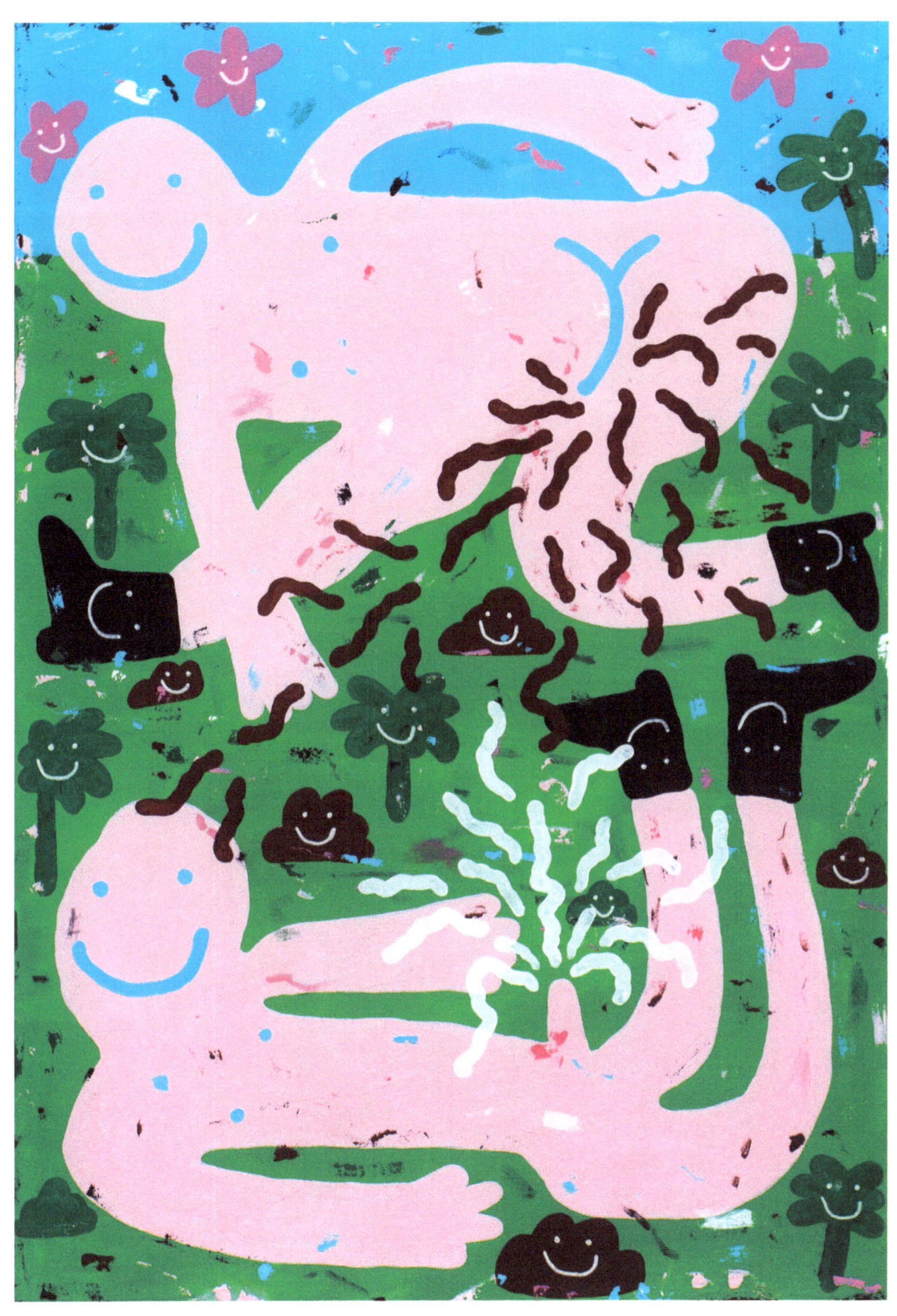

Philip Gerald
Playing with friends in the garden, 2017
Acrylic on canvas
27 x 40in.

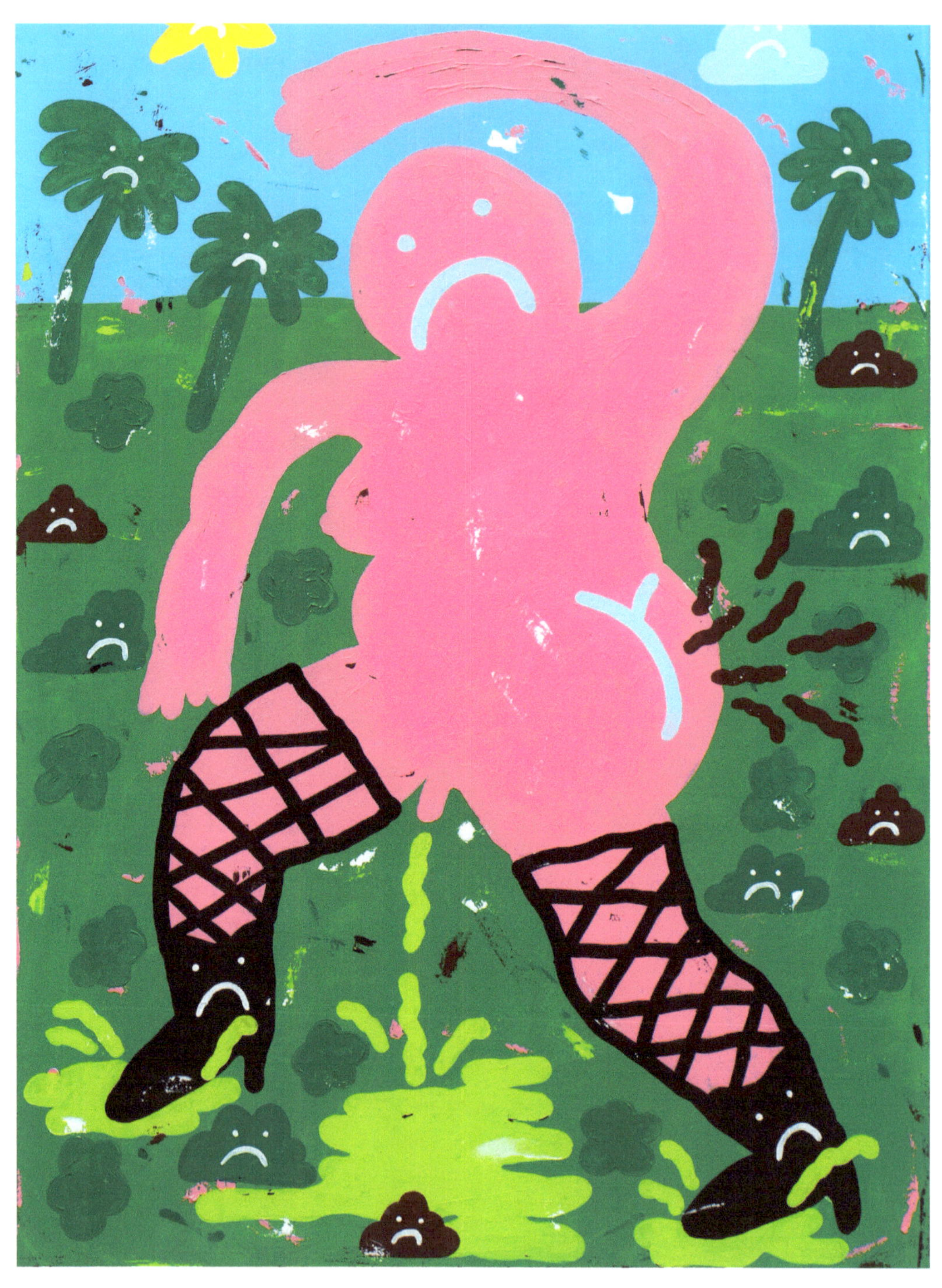

Philip Gerald
Rain Dance, 2017
Acrylic on canvas
27 x 40in.

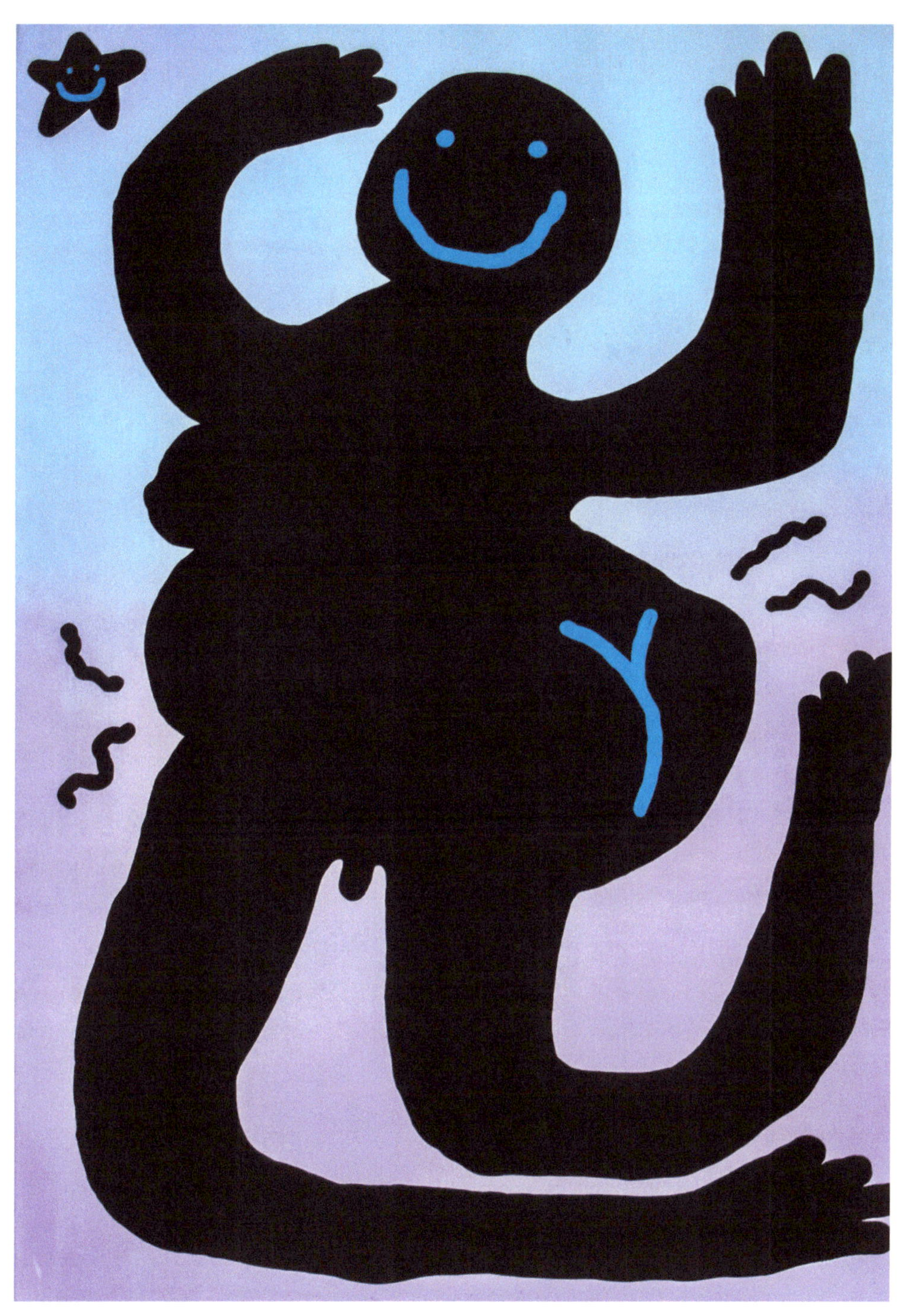

Philip Gerald
Pooper, 2017
Acrylic and oil on canvas
27 x 40in.

Juan Granados

Lubbock, Texas

Art affects everyone differently but serves as a universal language. My work reflects a life of need, growth, and change. Through my work, I attempt to communicate experiences of my past and present environment. I create art in order to share memories both past and present visions of places I've been, concerns about the environment, and observations of the human condition as well.

To do this, I use many different elements from my life and experiences. Subject matter may be difficult to separate and identify, but I try to create work that embodies an intuitive gestalt or the flow and response around an idea.

My reasons for using clay are simple and basic. Clay allows me the total freedom to create work that shares its connections to my background and my experiences of working with the land.

I believe that our past, present, and future conditions and our environment exert considerable influence on our sense of being. In turn, our experiences also affect who we are. My language echoes the origins of the earth. I have worked the land in various parts of the country and have harvested many types of crops and produce. All of this is part of me, and I have enjoyed celebrating these experiences of cultivation. Now I enjoy cultivating clay as a means of expressing ideas connected with human sustainability.

When I first began working as an artist, I found myself struggling with some of the basic art materials; but luckily I began using clay. As I continued to experiment with the versatility of

CONTINUED ON PAGE 130 →

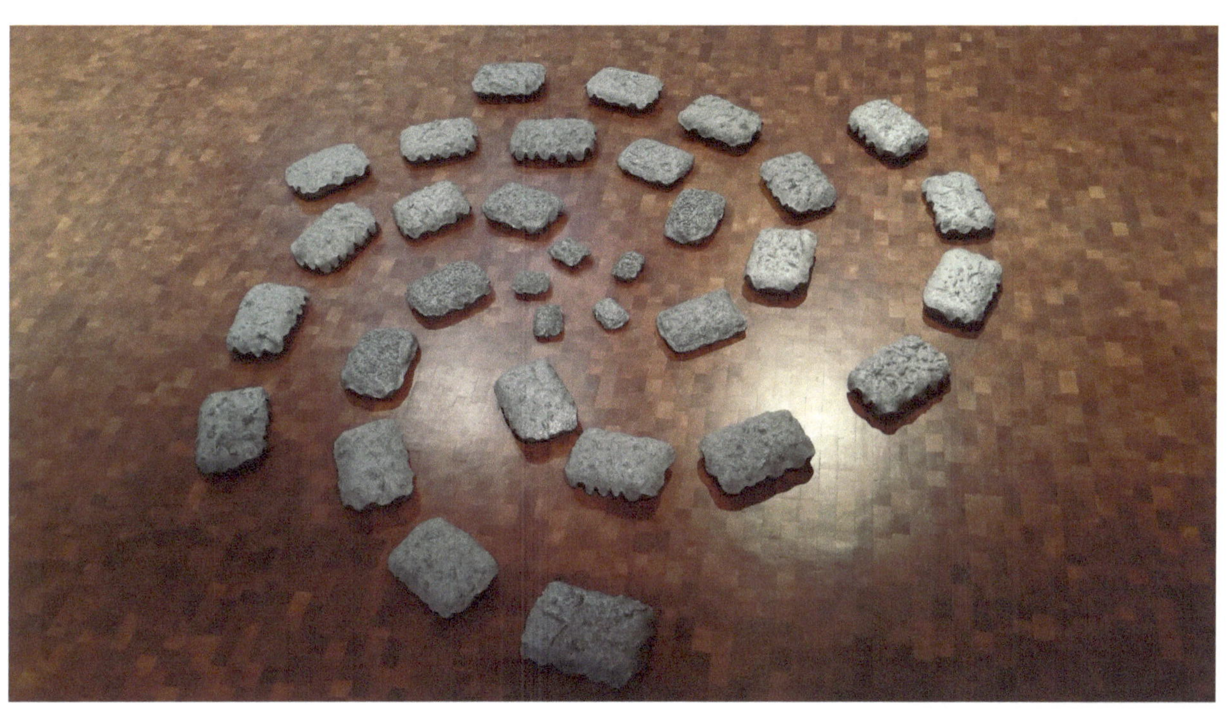

Juan Granados
Galaxia, 2015
Low-fire clay and glaze
420 x 420 x 11 in.

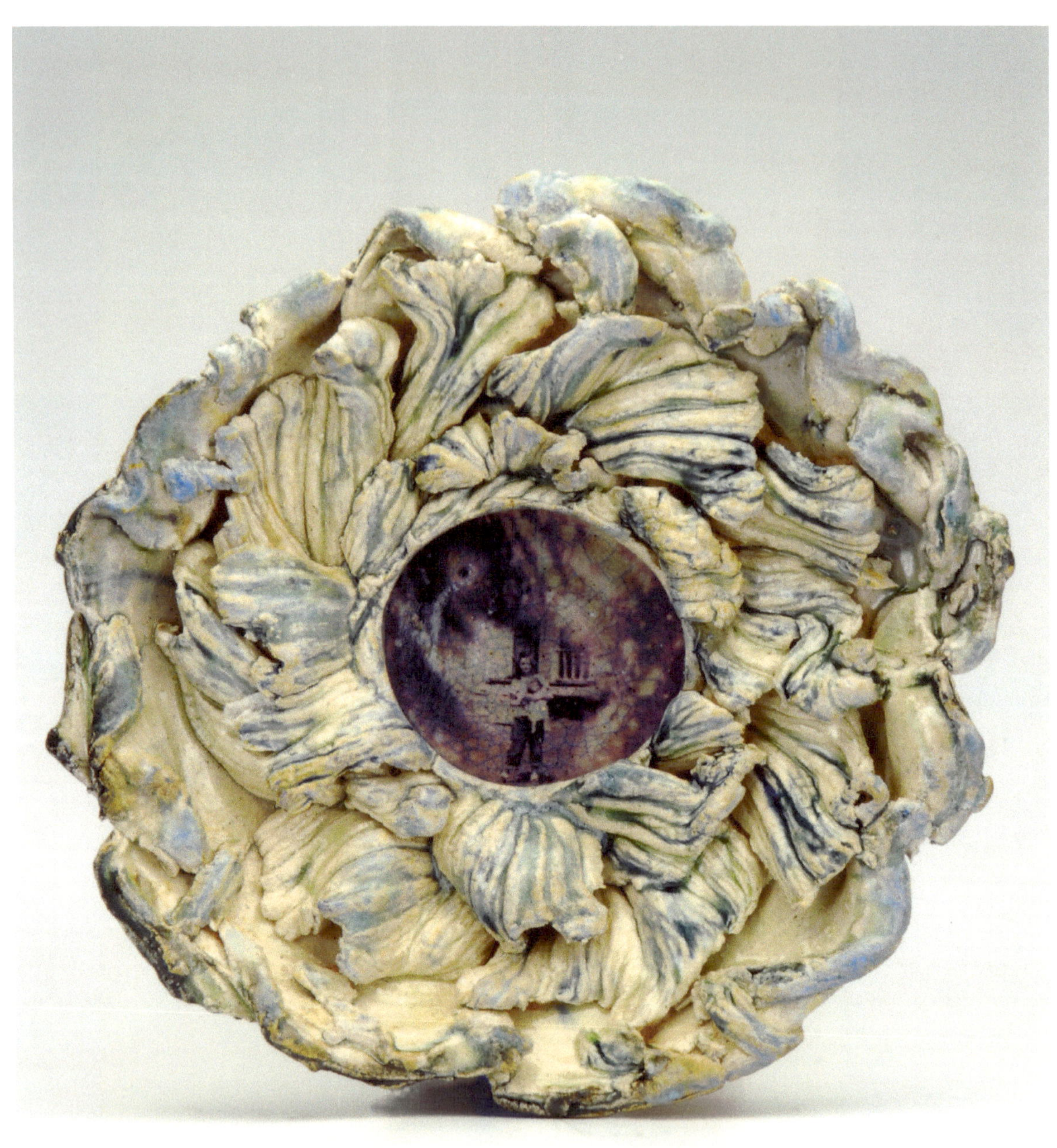

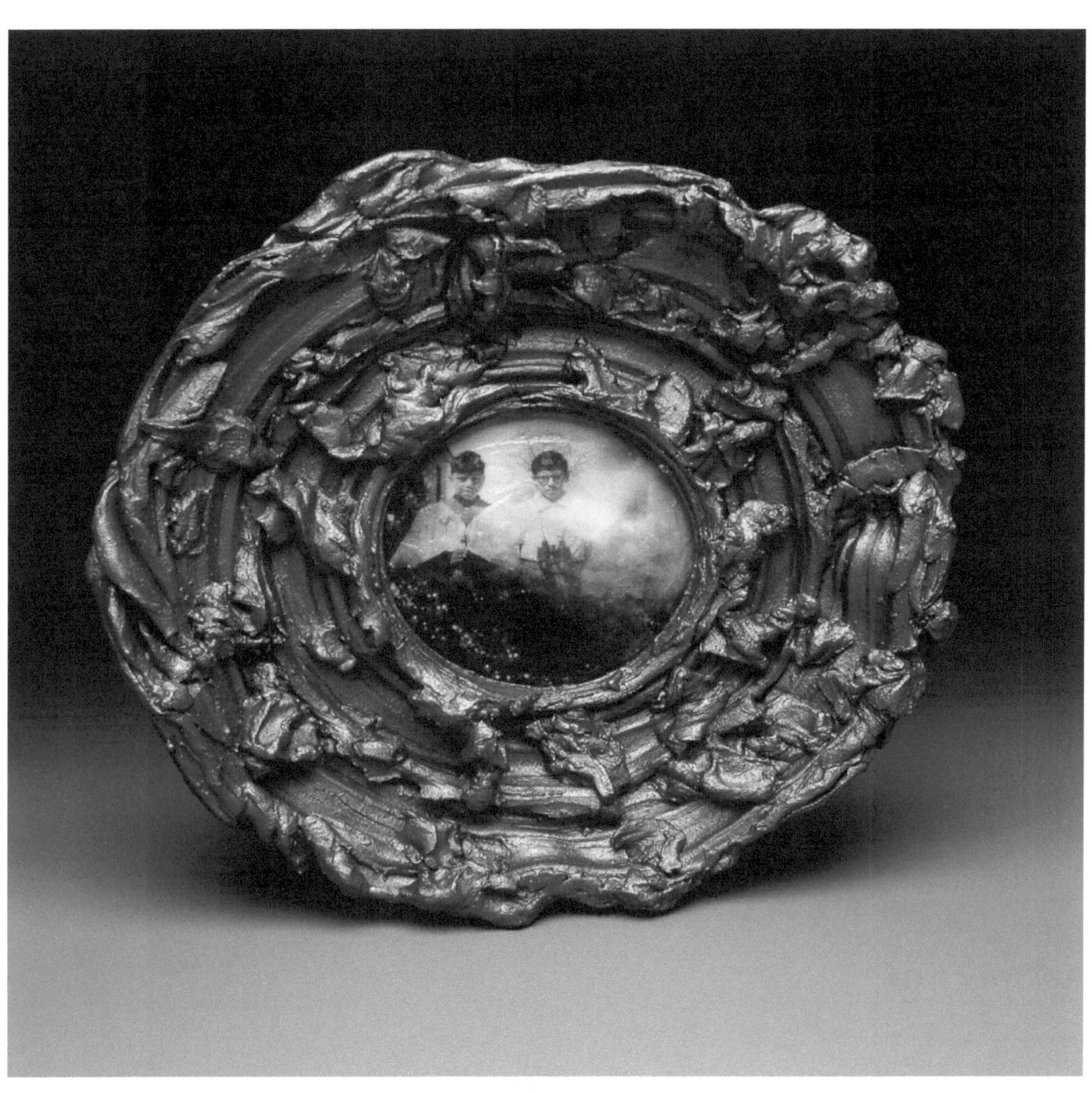

Juan Granados
Buscar: Parte Dos, 2013
Stoneware and metallic oxide pigment, and photo-image transfer
11.5 x 11 x 2.5 in

Nicole Havekost   *Rochester, Minnesota*   nikimade.com

For several years, I have been making figures that are doll-like in form. These stitched and painted bodies, with fragile limbs of sewing and cooking tools, began as an experiment with materials and found objects. These early figures had me excited about the potential of the process; the process of making bodies I had never seen but knew so well. I made another and then another, and somewhere along the way I started making myself.

These bodies feel like me; they are places where I can explore those feelings and desires I don't want to know. The bodies I make can be bloated, unmoored, unseemly, and disfigured. These bodies are allowed to be what I am not. Yet, these bodies also follow a strict set of rules. There is a precision and exactness to their forms that does not allow for a complete and total loss of control. This work is obsessive. There are forms, materials and marks that repeat over and over again. There is an inherent restriction and discipline to the process and outcome that mimics much of my physical experience. I can explore the visual embodiment of a felt sense; I can create a physical representation of my inner dialog. The making of these bodies is the best way for me to come home to my own.

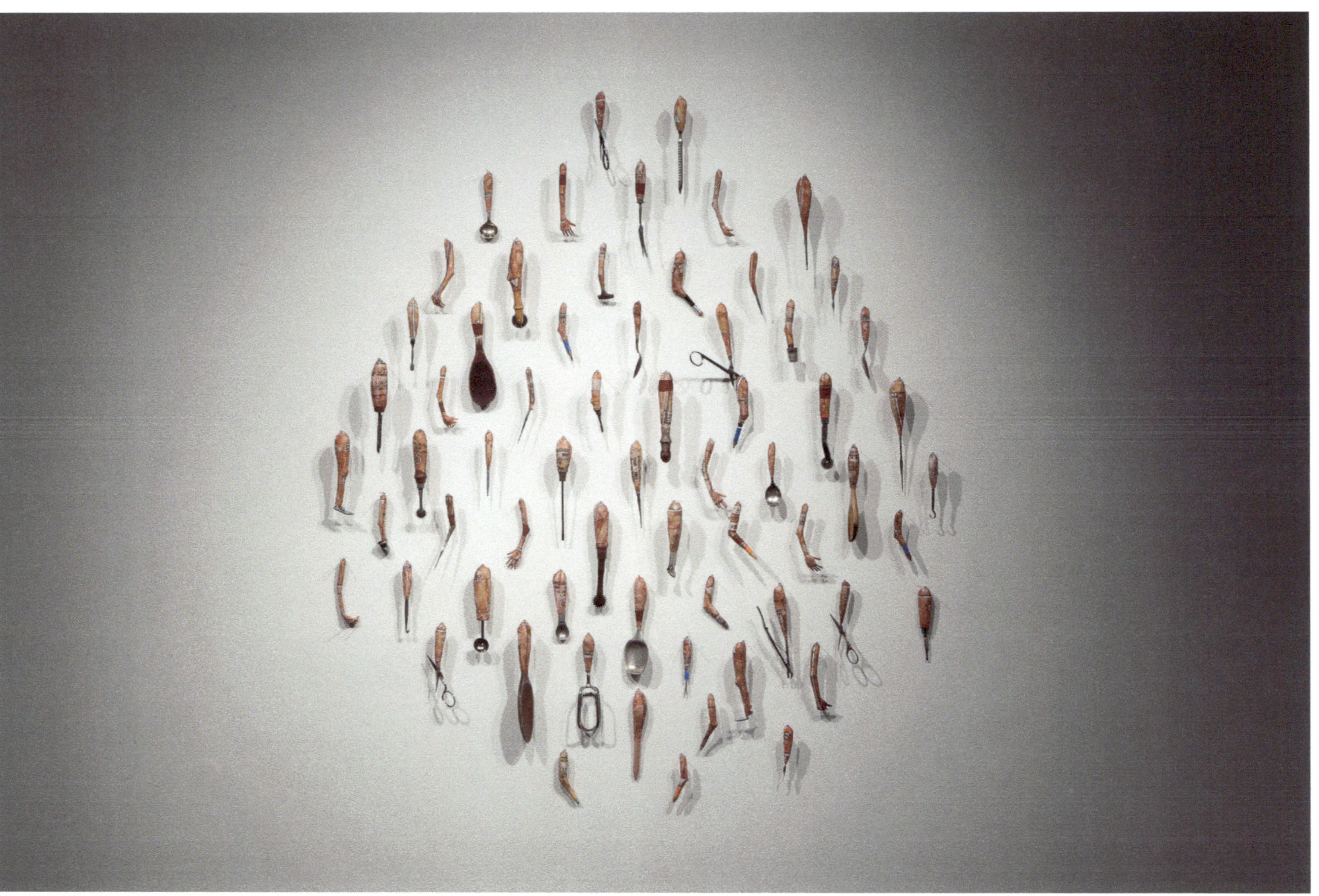

Nicole Havekost
Limbs, 2013
Mixed Media: Paper Clay, sewing pattern paper, acrylic paint, ball point pen, cotton thread, sewing hardware, found objects
54 x 48in.

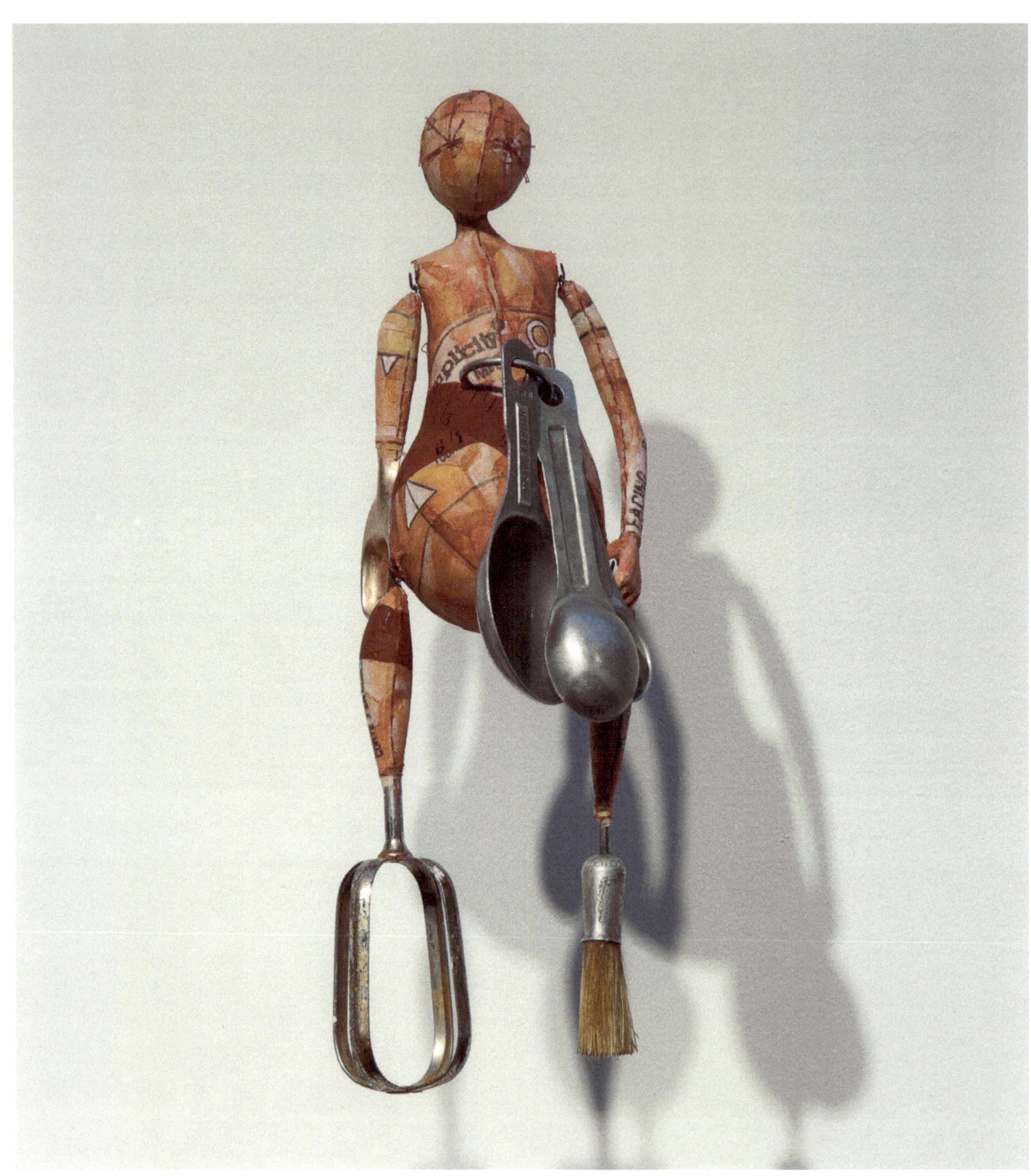

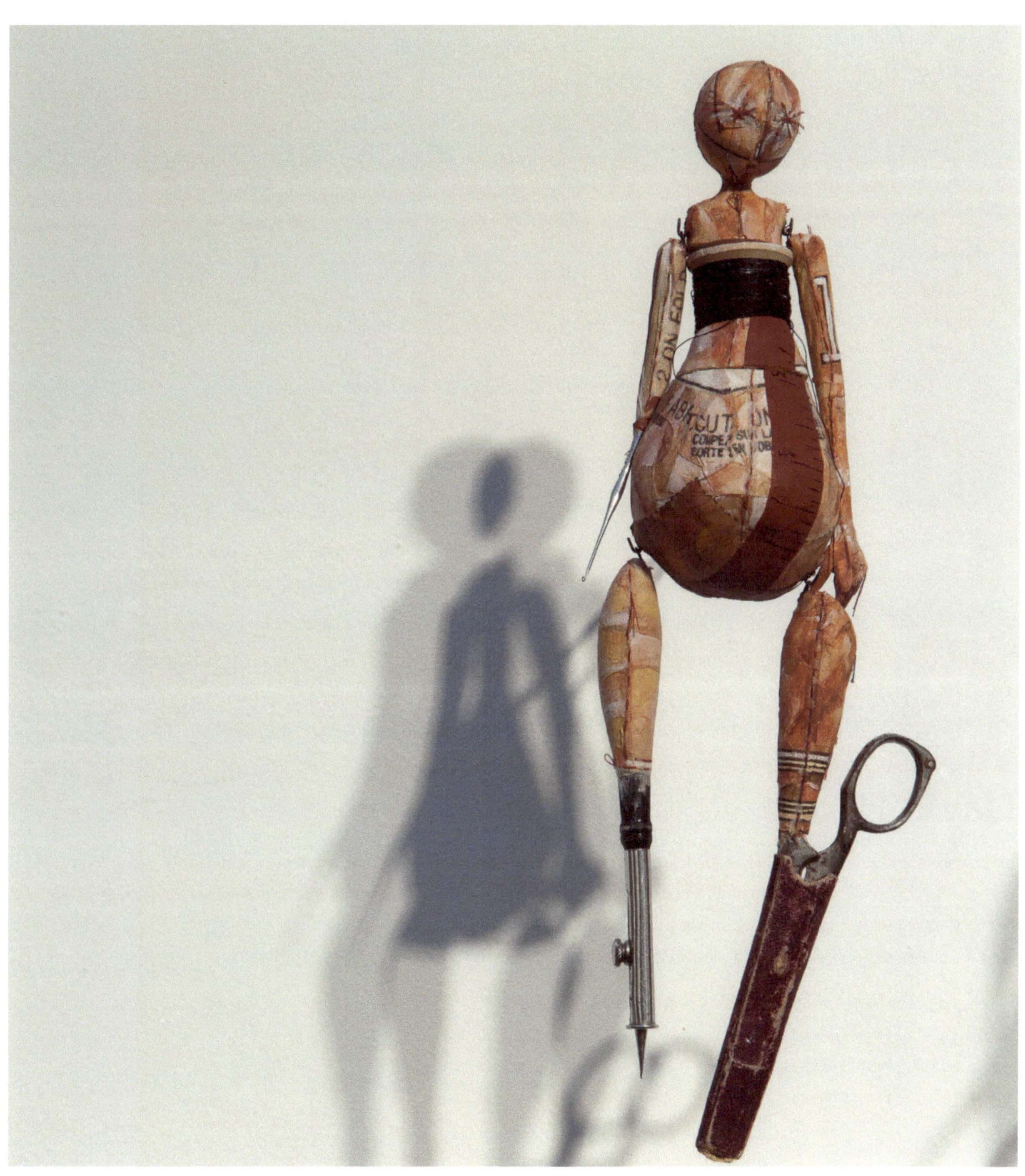

Nicole Havekost
Spool, 2013
Mix media and found objects
11.5 x 1.75 x 1.75 in.

David Heo

Chicago, Illinois   davidheo.com

My practice is a mixture of personal narratives and being voyeuristic. This duality is a reflection of my experiences and observations on moments of, casual intimacy, nightlife culture, pleasure and leisure and grandiose or mundane desires. I usually describe my work as a visual manifestation of the weekend.

I've always been captivated with the idea of people looking forward to decompressing or relieving themselves. It's wild to see how people enthusiastically attempt to chase the idea of "fun." The energy that comes out during the night is so contagious and sincere, and that energy is what influences my work.

I depict this energy using intensely vibrant colors, objective forms and figures that are usually presented in uncommon contexts and compositions. The rhythm of nightlife and desires is the foundation for my work. From my experience, time never feels linear and composed when you go out. It's always fading in and out, swaying and dancing. Your eyes embrace so many details of the night and before you know it, it's late and you want to go home and sleep. I think this example of physical sensation is one of the many influences for how my work is composed, structured and presented.

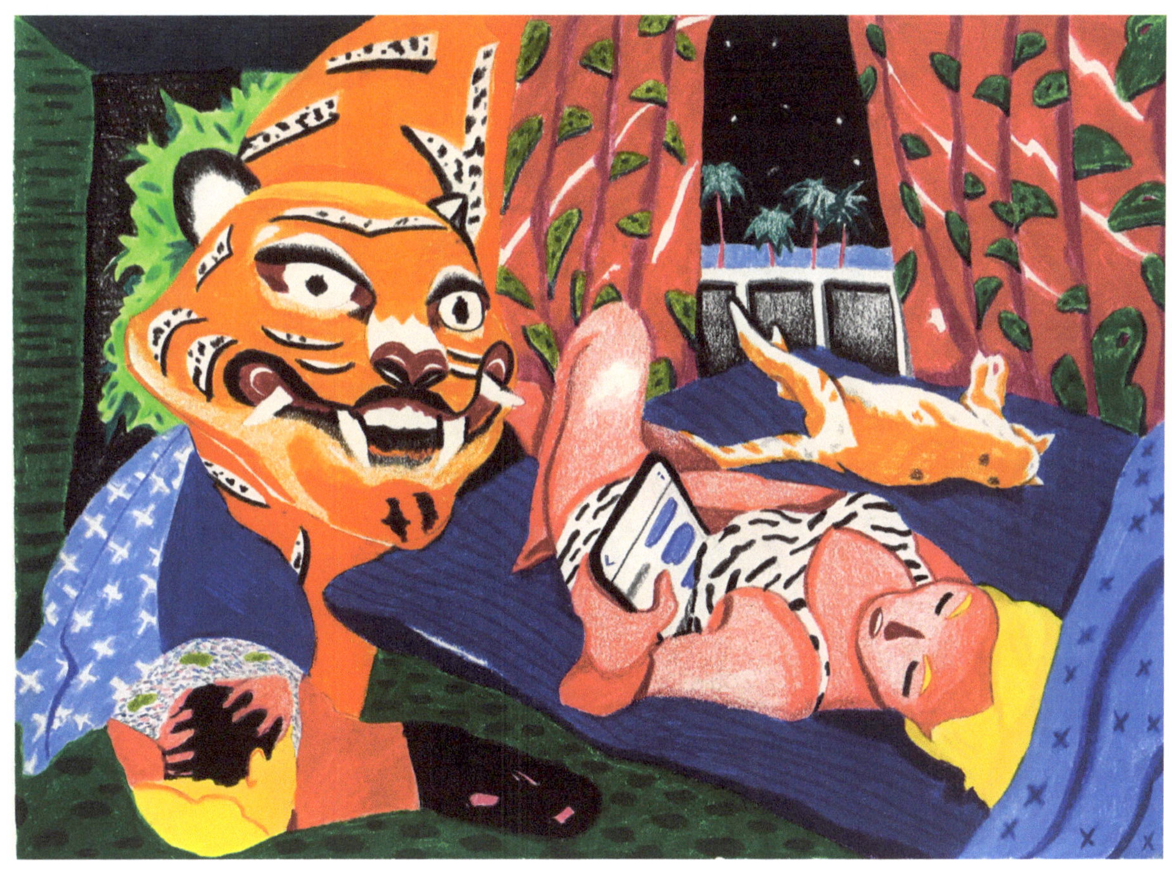

David Heo
Rebounds, 2017
Colored pencil on paper
8 x 11in.

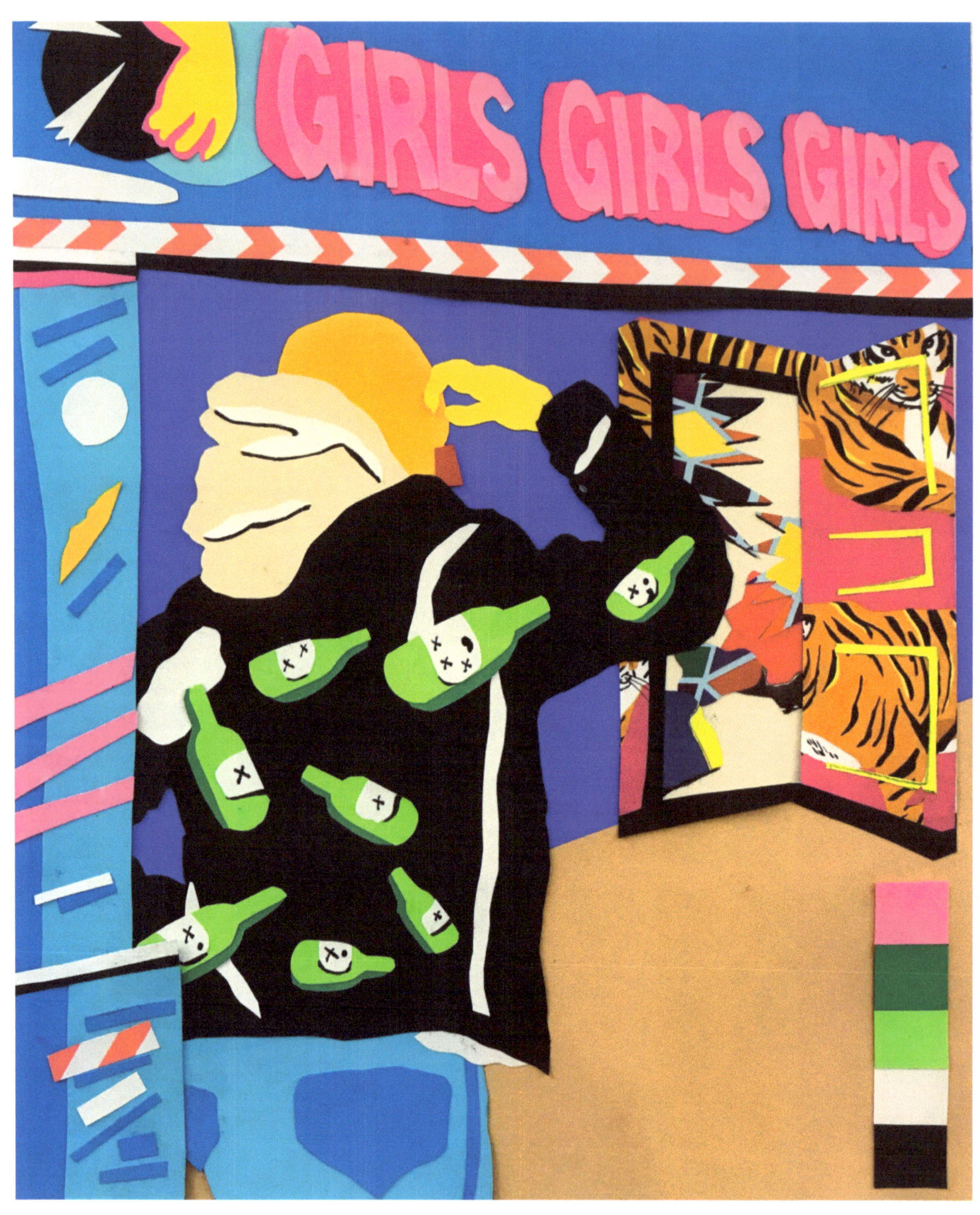

David Heo
Bustle, 2017
pigmented paper cutouts
9 × 13 in.

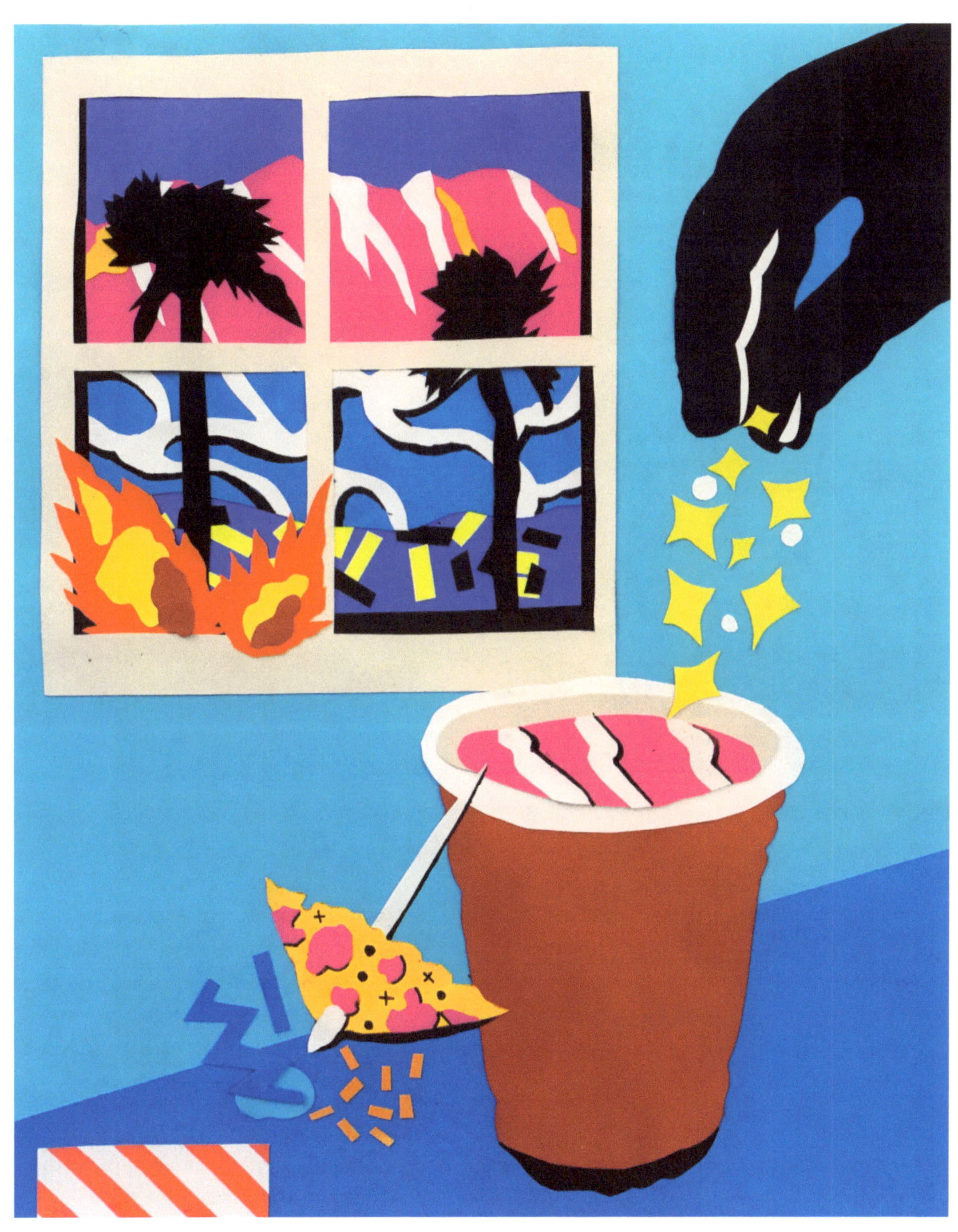

Katie Kameen

Richmond, Indiana   katiekameen.com

My sculptures are the result of discovering life in objects that have outlived their intended functions. I am interested in the potential of everyday objects to communicate with us, through us, and to help us communicate with others. I draw from my own experiences, relationships, and emotional growth to find new ways to communicate with old materials.

Our daily routines depend on an assortment of items. Our reliance on these objects becomes a source of both strain and neglect, causing us to value them less as they break down, and eventually discard them. Although they become forgotten, they remain imprinted with our memories. For this reason, my chosen materials originate from the 1950s to the 1980s, which coincides with; my parent's lives and my early childhood. Old tools remind me of helping my dad in the garage or gardening with my mom, and vintage cookware reminds me of my grandmother's kitchen. These recollections are triggered by both material and color. I use mid-century pigments, plastics, and fibers to create common ground between the dormant object, its past function, and the present viewer. As I discover the messages embedded in my objects, they transform into vessels of communication, each one bringing its own story and culminating with a larger abstract message. Instead of acquiescing to the end of their usefulness these items embrace their beauty, captivate our attention, and incite our memory and imagination.

I gravitate towards things that have or had a function; they are not purely decorative. Though they are no longer actively used, they continue to speak about our habits, and by giving them a new purpose they can simultaneously communicate their history and embrace their future. CONTINUED ON PAGE 130 →

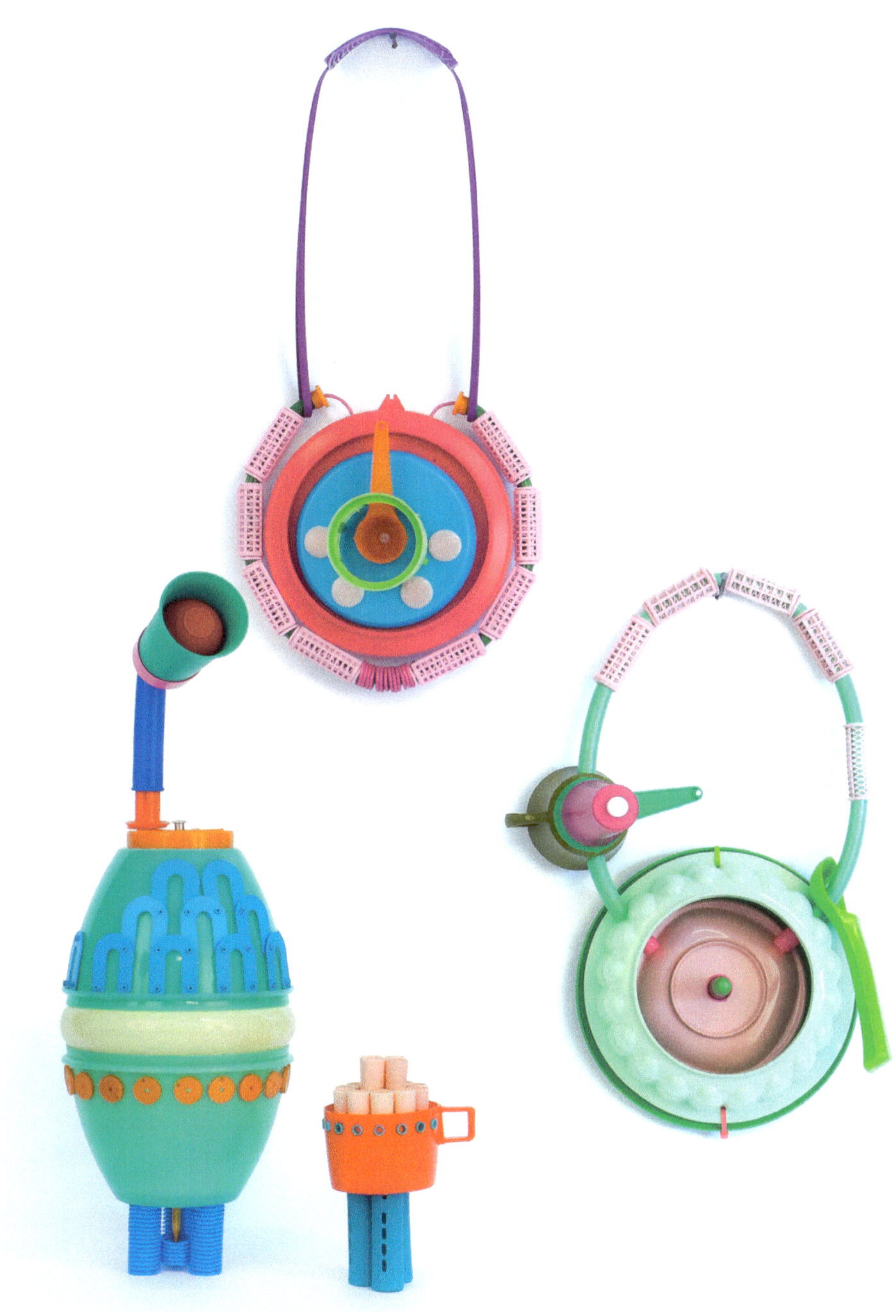

Katie Kameen
Posture, 2017
plastic objects, rubber tubing
dimensions variable

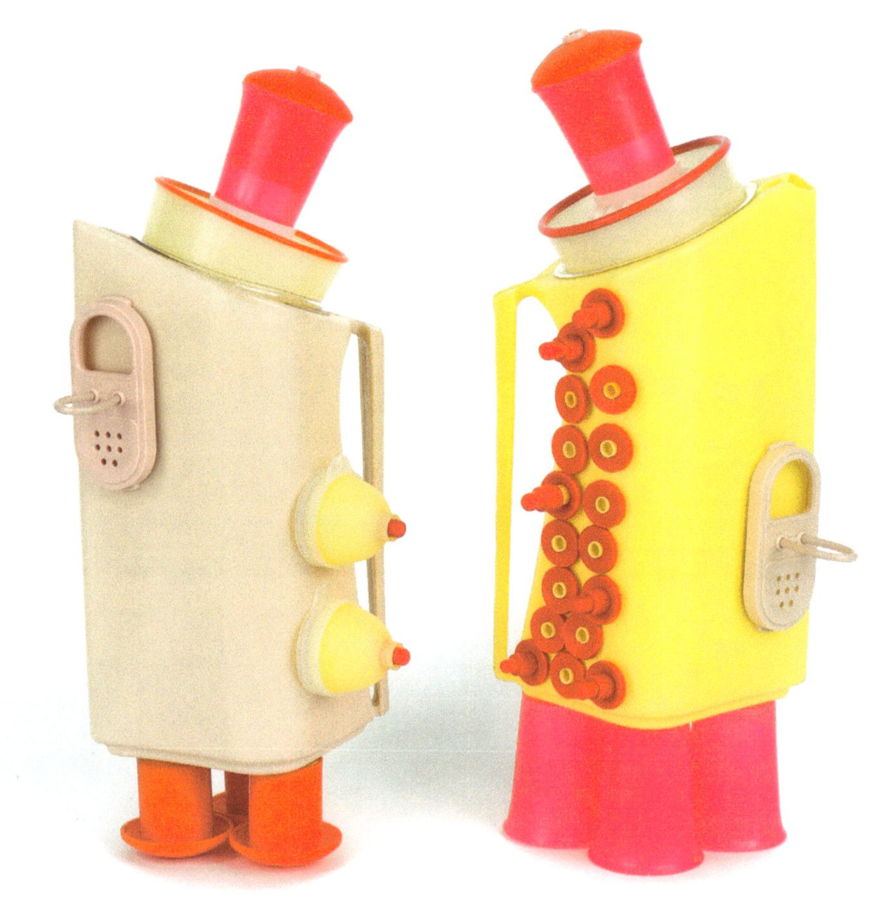

Katie Kameen
Encounter, 2017
Plastic objects
17 x 16.5 x 7in.

Friend of The Artist

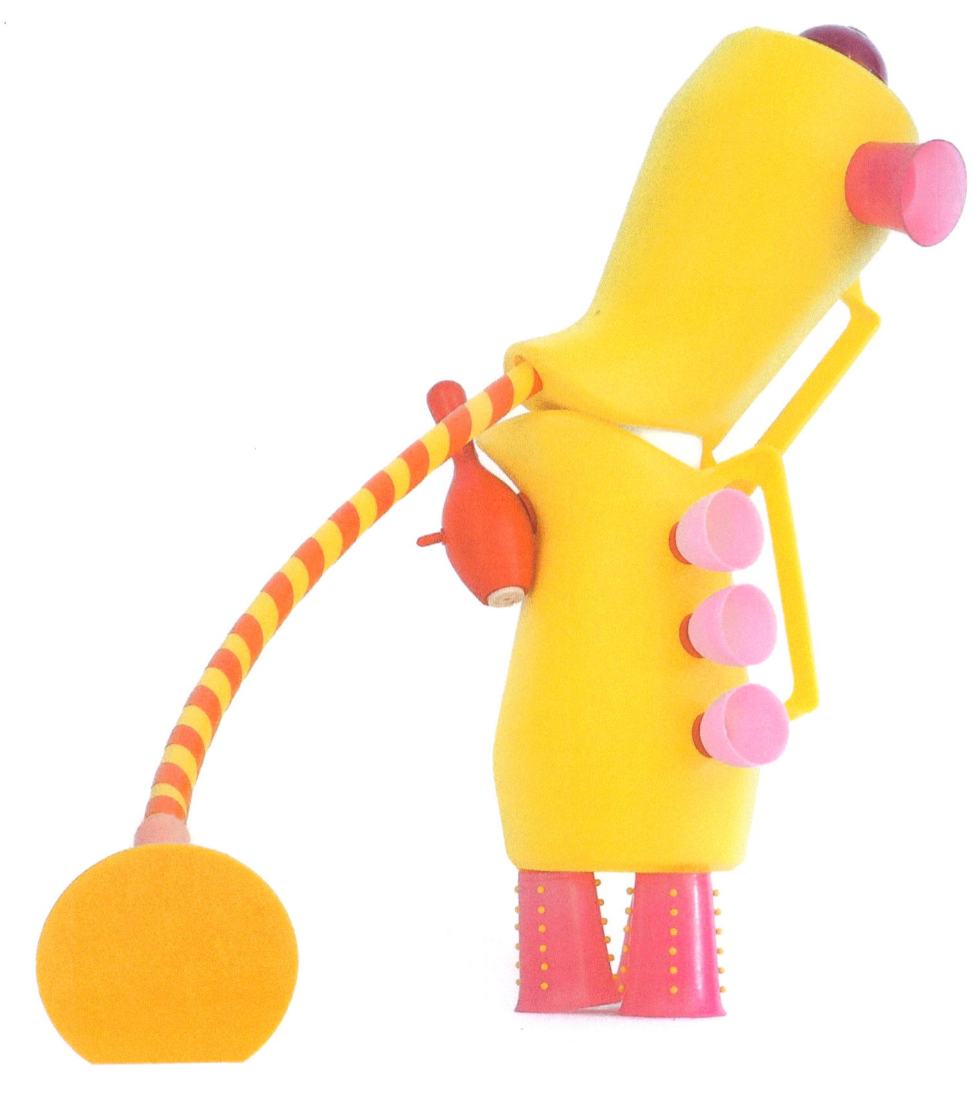

Katie Kameen
Straw, 2017
plastic objects
z25 x 30 x 26in.

Lara Nasser

Brookyln, NY   aranasser.com

There are direct breaches of social code: the deviant, the revolutionary, the ones incapable of abiding. I'm interested rather in those who cooperate most of the way. Using our differences as measuring sticks and etiquette as a lifebuoy, we usually bob peacefully over uncomfortable situations. Familiar symbols like warning signs and name tags organize us further. Most of us have schedules and habits, jobs and memberships. But these cozy structures themselves cause anxiety when their participants try and fail.

Living between Beirut and New York, I often observe a contrast of strategies for maintaining (or resuming) societal norms. Conflict arises, accompanied by embarrassment, hesitation, botched attempts and power struggles. As these tensions spill over invisible walls meant to keep us regulated and safe, there is an opportunity to question those walls. There is also usually an opportunity to laugh. From the macro level of political turmoil to my own personal insecurities, I playfully recreate these systems and their participants as we tumble through a sliding scale of breakdowns.

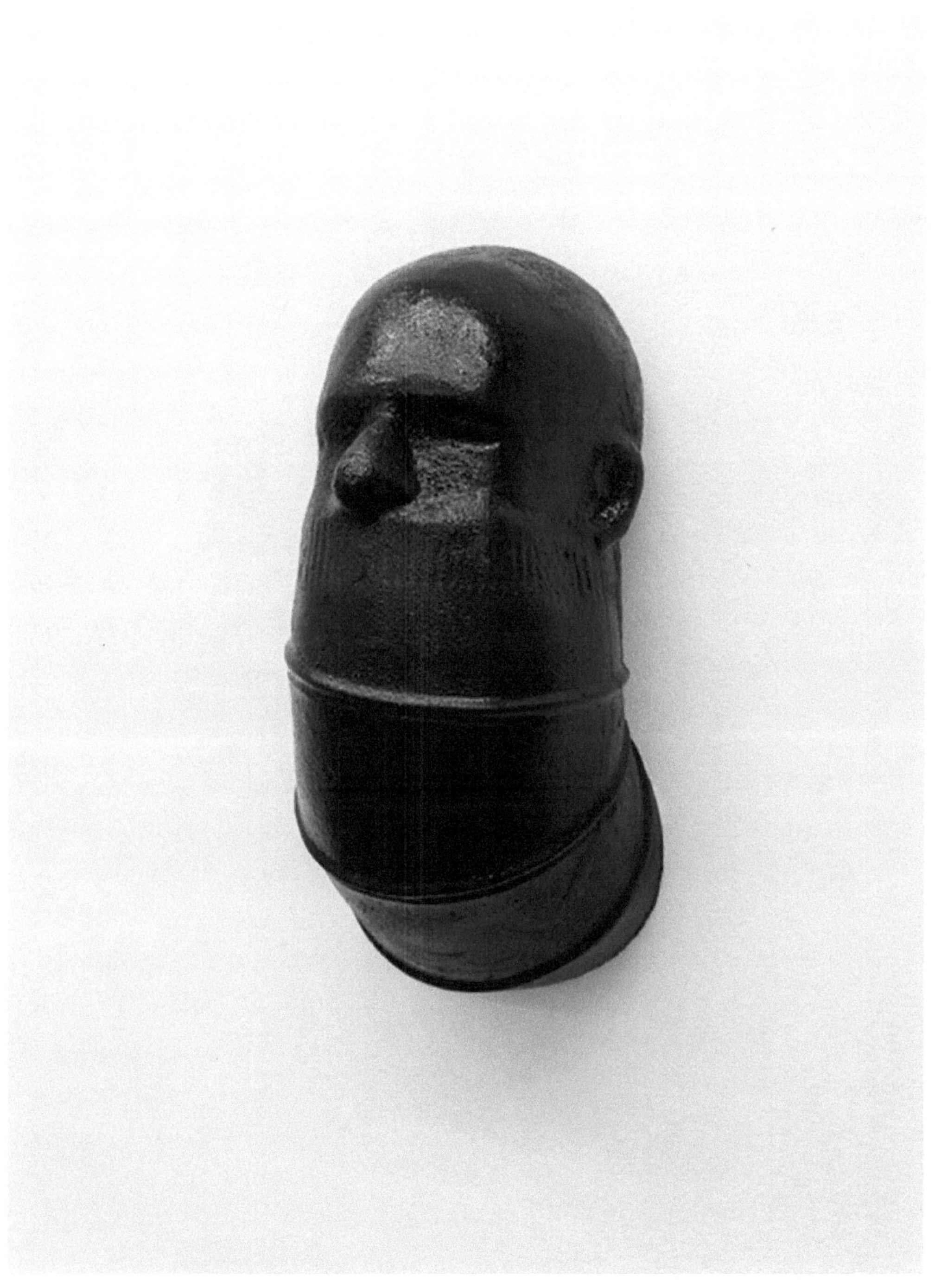

Lara Nasser
Agrippa, Is That You?, 2017
Plaster, shellac
16.5 x 7.5 x 8in.

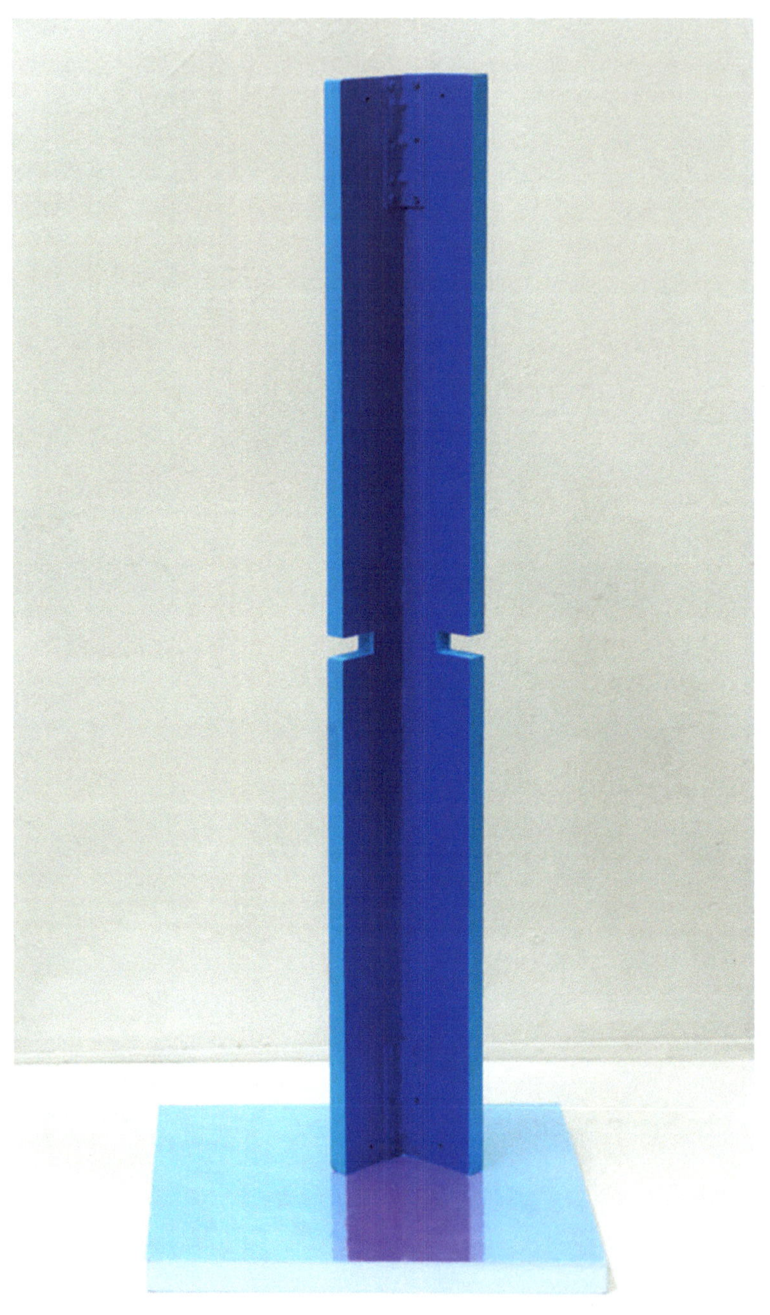

Lara Nasser
Pseudo-Seneca / Self-Sabotage; 2016
Wood, paint, mylar
31.5 x 12 x 12in.

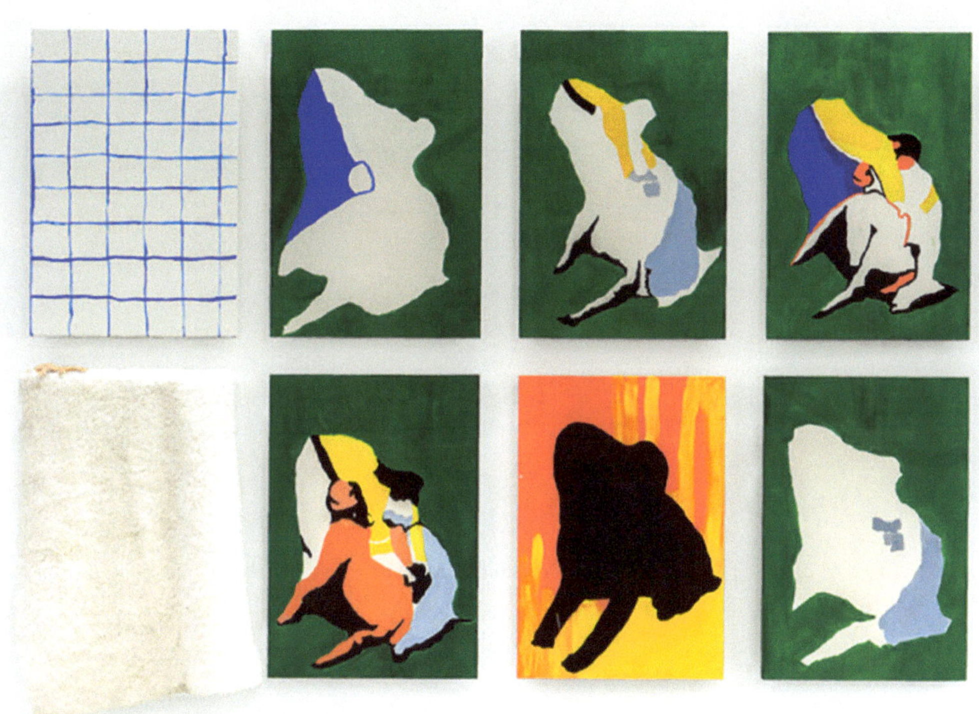

Lara Nasser
Shear, 2016
Acrylic, shellac, fake fleece on canvas;
8 paintings (12 x18in. each)

Esteban Pulido

Los Angeles, California   esteban-pulido.com

In analyzing the techniques of police in big cities, Jonathan Rubinstein points out that the "patrolman learns that he has the right to stare at anyone for as long as he wants" because officers look at people for insight into their intentions in ways that civilians cannot. Photography offers a similar right. It allows the viewer to stare, to look with a held gaze and burning intent, to see the topography of a person's skin, the accumulations under their fingernails, every stray piece of hair. We look as if by staring we can actually reveal something about them.

As an artist working in photography and interested in creating concrete yet theoretical photographic objects, I prod at and with photography to create highly detailed images that present the viewer with what Hal Foster via Ben Lerner calls "the utopian glimmer of fiction." The photographs don't deconstruct reality; they are built-up images that signify more than what they directly represent.

They are what Jeanne Randolph calls amenable objects. Their meaning is neither explicit nor disguised; the viewer's reading neither reality nor fantasy; the evidence presented neither inner nor outer. The photographs offer no reassurance; they will absorb any story, including the next contradictory story.

Esteban Pulido received an MFA from the School of the Art Institute of Chicago in 2012 and a BFA from the University of Oklahoma in 2009. His work has been exhibited in New York, Chicago, Kansas, Oklahoma, São Paulo and most recently in a solo exhibition in Los Angeles. Pulido was born in Venezuela. He lives and works in Los Angeles.

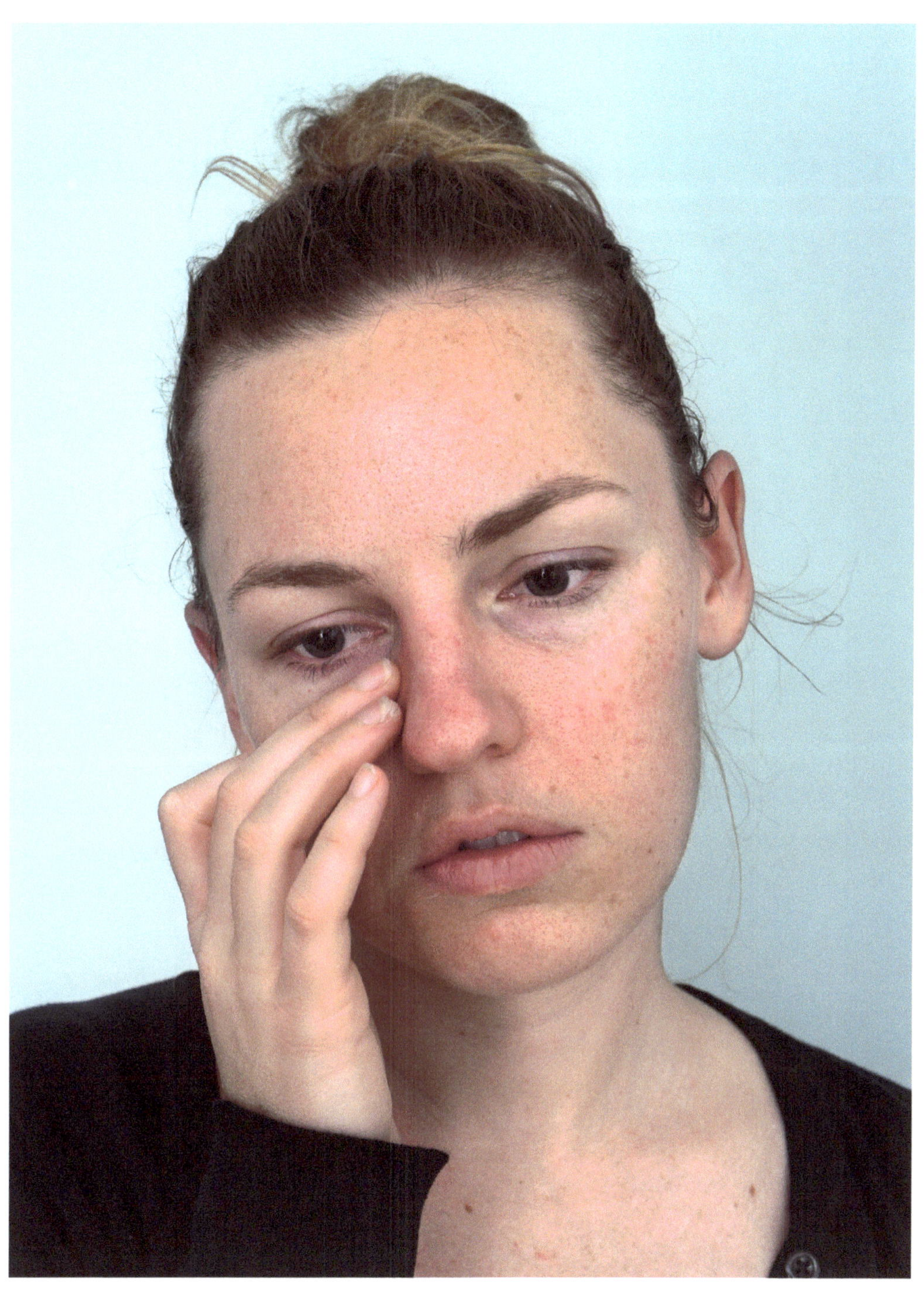

Esteban Pulido
Patrolmen 2, 2017
pigment print
17 x 23in.

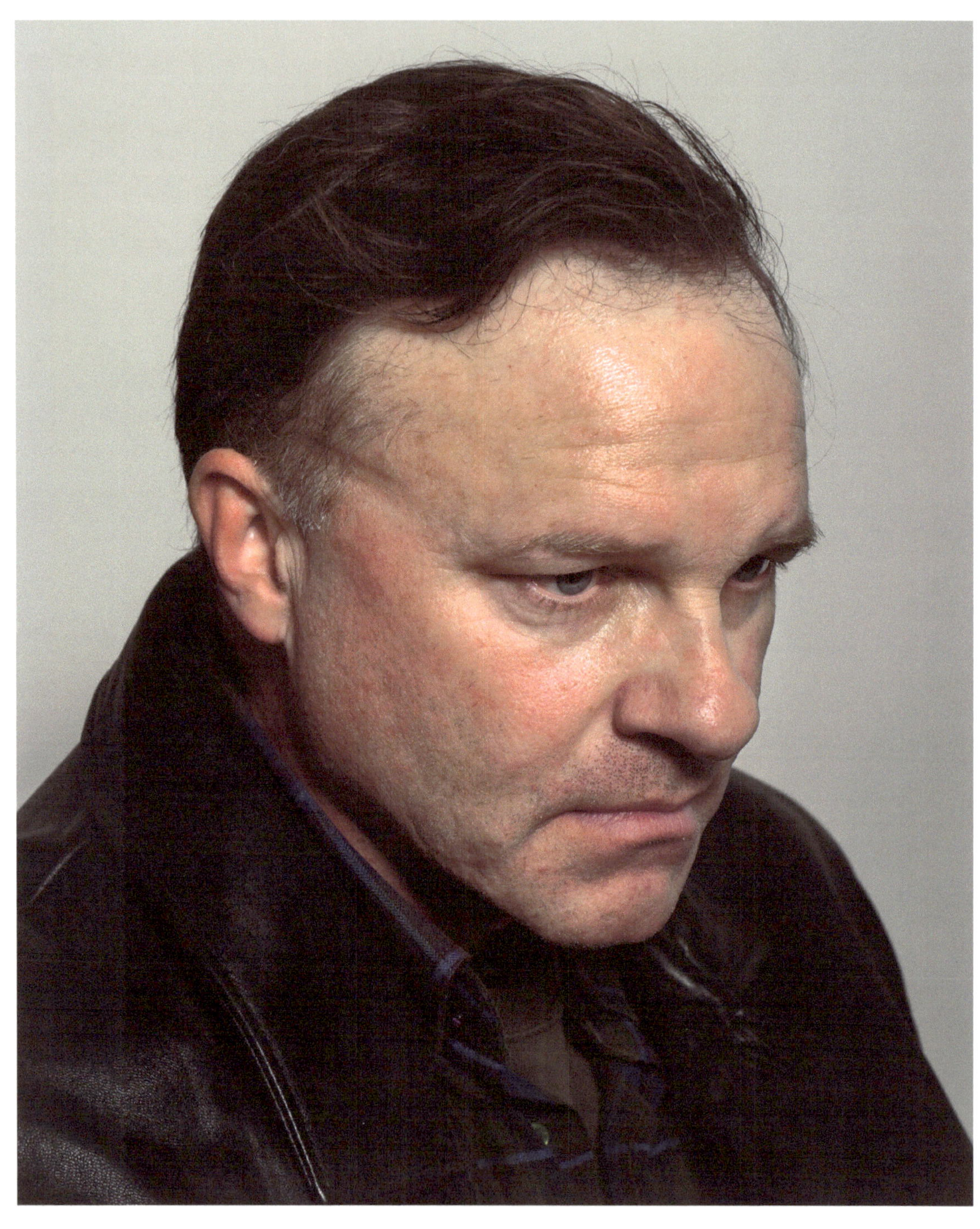

Esteban Pulido
Patrolmen 2, 2017
pigment print
19 x 23In.

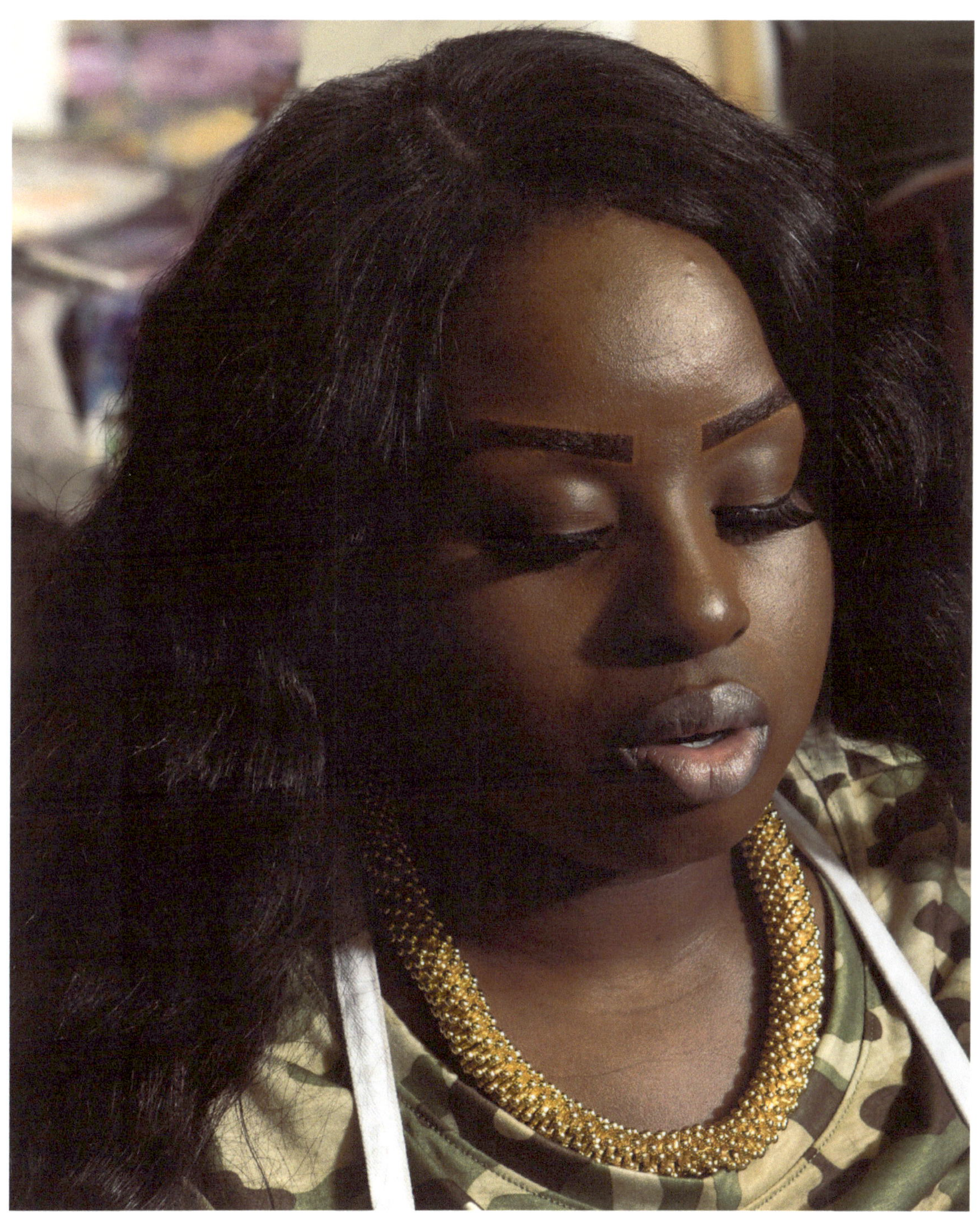

Esteban Pulido
Actual Gain, 2014
pigment print
30 x 40in.

Mary Raap   *Brooklyn, NY*

My current work focuses on exercises in labor and form, including interactions
between historically gendered media or approaches, such as feminine
sewing and masculine abstract painting. I'm interested in investigating the
assumptions around production and bringing nuanced attention to ideas
around "women's work". At turns looking at textiles, weaving drafts, minimalist
and abstractexpressionist work, the resulting compositions remind me of the
body, movement inenvironments, and complex ecosystems.

I think of gender expectations that have been shifting and the changing forms
of female-identifying l abor and wonder where I fit in the current world or in
my family: my grandmother, a farmer and teacher who had eight children; my
mother, a small business owner who also had eight children, and then myself—
on a different trajectory. I'm interested in envisioning a connection between
my sewing-painting-labor and that of my foremothers, while subverting the
stereotypically masculine act of abstract painting into a broader vocabulary.

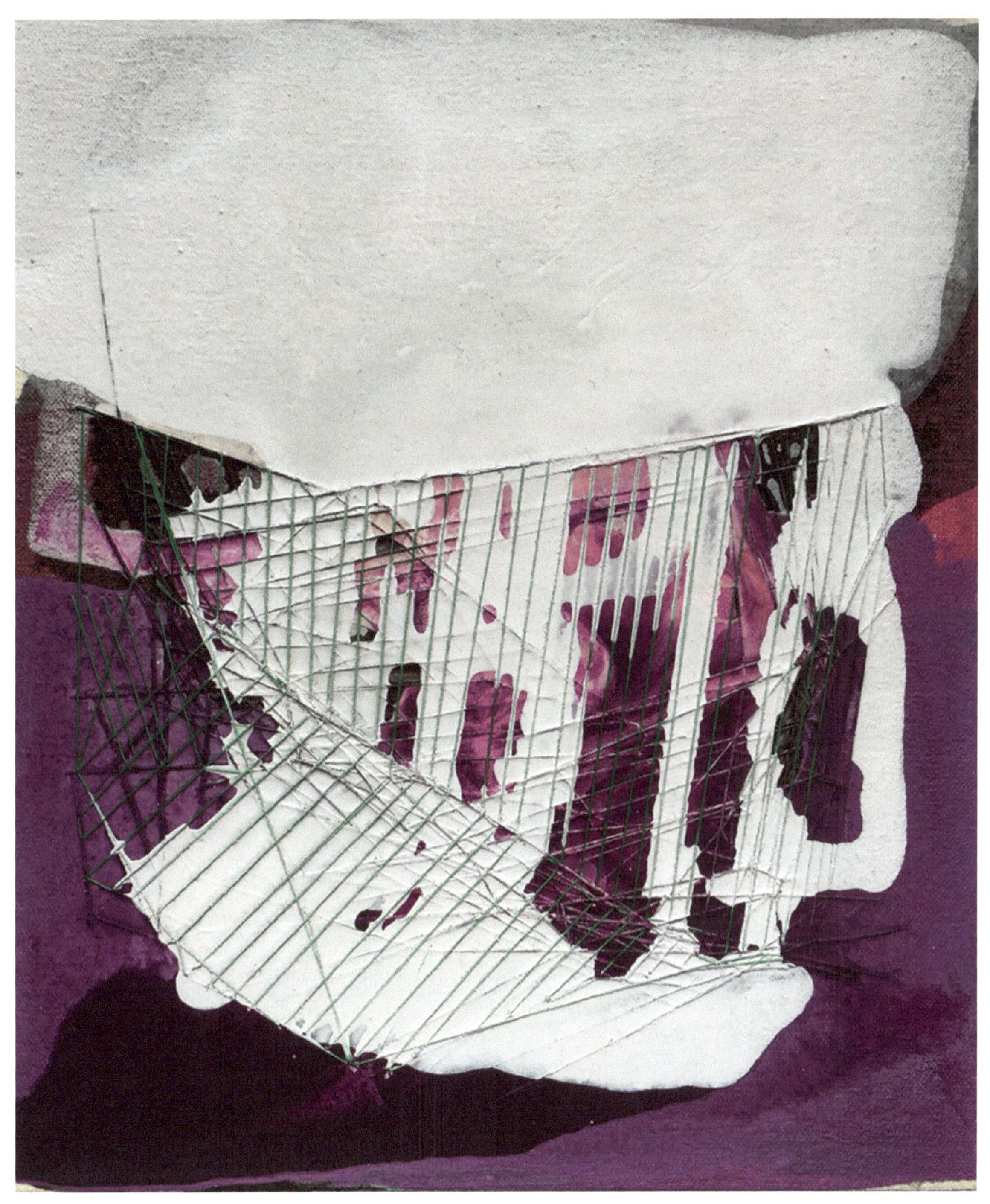

Mary Raap
Royal, 2017
Thread, acrylic, and gouache on canvas
8 x 10in.

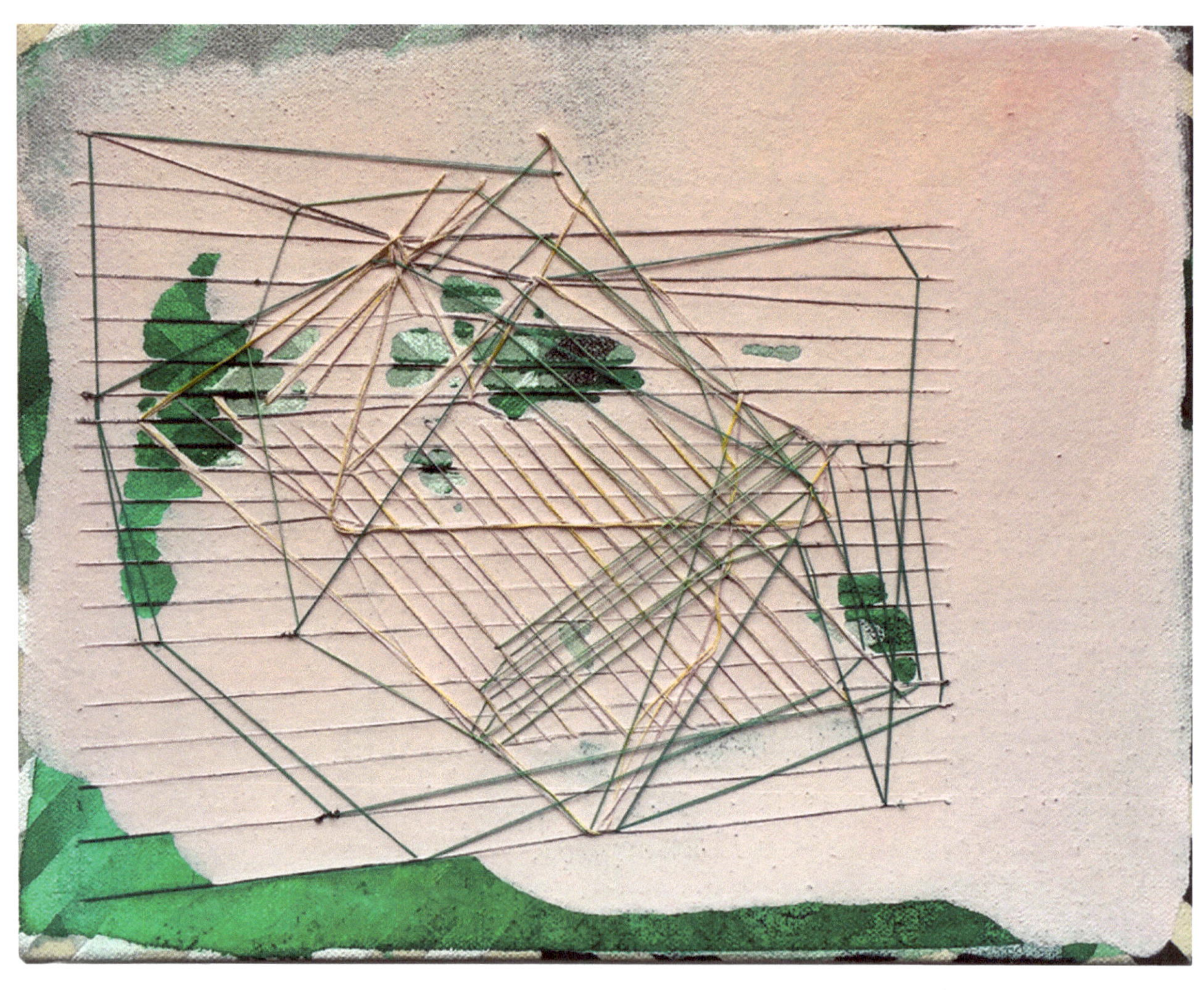

Mary Raap
Highline, 2017
Thread, acrylic, & gouache on canvas
8 x 10in.

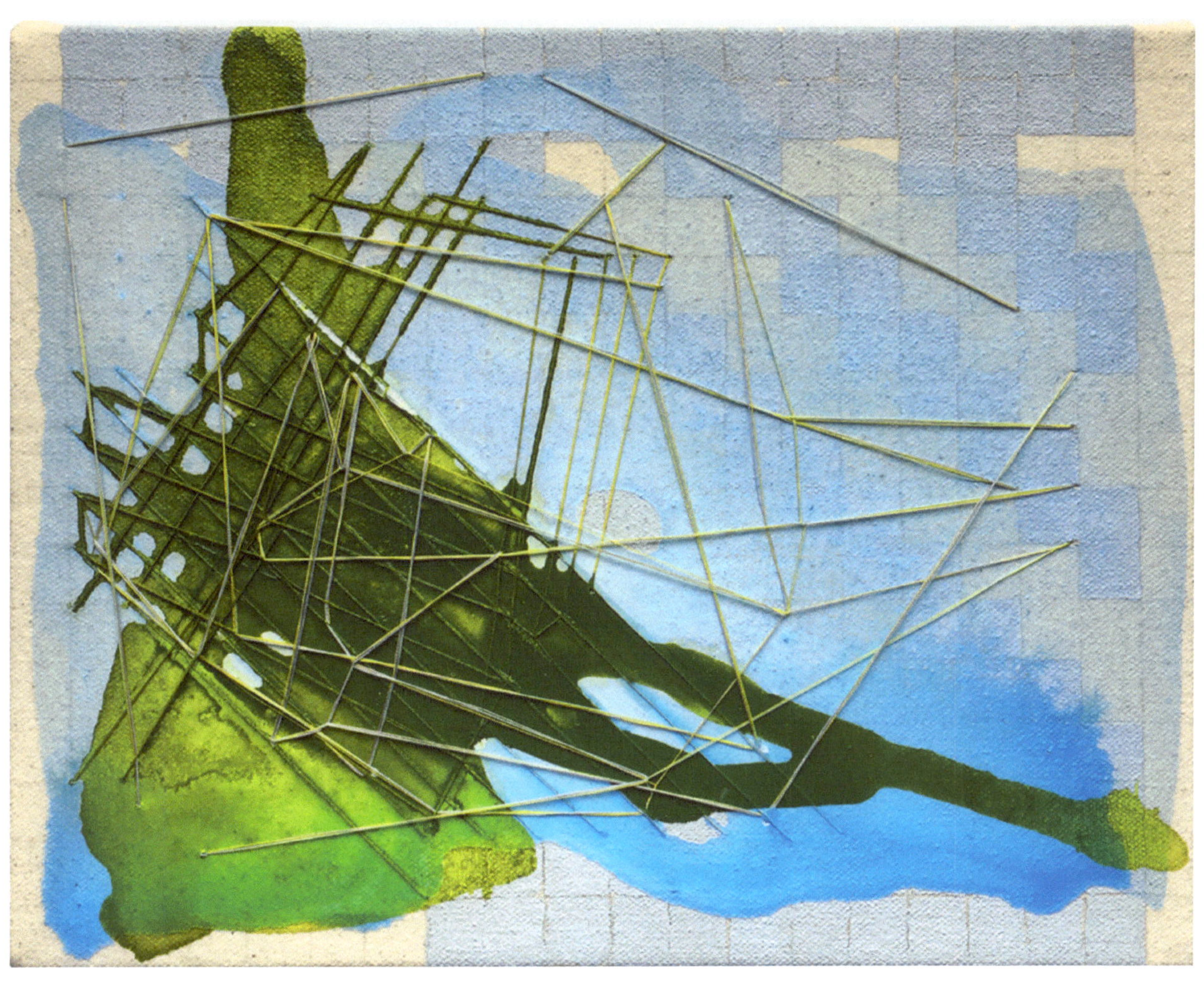

Mary Raap
Baby Blue, 2017
Thread, acrylic, gouache, and graphite on canvas
8 x 10in.

Anya Rosen

Aldie, Virginia anyarosen.com

My current body of work "Land For Sale by Owner: The Romance of the Exurbs" explores the rapid turnover of rural farmland to suburban homeland in Loudoun County, Virginia.

When I moved to Loudoun County I was disappointed. The sameness of the houses and the newness of the fabricated landscapes felt void of character. Machines worked diligently in the background, shredding the natural habitat mindlessly, shaping the monotonous scenery that was unfolding in every direction. Yet, there was a level of transparency to the region that surprised me, as if you arrived at a restaurant and saw dirty cookware scattered about the dining room. Neon orange fencing, stacks of plywood, and road work signs broke the continuity; empty plots sat awkwardly midst rows of finished houses like gap teeth.

It was by way of this transparency that I was eventually able to embrace my new home. After months spent watching my surroundings evolve, I came to value the opportunity of living in such close proximity to this radical overhaul of the landscape. I was witnessing a pivotal moment in the history of the place. I was able to see simultaneously what the land once was, and what it was about to become.

I am driven by the notion that death and birth are not discernible moments but processes. Still, my desire to capture evidence of these perceived singular occurrences is insatiable. I am afraid to die but equally afraid of living in denial of my mortality. Identifying the exact "time of death", however hypothetical, is a kind of paranoid reassurance that I, and the contemporary society in which I am a part, will one day cease to exist. My obsession with collecting evidence indicating a passage of time serves as a reminder that the world will continue on.

My work regards the absurdity of permanence in the natural world.

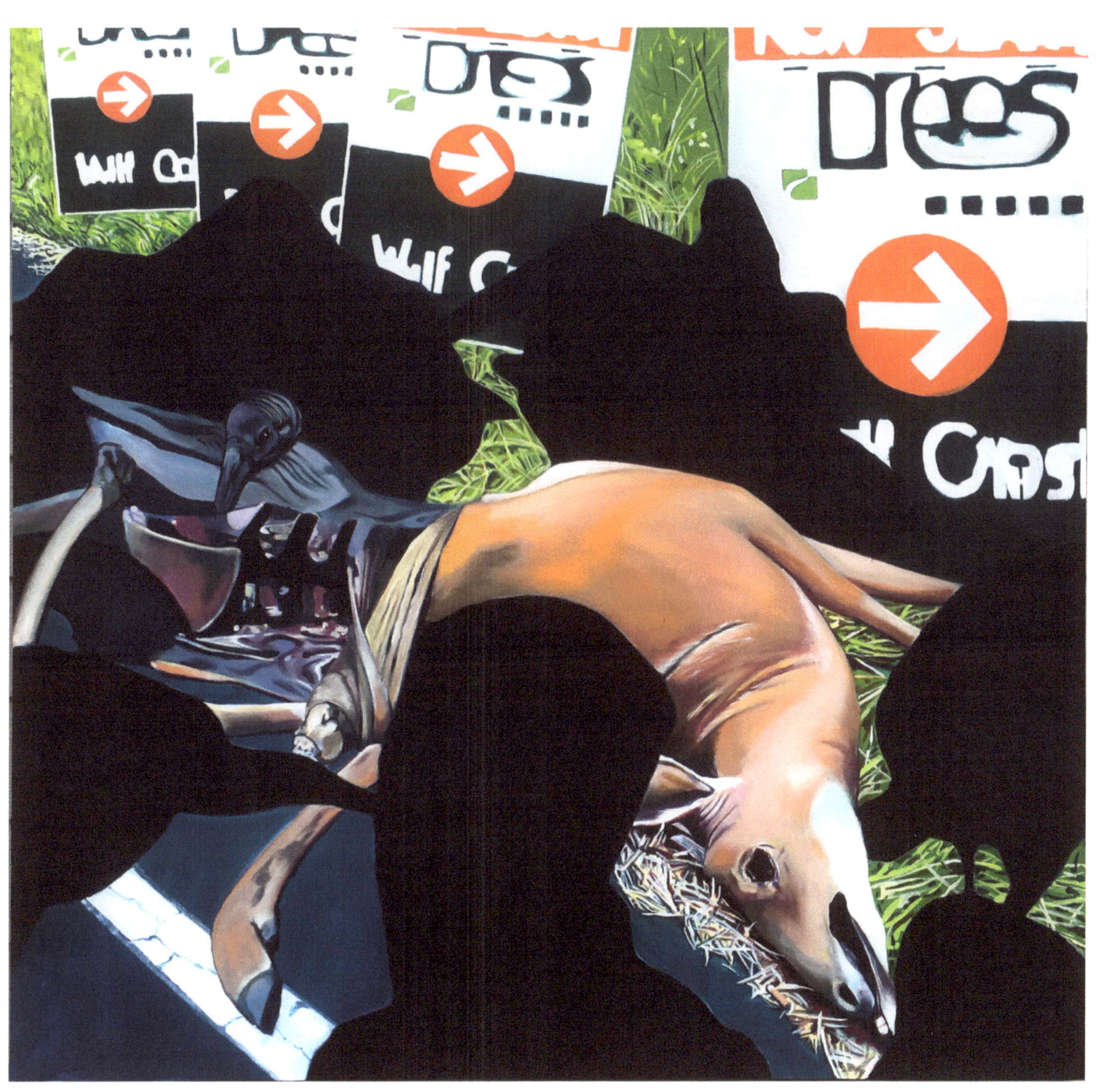

Anya Rosen
The Wake, 2017
Oil on canvas
60 x 60in.

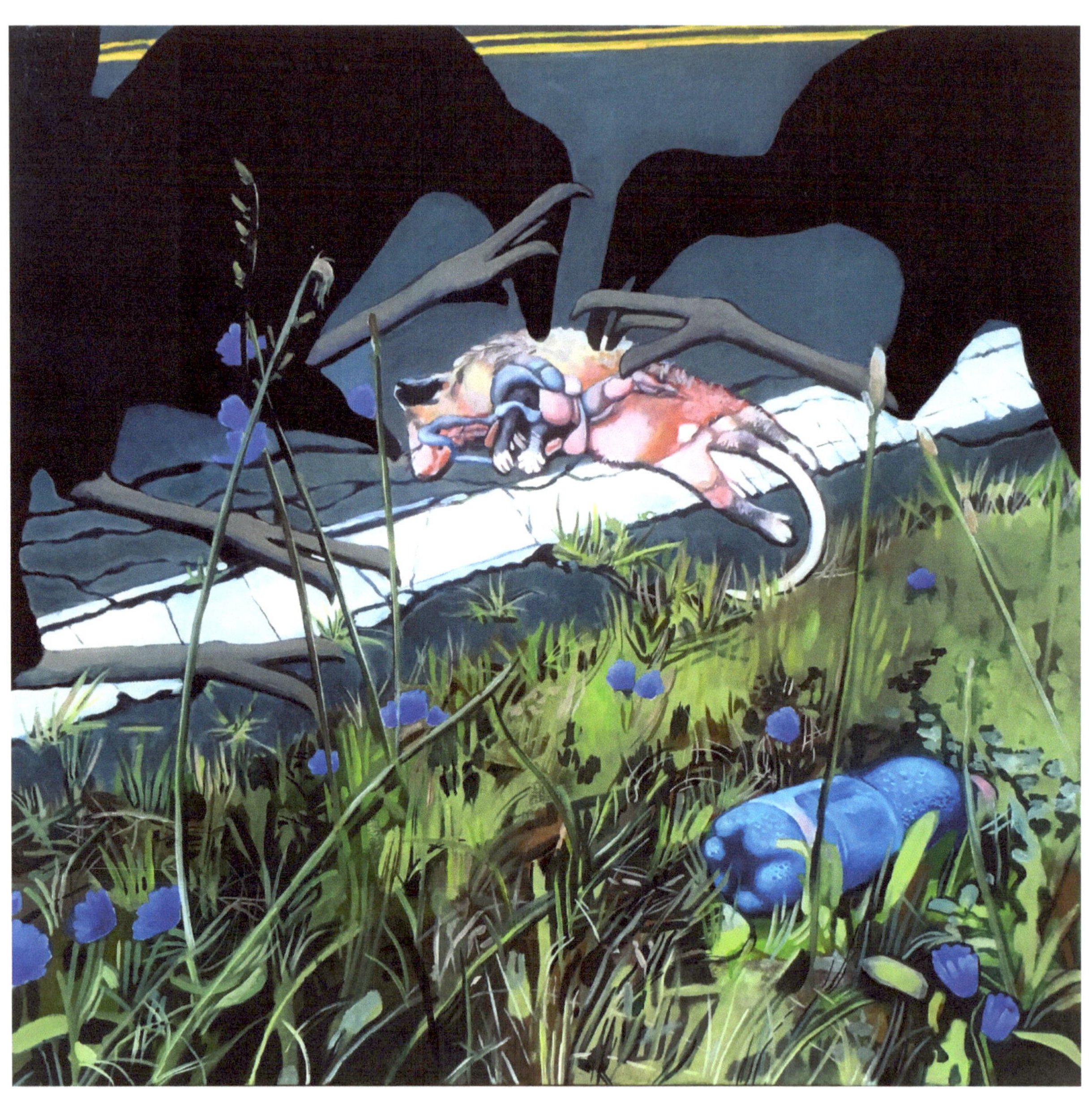

Anya Rosen
Chicory Flowers in Late Summer, 2017
Oil on canvas
48 x 48in.

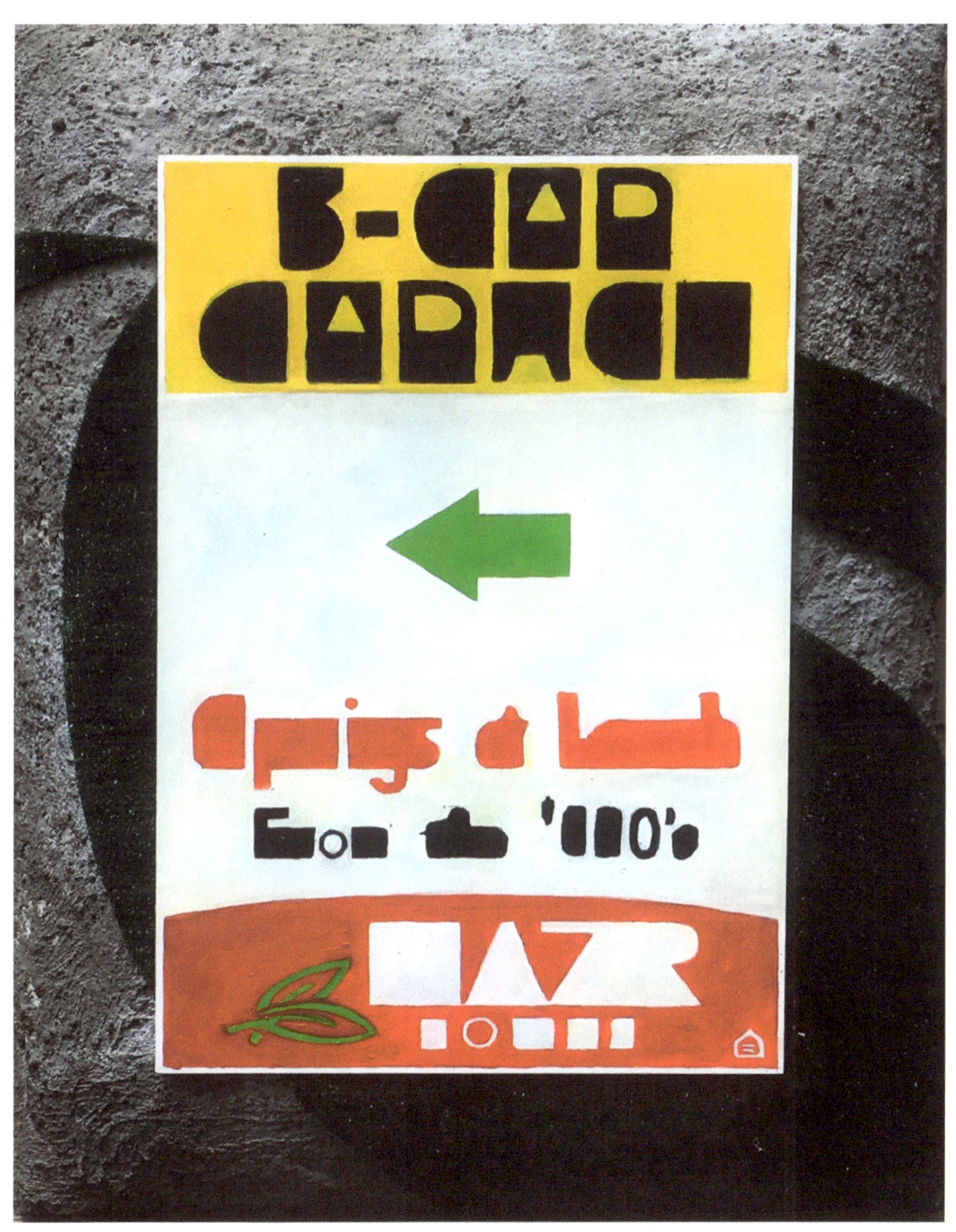

Anya Rosen
3 Car Garage, 2017
Oil paint on wood panel, wire mesh, plaster, fabric, wood, concrete,
sand, asphalt, astroturf
48 x 36 x 4in.

Hyunjung Rhee

Brooklyn, New York   hyunjungrhee.com

There are always failures in communication systems. When I moved to New York, dis-communication and misinterpretation followed by the linguistic collision caused extreme confusion and frustration. This condition of failure became central to my investigation. I am interested in creating mechanized sculptures; each programmed to reinterpret sound or text, endlessly operating to create and examine glitches in systems of communication. The material used and specifically made for the installations, such as receipt printers and motors continuously transpose into ever-changing metaphors touching on the sense of impossibility. My work is continually operating; there is no start or end. As they repeat again and again, machines in my work reproduce meaninglessness, hinting at the enormous failure of communication processes.

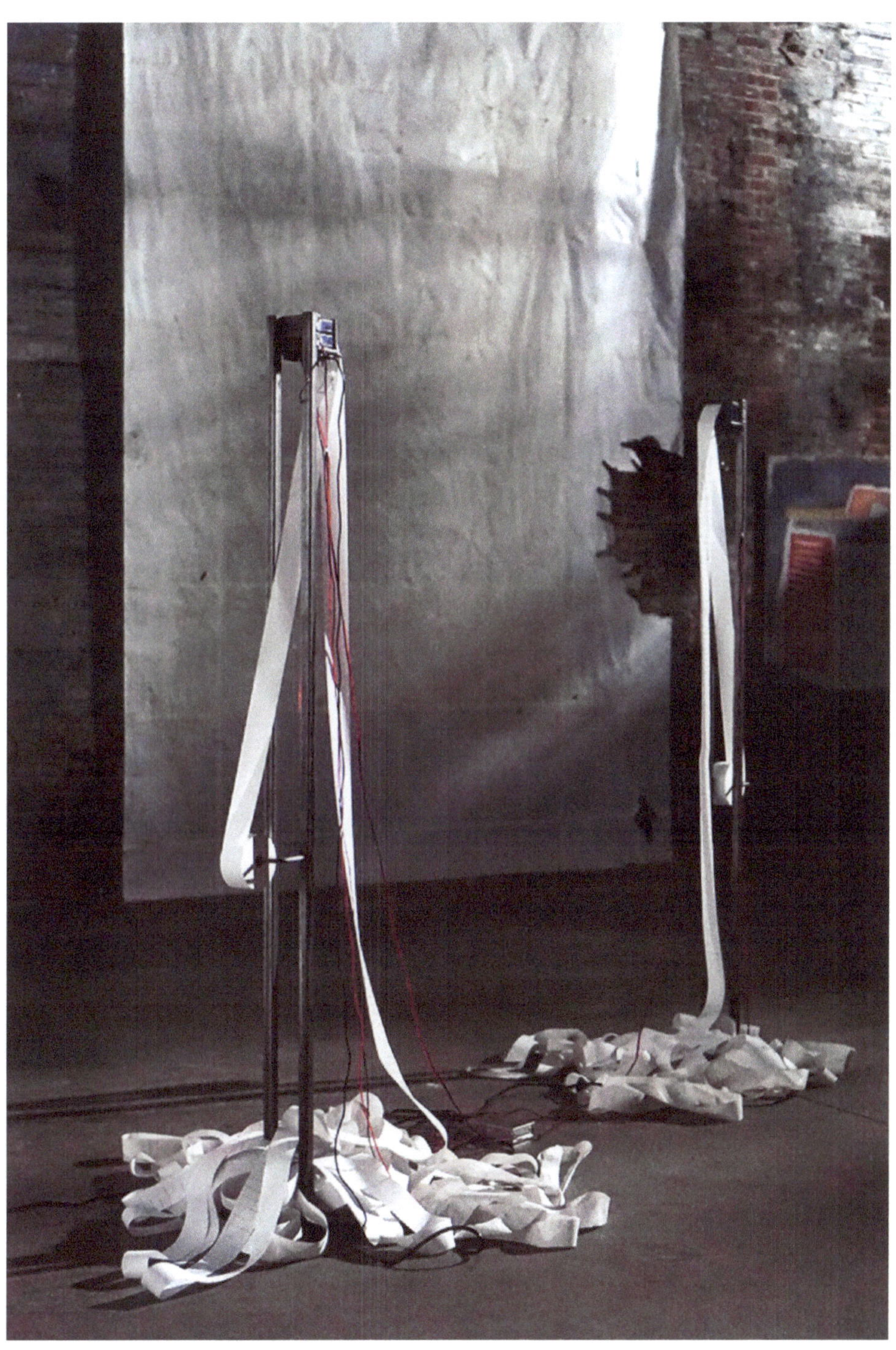

Hyunjung Rhee
The Increase Of Margin Of Error—Or Chaos, 2016
Two receipt printers, two metal structure, thermal
paper, Arduino (programming board)
dimensions variable

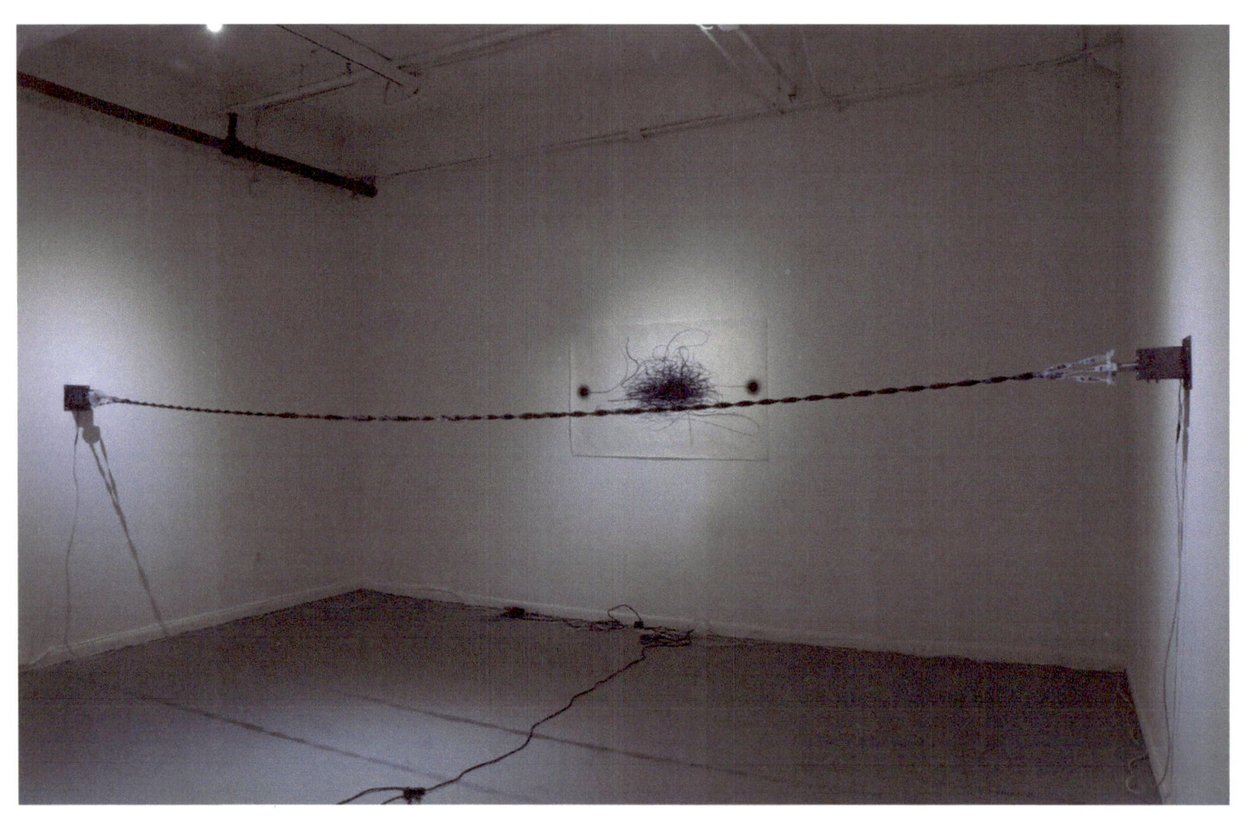

Hyunjung Rhee
Entangled Descriptions, 2017
Stepper motors, Arduino, plexiglass discs, texts
written of plaster, translucent silicone bands,
Dimensions variable

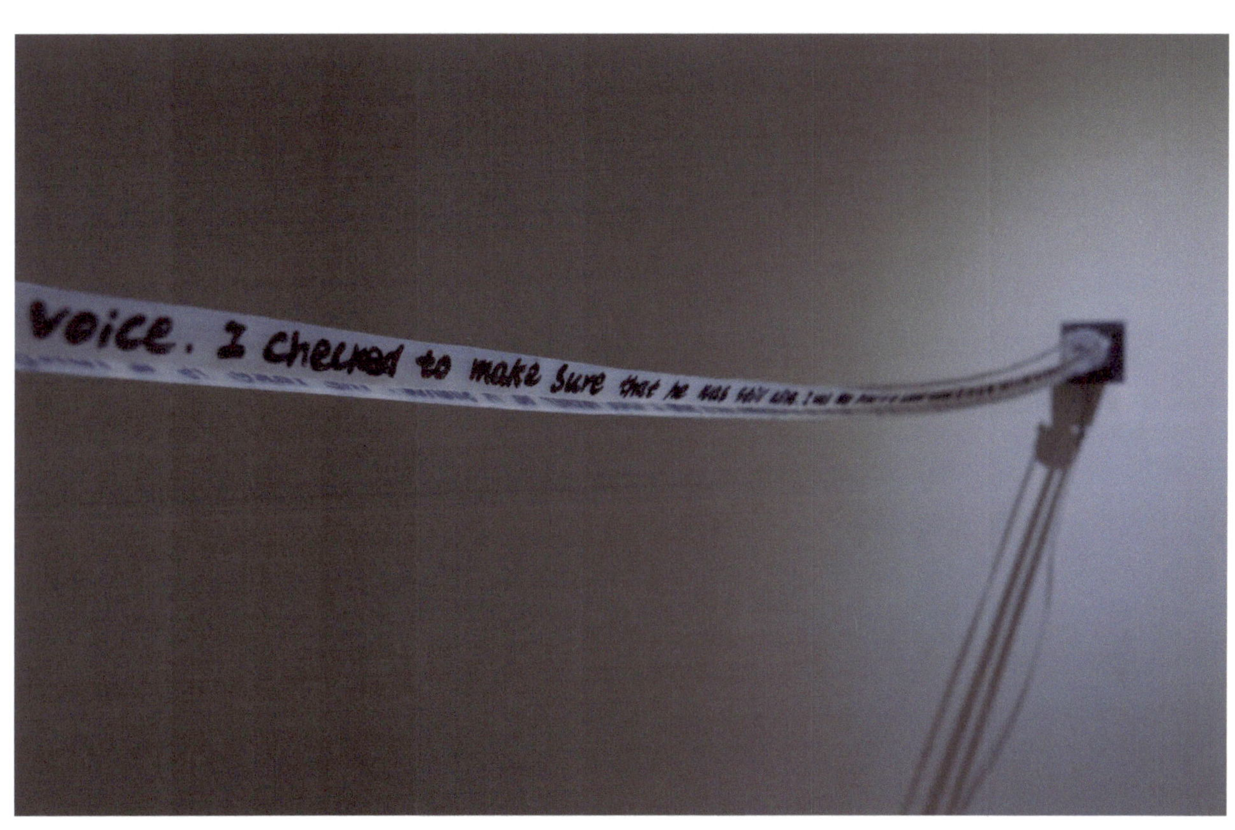

Hyunjung Rhee
Entangled Descriptions, 2017
Stepper motors, Arduino, plexiglass discs, texts
written of plaster, translucent silicone bands,
Dimensions variable

Anna Rotty

San Francisco, California   annarotty.com

My work aims to explore the tension between resistance and acceptance of change. I am interested in the relationship between maintaining control, versus surrendering to process and material. I am inspired by the dialogue between two forces, their influence on each other, and the impermanence of it all.

Since moving far from home, I photograph my family in rare moments of stillness. As the prints slowly dry, I allow the photograph to distort and change due to environmental forces, similar to how a mind treats a memory. The ink of the print spreads across the paper, often outside of the original boundaries of the camera's frame, creating an abstraction. Dust, hair, movement, gravity and air impact the final piece. I attempt to blur the line between representing a captured moment in time and the feeling that moment generates as time passes. In a world saturated with immediate imagery, I hope to slow down the image to create moments of reflection.

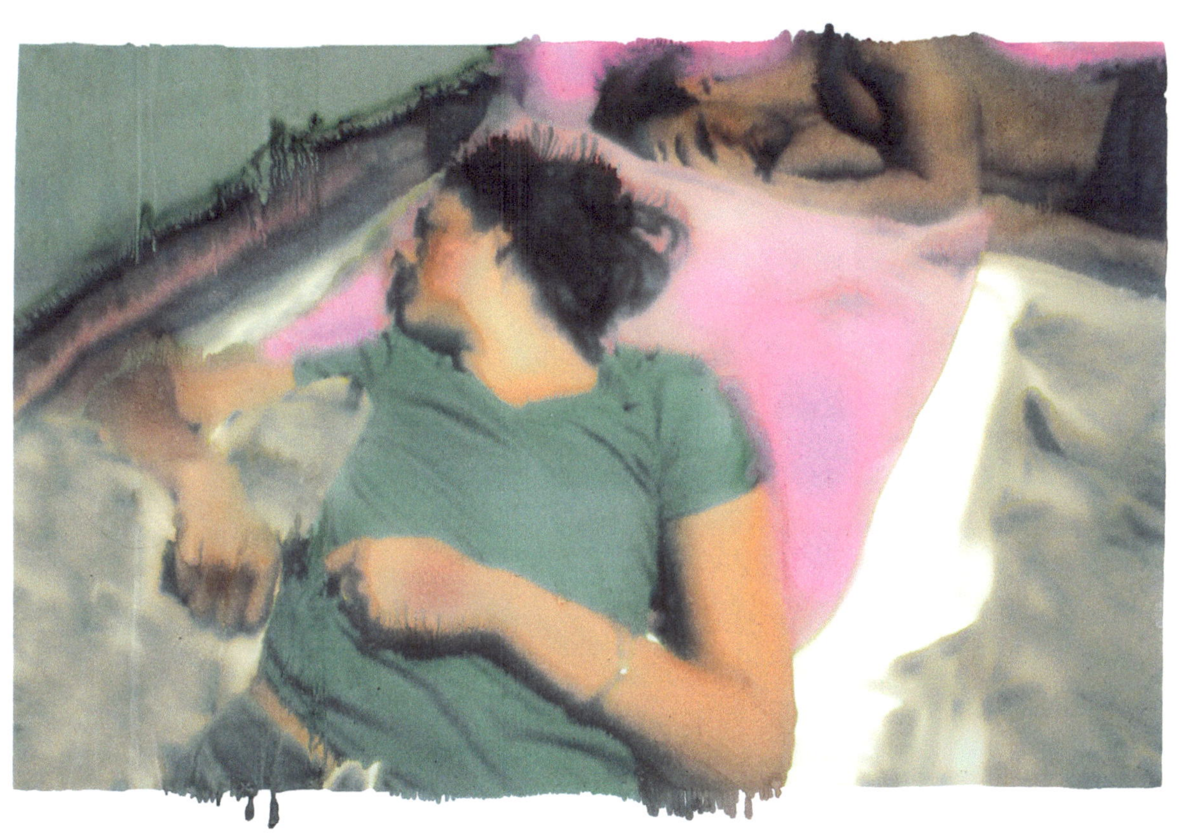

Anna Rotty
Melanie and Jake, 2016
Digital photograph on paper
30 x 40in.

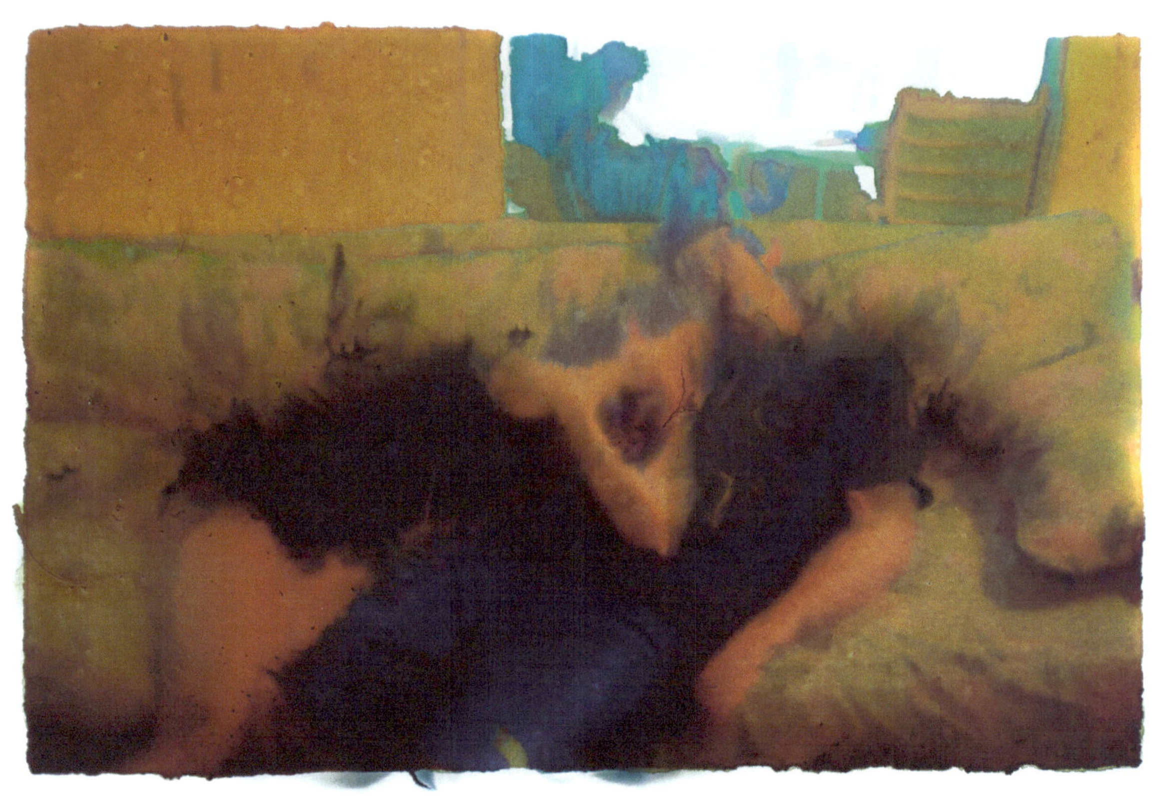

Anna Rotty
John and Michaela, 2016
Digital photograph on paper

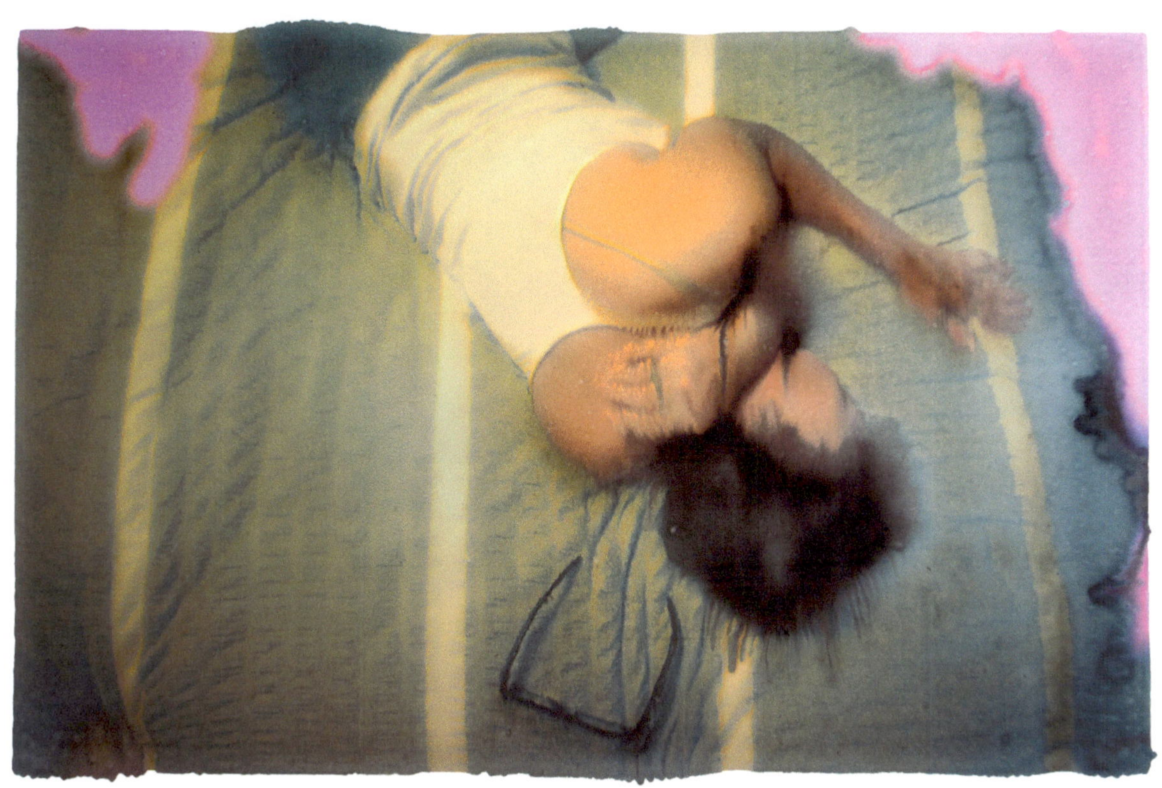

Anna Rotty
Mom Sleeping, 2016
Digital photograph on paper
30 x 40in.

Rajab Sayed

Houston, TX　　　rajabalisayed.com

Born to a Filipino mother and Pakistani father, I spent my childhood navigating two distinct cultural identities. I graduated from the National College of Arts, Lahore in 2013 with a Distinction in Fine Art, presenting an interdisciplinary thesis project in painting, video installation, and photography titled "Pretty Young Things". I also attended Augustana University in Sioux Falls, South Dakota and travelled the American Mid-West as a Fulbright Scholar. I now live in Houston, Texas with my husband and 3 dogs after graduating from the University of Houston's MFA program under the tutorship of contemporary artists Aaron Parazette, Gael Stack and Rachel Hecker.

My paintings create a dialogue about identity and representation within the history of painting. I co-opt visual cues from historical paintings to express personal mythologies, placing male figures in compositions traditionally associated with female genre paintings, or leaving figures out of compositions to reflect on human presence in absentia. The paintings are detached observations but contain certain elements of wit and humor. There are reflections of romantic possibility, observing couples and other interpersonal relationships. Visual devices such as color and mark run through a series of paintings to continue the narrative. My handling of paint has an urgency that races to capture the details of time and space, fine-tuning visual elements to create psychological realism.

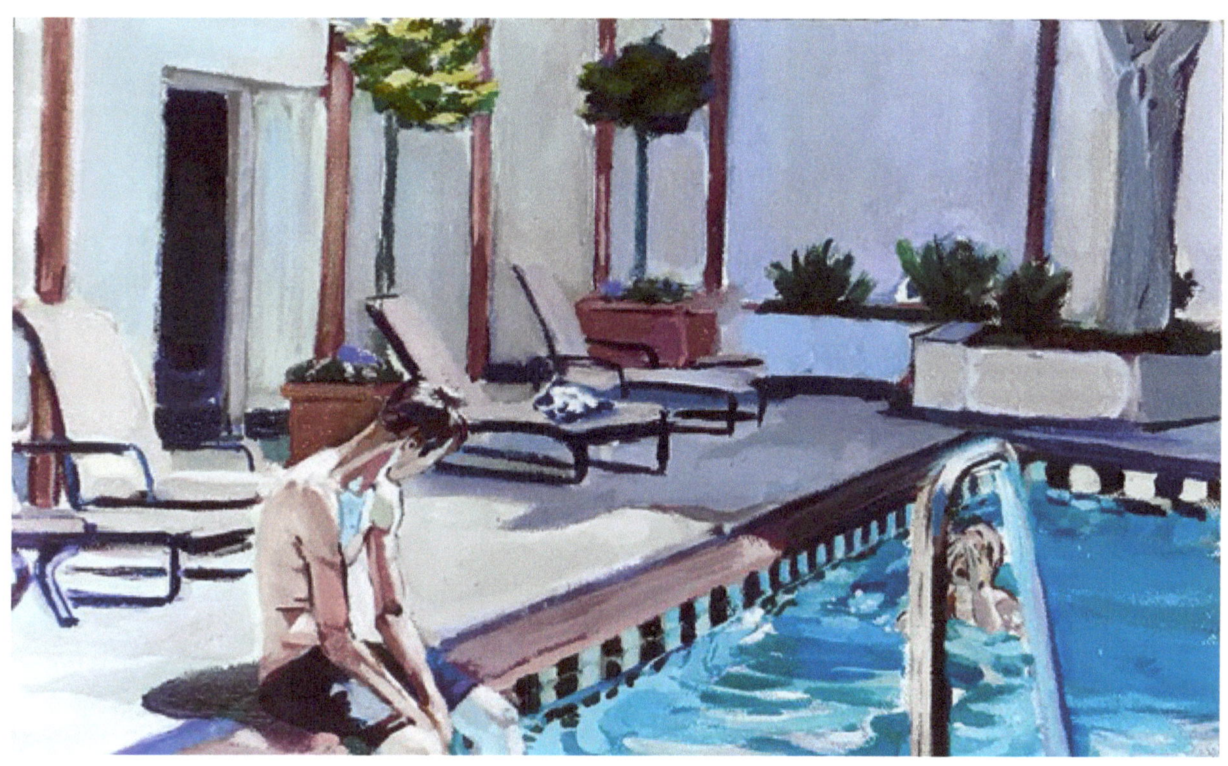

Rajab Sayed
Poetry is no place for a heart that's a whore, 2017
Oil on Canvas
9.5zzz x 15 in.

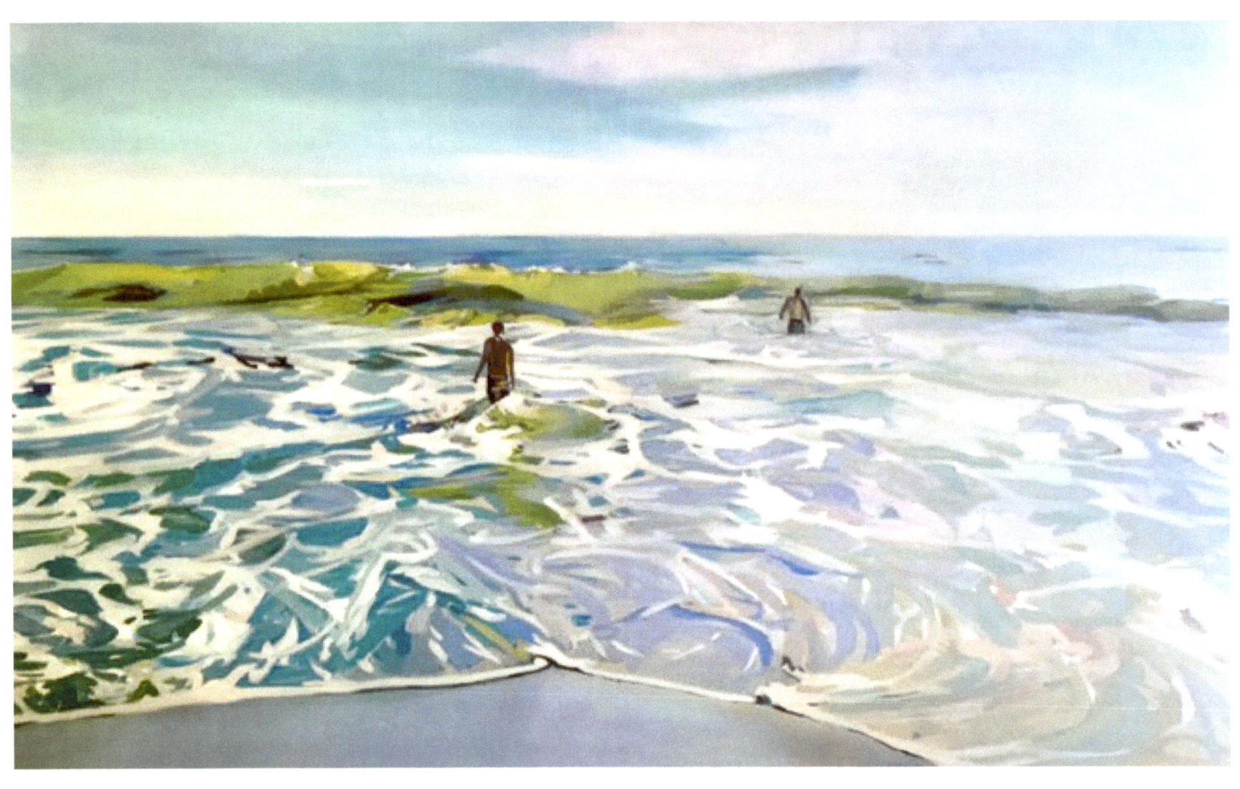

Rajab Sayed
Call me by your name, 2017
Oil on Canvas
60 x 96in.

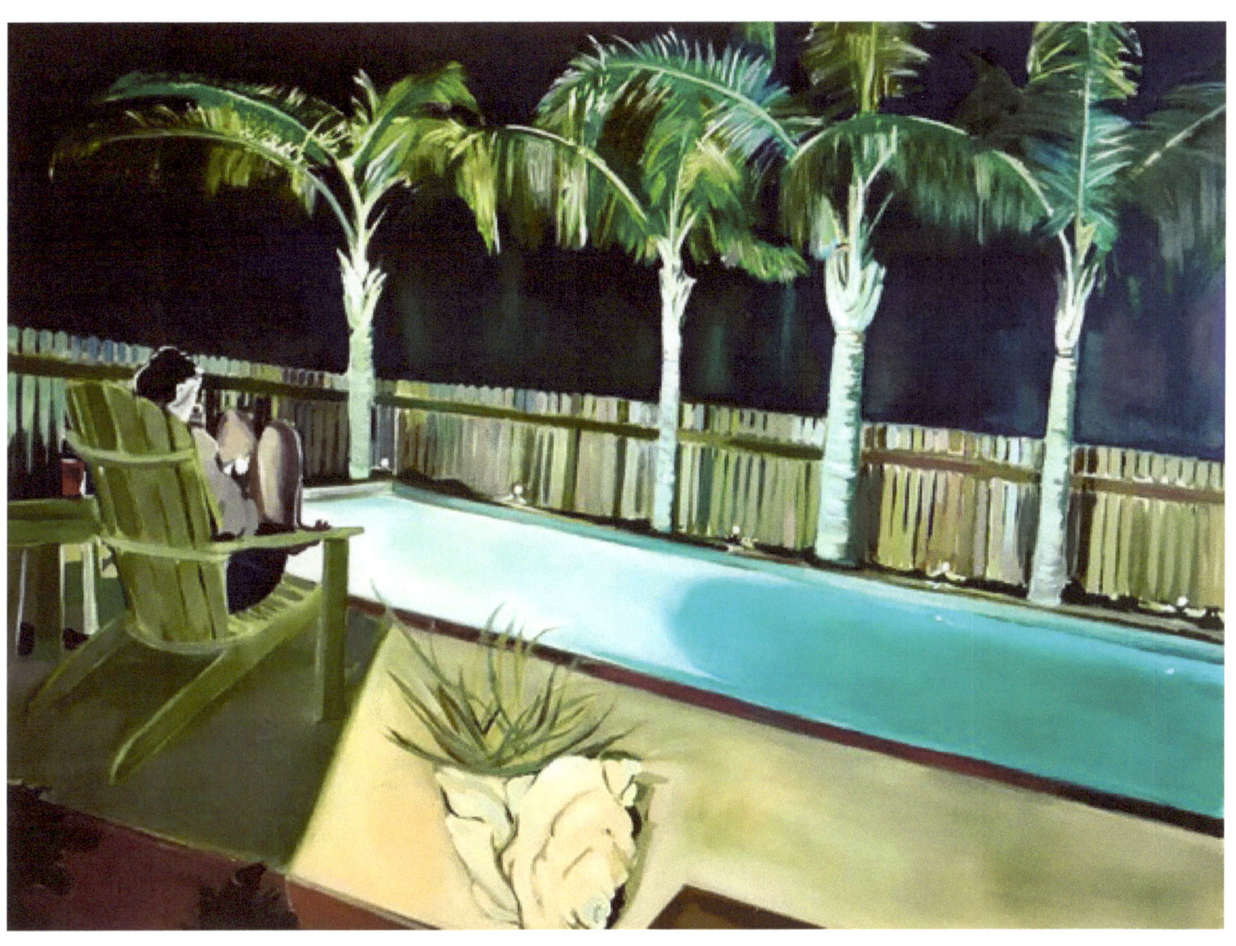

Rajab Sayed
Ophelia (Reprise), 2017
Oil on Canvas
58 x 70in.

Evan Sheldon

Dallas, Texas　　evansheldon.com

What is a photograph? Is it an accurate representation of what things were like at a certain time and place? While that may have once been the case, it is no longer. What can we rely on as truth in an age where the look of something on the surface is more important than its actual content?

In an effort to call attention to the death of the photographer as arbiter of truth, I've created what I believe to be a new process of "light painting" that photography is often the medium for. By making use of traditionally essential elements of photography, light and chemistry, I automate non-objective imagery without the use of a camera, in a painterly mode of mark making.

The results of this intuitive light painting are what we would call a chemigram, a process coined in 1956 by Belgian artist Pierre Cordier. However, chemigram-like images have been created and experimented with by photographers and scientists as far back as the 18th century. They are usually created using standard gelatin-silver paper and resists that are applied to the paper to selectively mask development. The paper is then placed in developer and fixer, back and forth, in either order, until the paper's chemistry is exhausted and a final composition is fixed.

After the analog chemigram is created, I digitize it by scanning it and opening it in a widely used contemporary photographer's tool, Photoshop. I then select what can only be described by photography theorist Roland Barthes as the "punctum," those poignant details of a photograph that stand out, stick in your mind, and force you to continually recall said photograph. The punctum of these curi marks left by my painterly performance often comes from compositions that allow the viewers' eyes to continually move around the canvas, just as a traditional photograph might do. While the punctum may jump out from each

CONTINUED ON PAGE 130 →

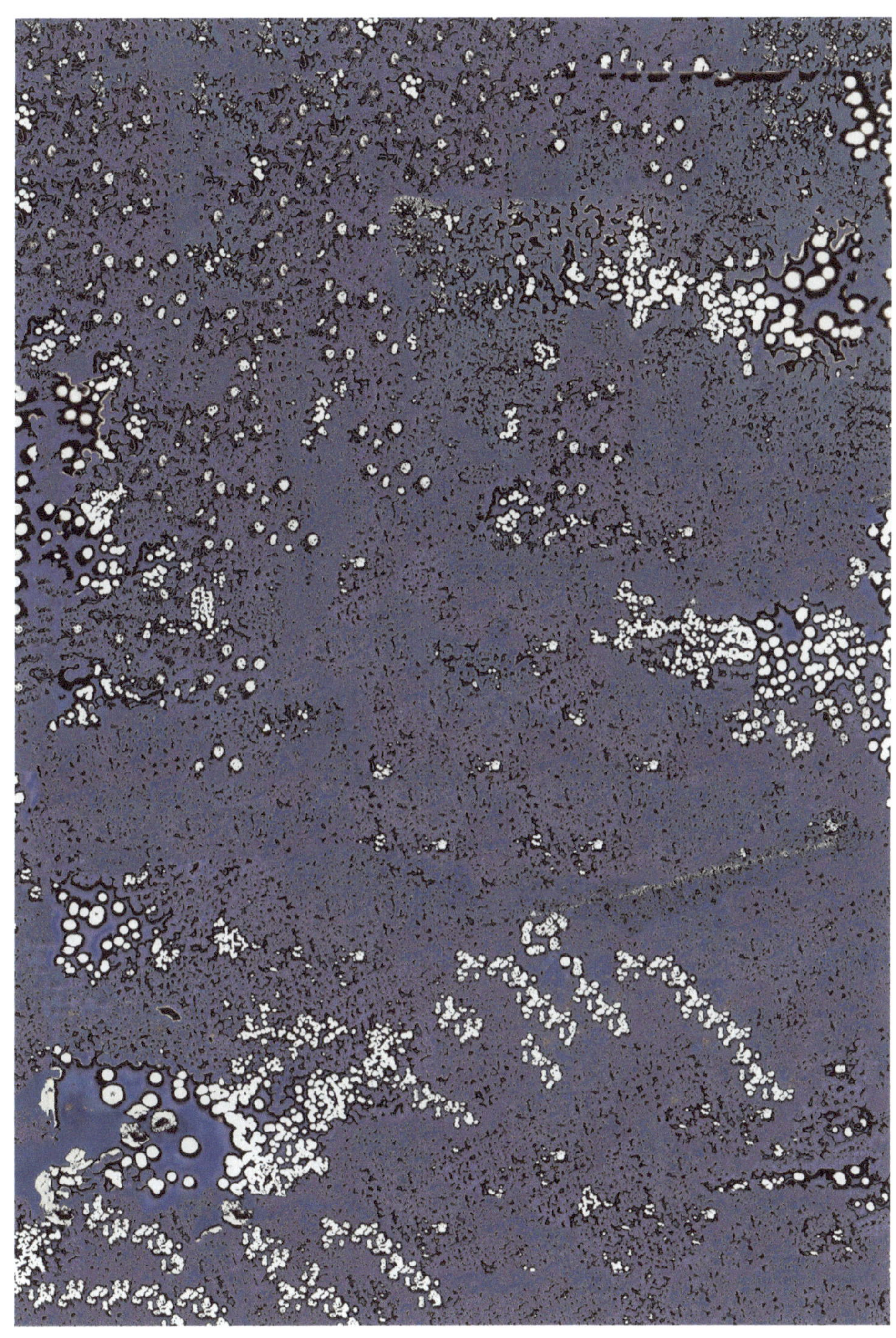

Evan Sheldon
8b, 2017
Content-Aware chemigram on archival ink jet paper
60 x 40in.

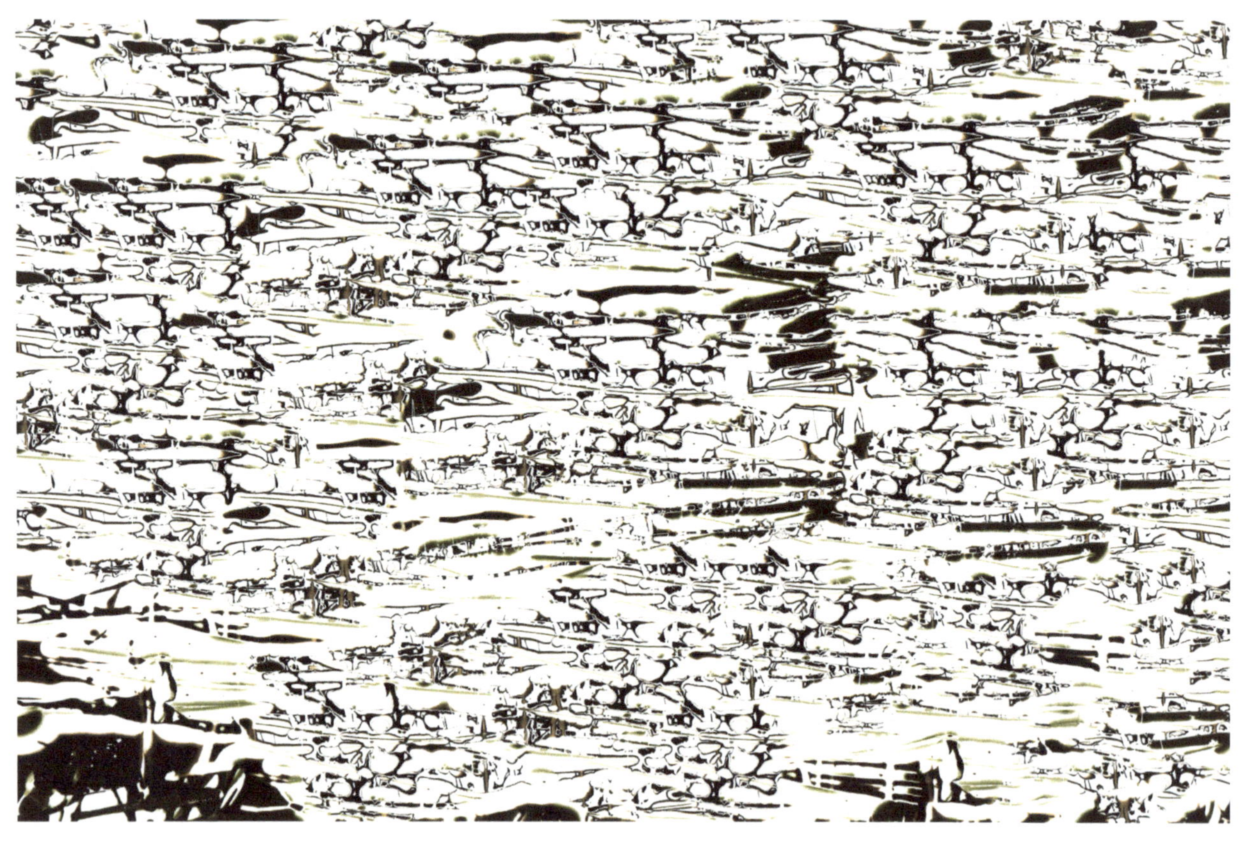

Evan Sheldon
2a, 2017
Content-Aware chemigram on archival
ink jet paper
40 x 60in.

Friend of The Artist

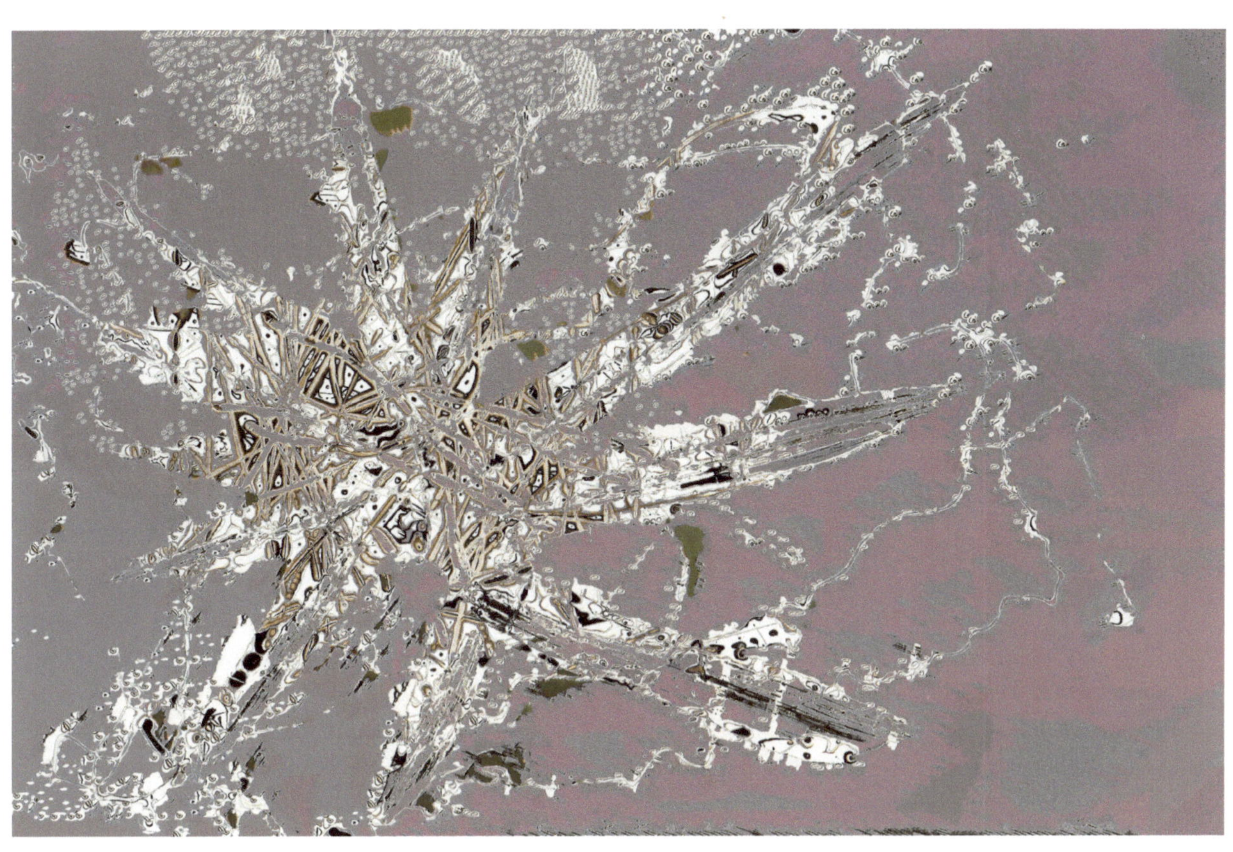

Evan Sheldon
5a, 2017
Content-Aware chemigram on archival ink jet paper
40 x 60in.

Wei Tan (Tatawa) *Kuala Lumpur, Malaysia*

Tatawa (Wei Tan, b. Malaysia, 1991) is a mixed-media abstract artist. With a background in music composition, she completed her Master's degree in Music Technology at New York University. In summer 2015, while developing work on image-based experimental sound art, Tatawa started exploring the world of abstract painting – first collaborating with her teacher Gina Bonati and then experimenting on her own, drawing inspirations from the great Abstract Expressionists to today's cross-disciplinary, multimedia artists. Since then she has become a full-time artist and has exhibited in New York, London, Florence, and Berlin.

Tatawa's art is an act of self-revelation through improvisation. Each artwork is a journal entry where outer influences are purged and inner responses are confessed. Like making soup, materials are thrown onto the canvas and mixed together through spontaneous gesture. Often a period of mindless doodling is carried out before the painting emerges with an unexpected coherence. Influences of sight and sound are exposed: the colour of a coffee mug, the shape of a distant hill, the meow of a cat, the piano playing next door. The process of improvisation allows each layer of influence to be shredded until the limitation of habit is revealed. This limitation is then challenged so that each painting is a set of broken habits. Tatawa's commitment to authenticity results in an inconsistency in style. Each day a new character emerges and the old one disappears like shredding skin. The only constant is the desire to truthfully express the fluctuation of current states.

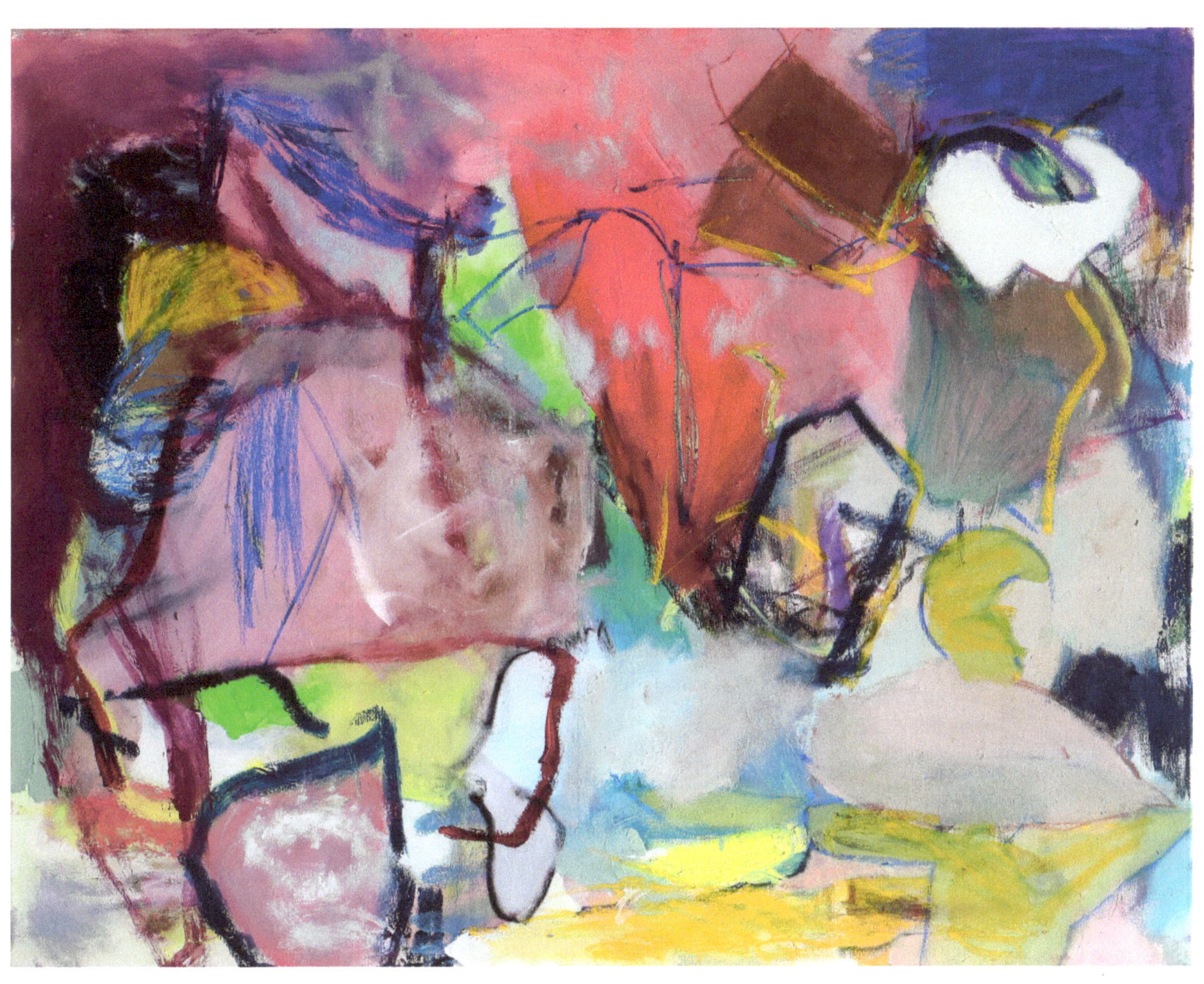

Wei Tan (Tatawa)
Late for the Dentist, 2017
Mixed media on canvas
31 x 39in.

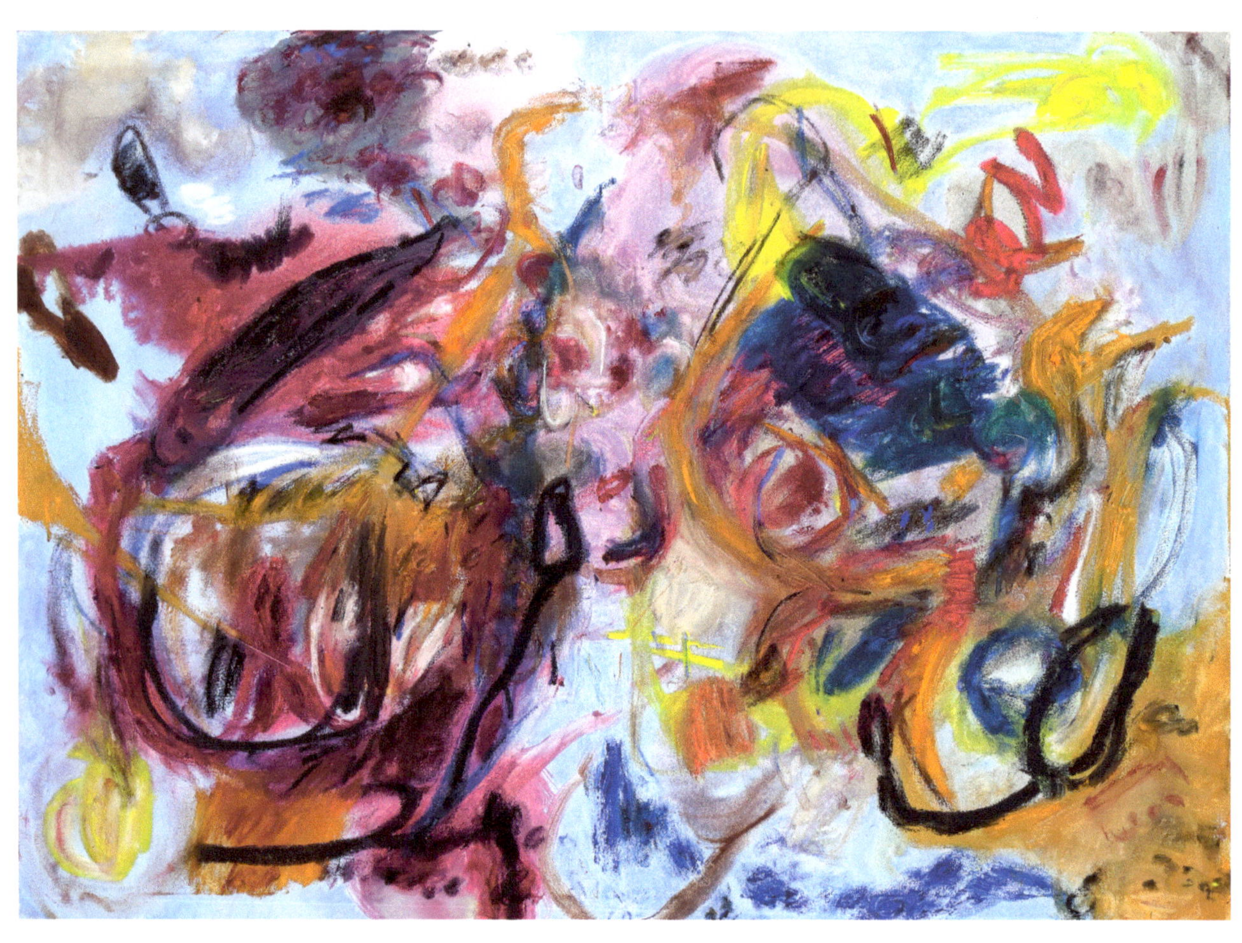

Wei Tan (Tatawa)
The Mechanics of Play, 2016
Mixed media on canvas
30 x 40in.

Friend of The Artist

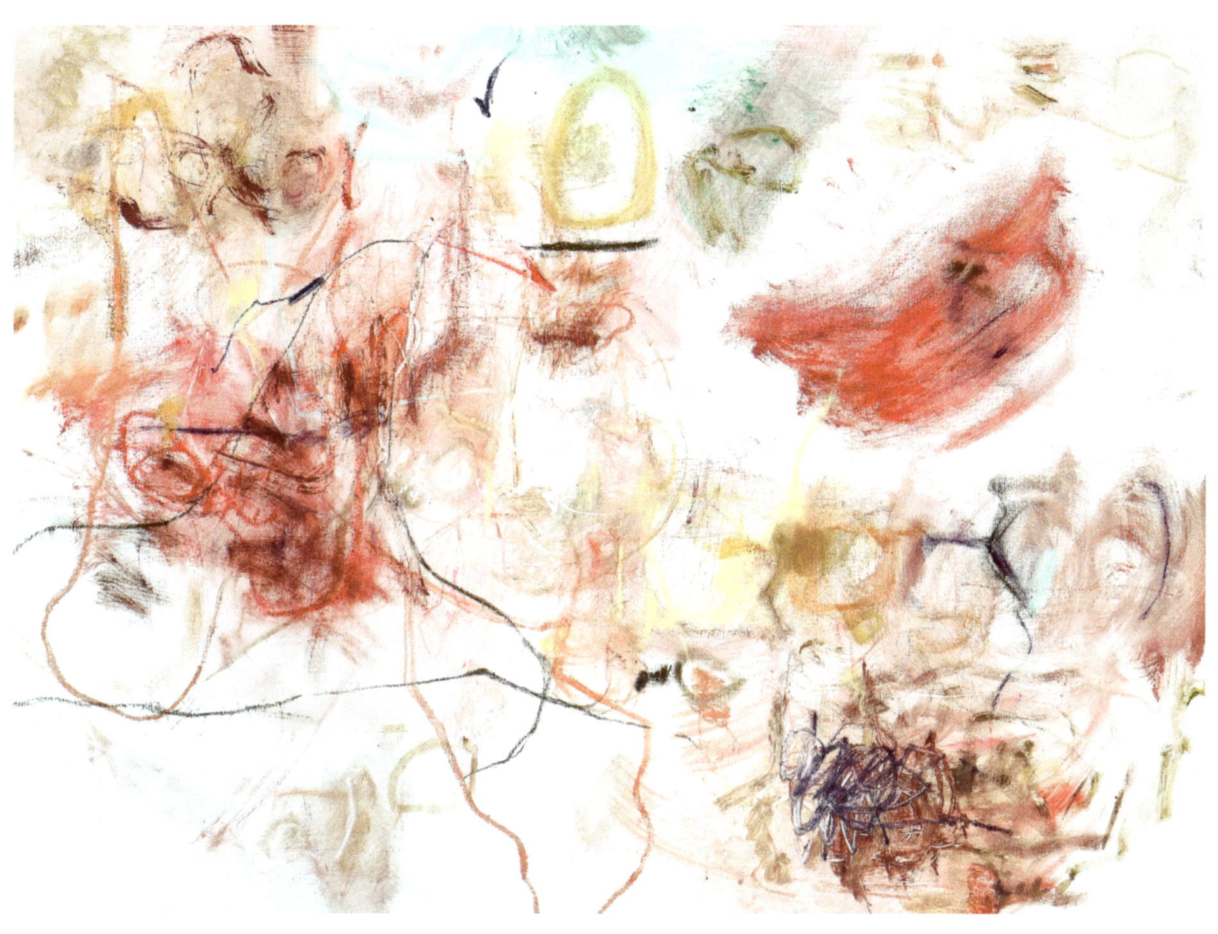

Wei Tan (Tatawa)
Abdomen, 2017
Mixed media on canvas
30 x 40in.

Sarah West

Miami, Florida   thesarahwest.com

My work explores spiritual seeking through our relationships with
the digital. My paintings reference Early Renaissance art, Photoshop
tools, computer games, hand-manipulated digital scans and stock
computer wallpaper. Recent paintings feature abstract glyph-like forms
that give way to a volumetric Renaissance space. These markings are
inspired by finger swipes on touchpads and smartphones, our grease-
stained traces of interaction with the screen a merging of tactile and
virtual fields. The searching intimacy of the hand in relation to its
digital device echoes the relationship we once held with illuminated
manuscripts, intended to simultaneously mesmerize and provide
an accessibility to the sacred. Through pairing sacred narratives
of the Renaissance with digital symbols, the work suggests the
spiritual undercurrents within digital technology in its potential for
enlightenment, transcendence, and evoking a sense of the infinite.

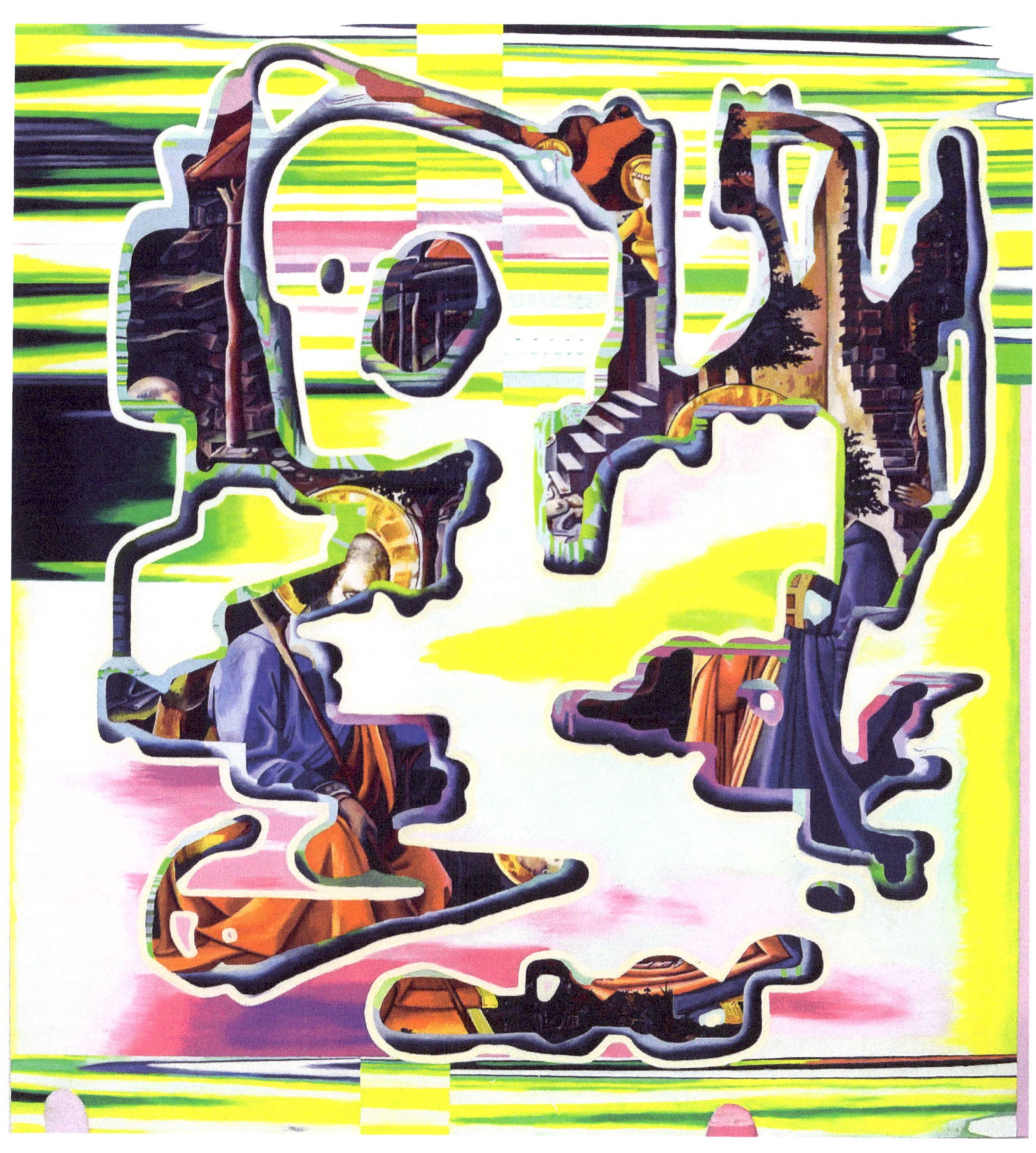

Sarah West
flickering veil, 2016
Oil on panel
44 x 44in.

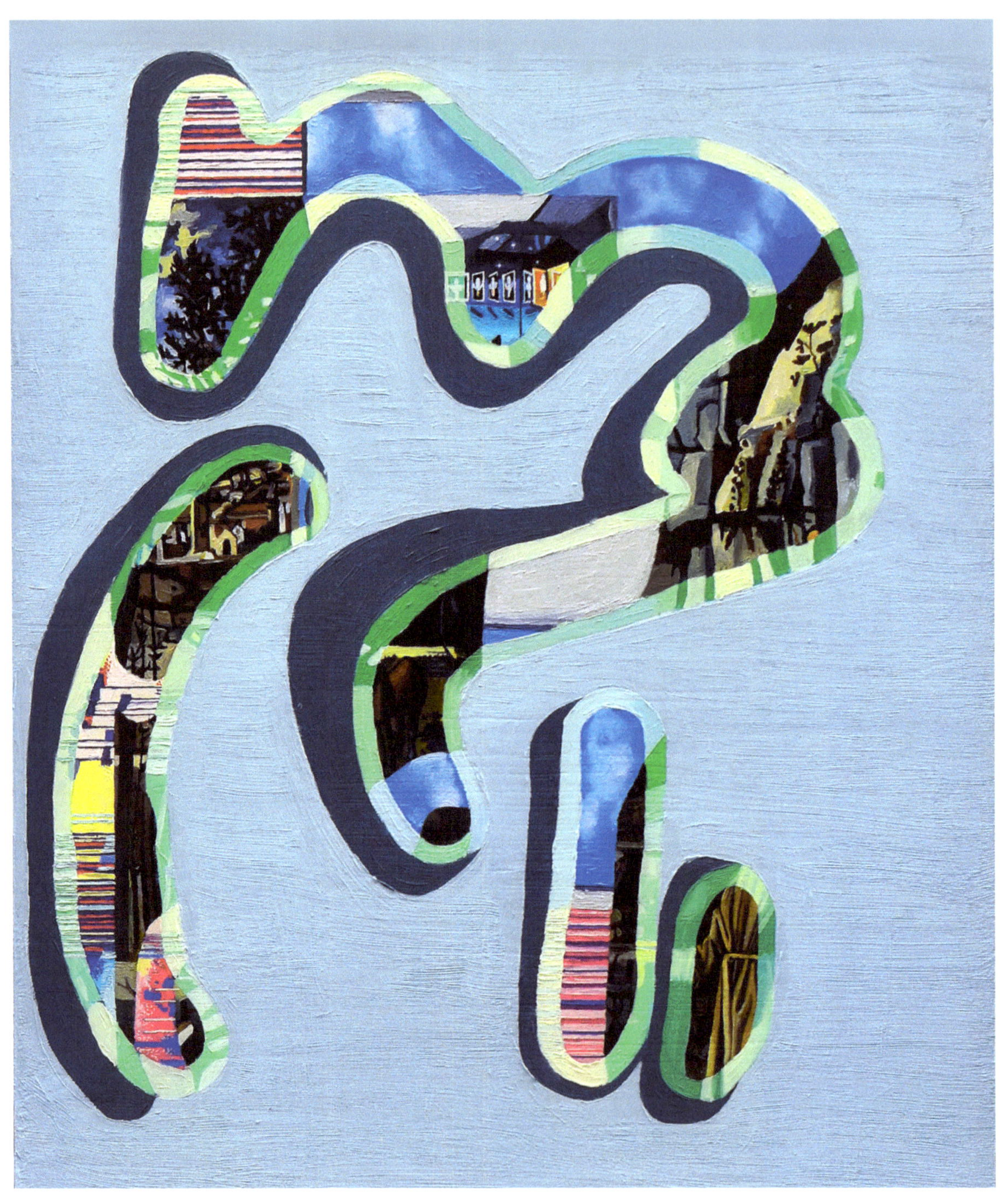

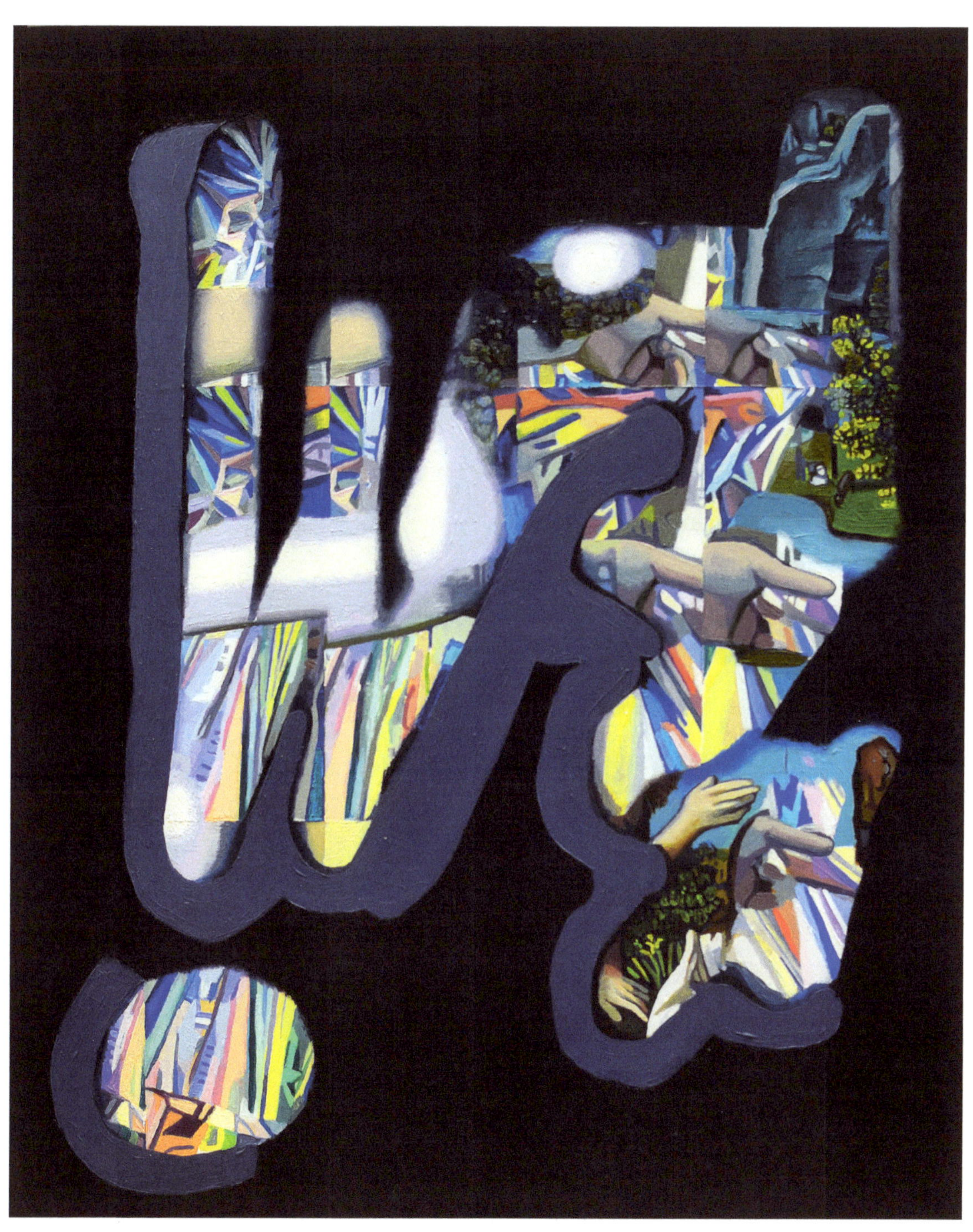

Sarah West
swipe II, 2016
Oil on panel
14 x 11in.

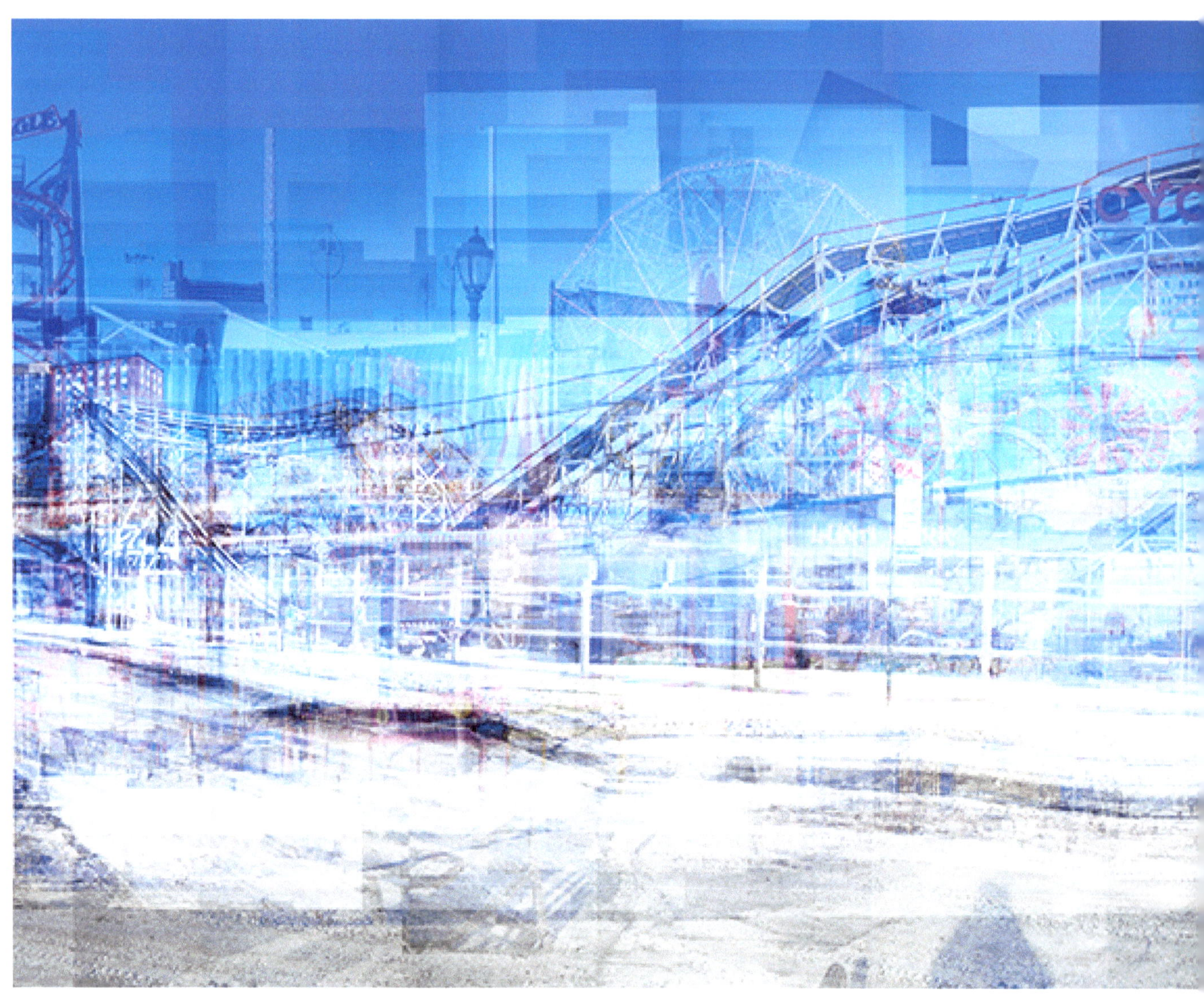

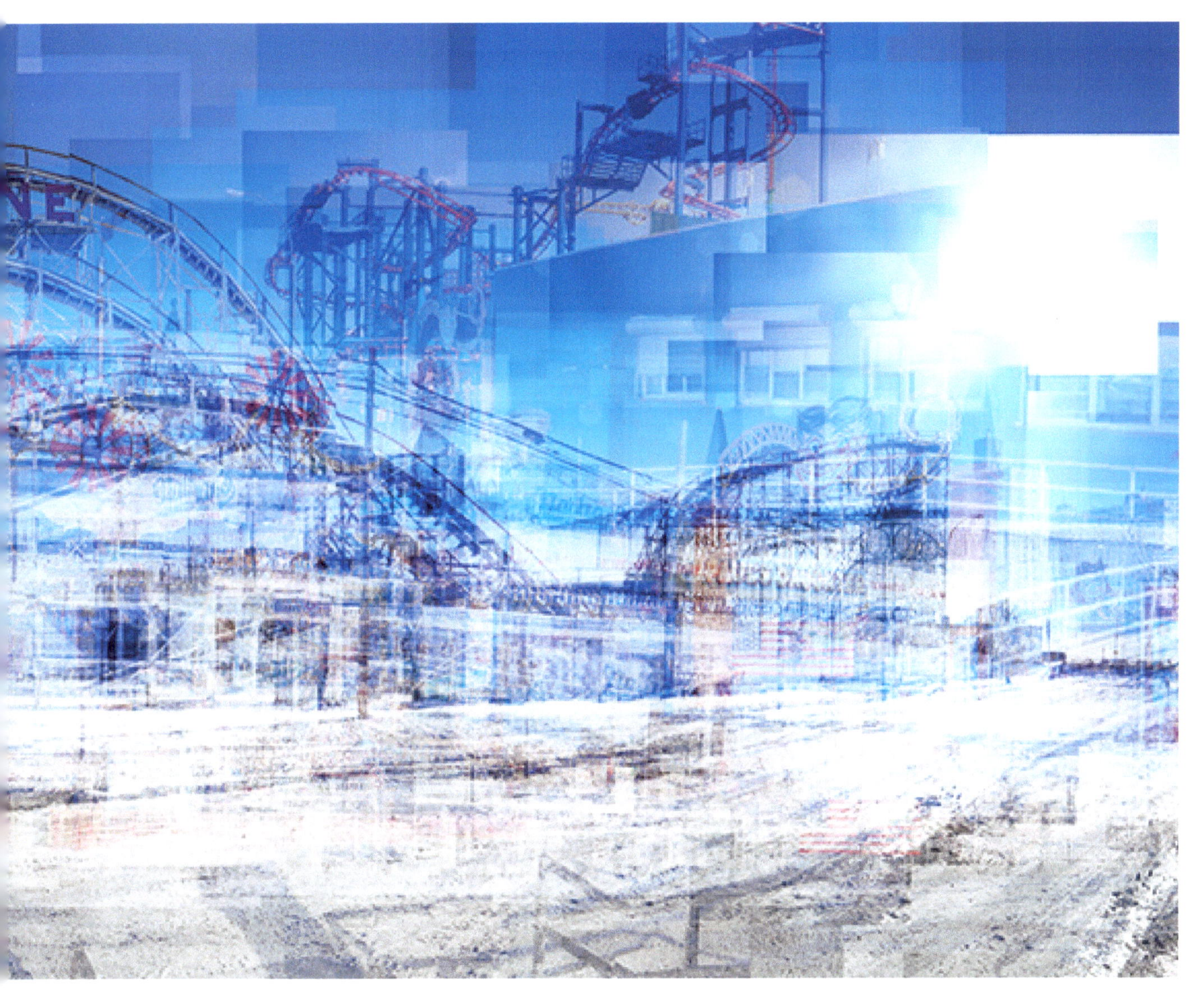

Gemma Lopez
Untitled Winter, 2017
ink jet print, detail

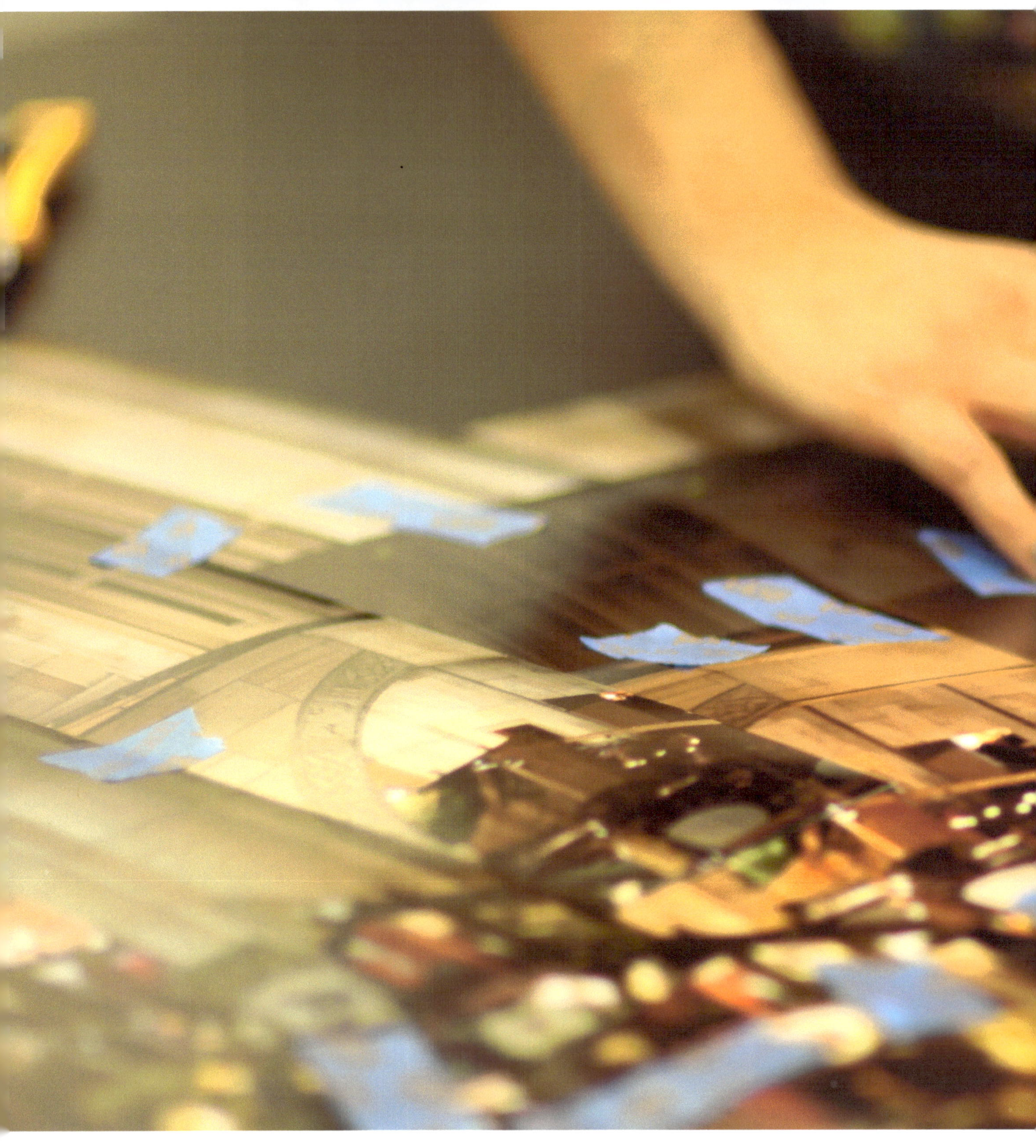

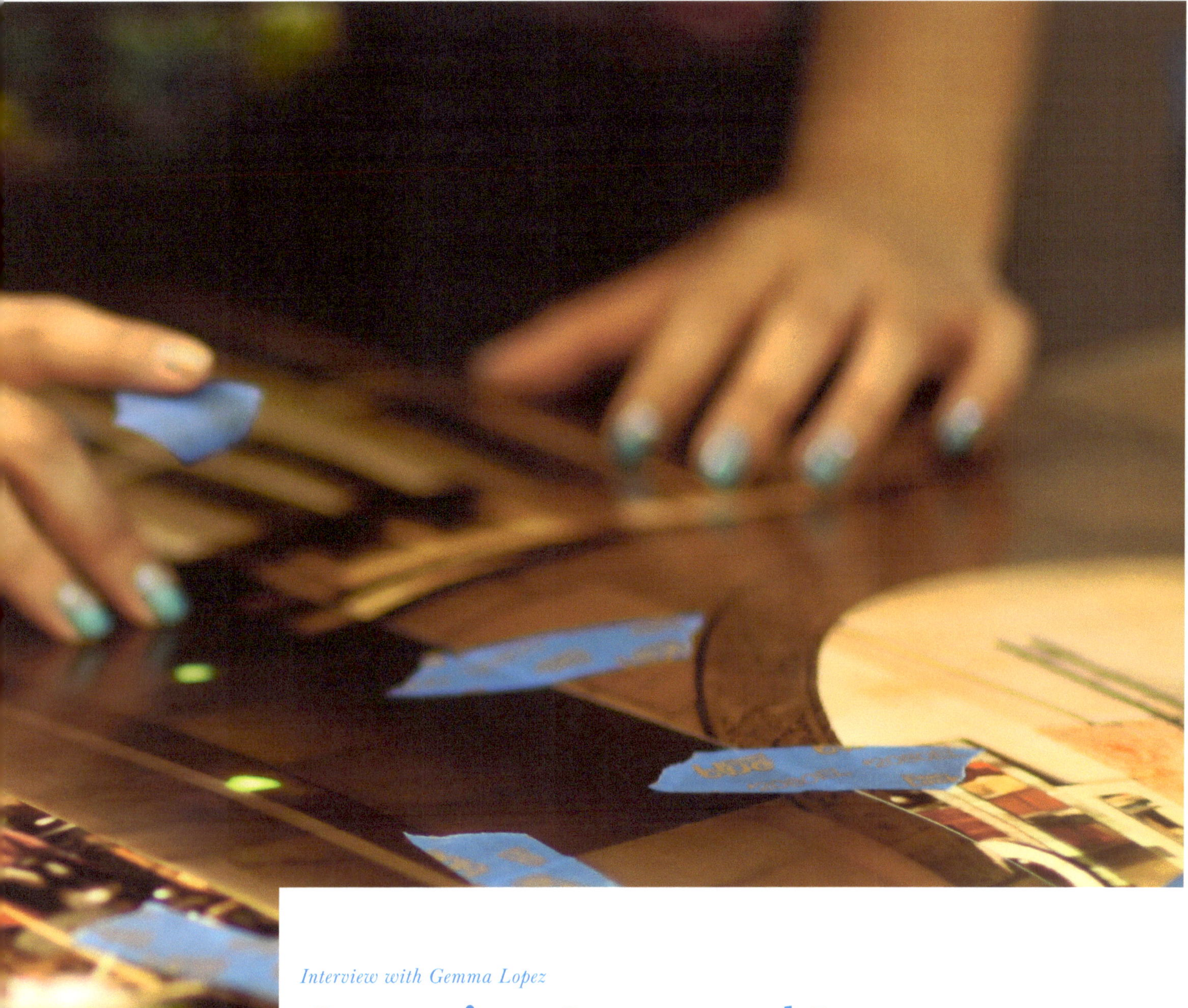

Interview with Gemma Lopez

Capturing Space and Passages of Time

Works by Gemma Lopez

Interviewed by Justin Archer

J: Gemma, you received an undergraduate degree in architecture before pursuing a post-baccalaureate and then a masters in photography. What was it that caused you to shift your interest from architecture to photography, and how has architecture affected the content of your work?

G: While studying architecture I was introduced to a variety of art mediums such as graphic design, photography, drawing, and screen-printing. After briefly working in the architecture field I realized that what I actually wanted to do was pursue a career in art. Getting exposed to different mediums in architecture school

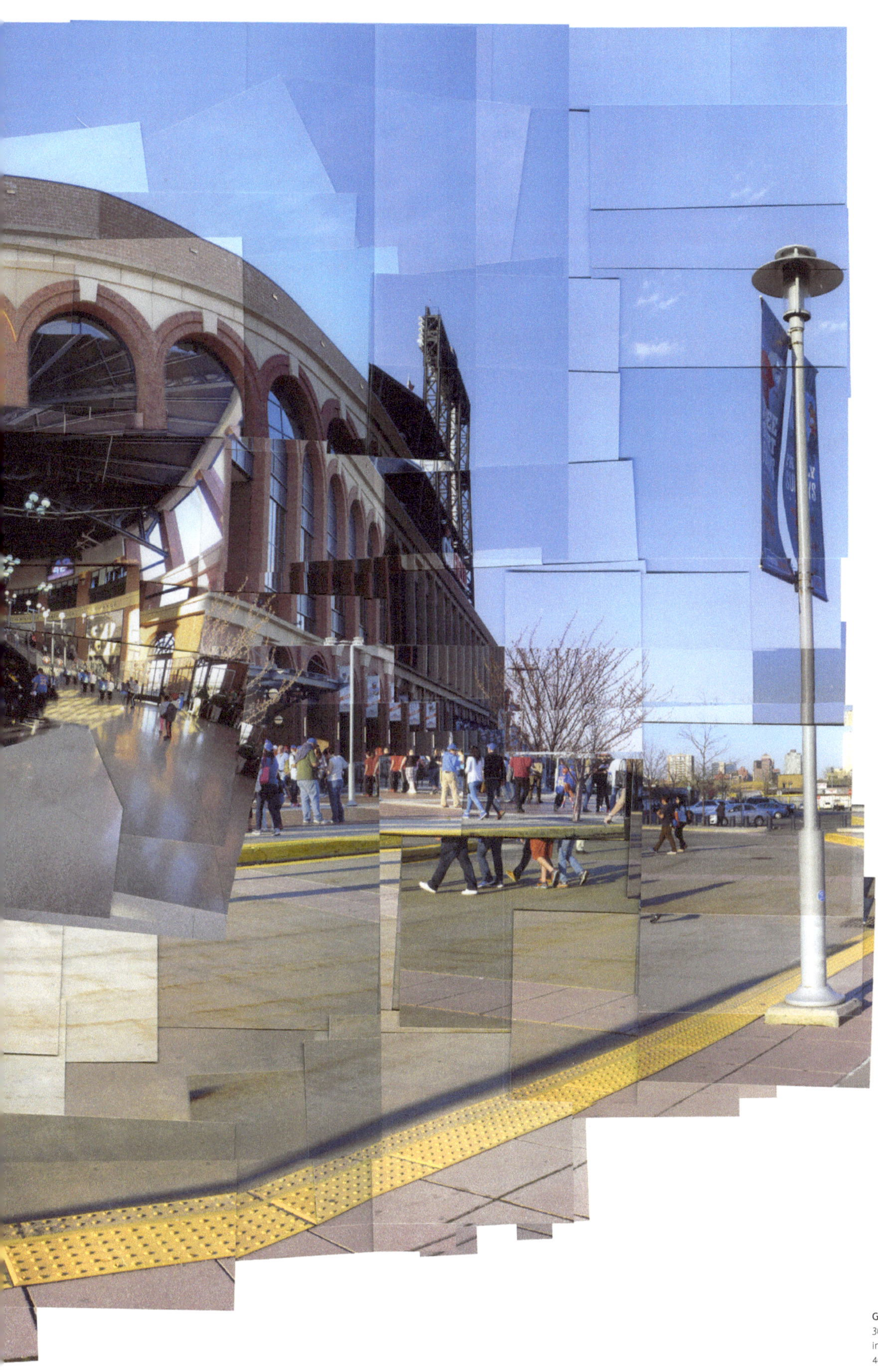

Gemma Lopez
30 Baseball Stadiums: Citi Field
ink jet print
40 x 30in.

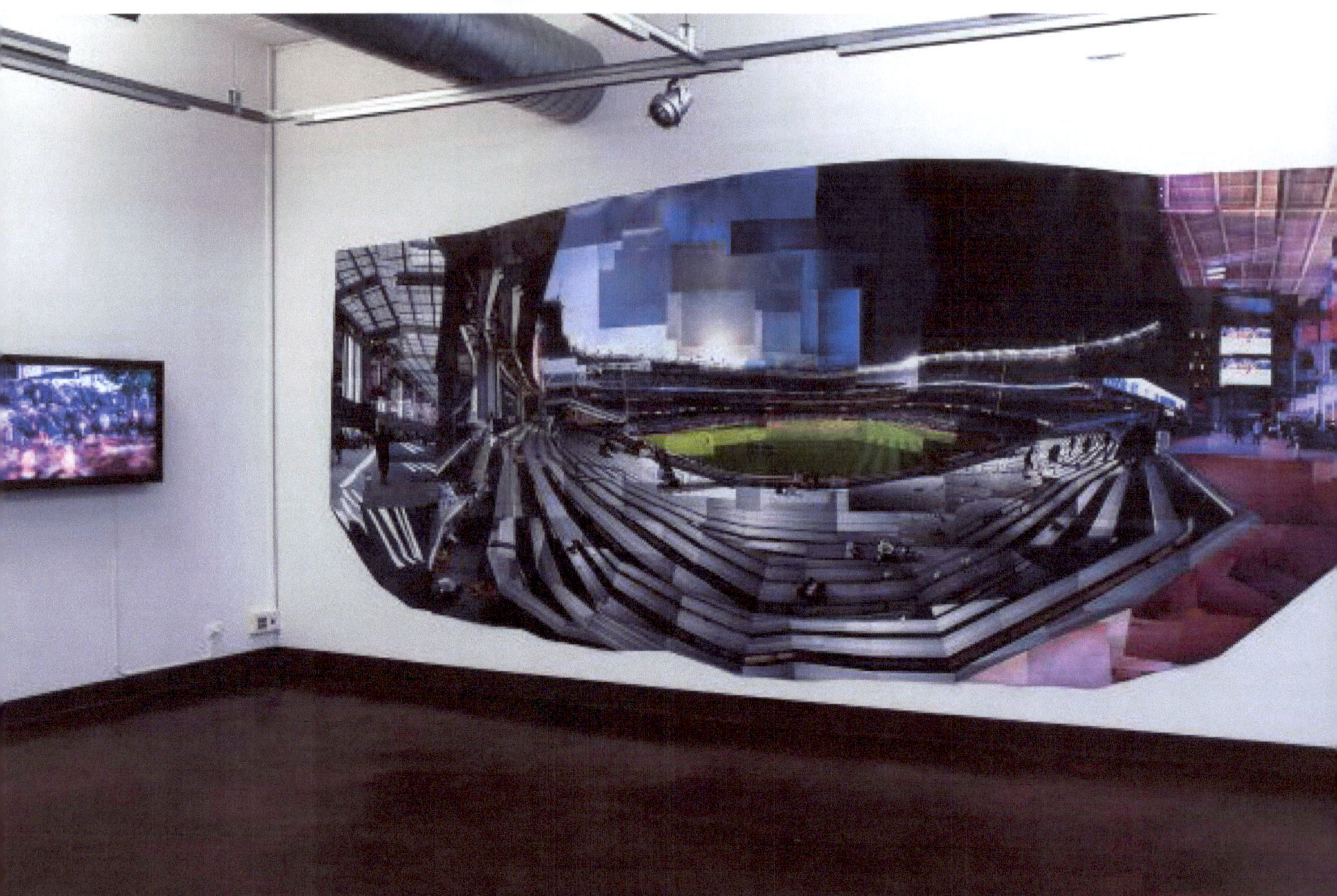

helped me zone in on photography. Even though I no longer work in the field of architecture I am still very interested in the design process and draw my ideas from architectural theory. Built environments are at the base of all of my art projects and my architecture training definitely influences the way I perceive spaces and the way people move within them.

J: The overall composition of your images focus on a large architectural structure compiled of several smaller photographs. I am curious how you make decisions about the larger composition. How do you determine which smaller images to work with to create the larger architectural photograph?

G: It consists of a lot of trial and error. In my process I group together the images that I've photographed on the same day and time. I then composite all the images together and begin the layering process to see what pieces work with each other. I consider perspective, where the sun is stationed, and in the "untitled" pieces I really try to focus on the volume of people to show the way the space is being occupied and not occupied throughout the year.

J: Photography has often focused on capturing or demonstrating an event as documentation of a moment in time. Does this line of thought influence your work? In using multiple images are you working to create a more authentic expression of a moment that a single photograph could?

G: I am interested in spaces that go through high volumes of activity to none. I photograph hourly during an event and by using multiple images in one composition I am able to portray the passage of time and its many occurrences. In the "untitled" series I photographed Coney Island (in Brooklyn) not only hourly but also seasonally. I photographed all 4 seasons to show the drastic change throughout the year. It's so alive during the summer and in the winter it's a ghost town, which changes the feel and look of the site.

J: I am interested in what your process looks like. You talk about analyzing, deconstructing, and reinterpreting certain spaces, can you elaborate on what all goes into that?

G: Before I photograph a site I do research on that particular location. For instance, I determine it's main attractions and research its peak and bottom hours of occupancy so that I know what to specifically photograph in order to best portray the site's character. At the site I take multiple images from different perspectives on an hourly basis.

G: The renderings and photographs we often see in architecture magazines portray the spaces as picture-perfect and dictate the way people should be using them. It's interesting to visit sites and see how they are actually used as well as how they fit in with their existing surroundings. Sometimes the architect's intention of how the building should be used fails and I like to depict the unexpected usage and in some cases, the decay of a space. In this sense- I am deconstructing its prestige image, reinterpreting it's real function and analyzing the way people transform it to be other things.

J: What type of photography do you utilize? Are your final images digitally composed or do you print and cut each one out to create your composition?

G: I like being hands on with the work I do so after a shoot, I print all the images I take and collage them by hand. This technique gives them a unique tactile quality. I then scan the collages and manipulate them digitally because I have more control of the overall composition.

J: You received your master's in photography from the School of Visual Arts in New York. How do you think that transformed the work you were making from the post- baccalaureate program you were a part of?

G: During the post-baccalaureate program I was conceptually re-exploring photography, being introduced to artists, learning new ways of analyzing information and refining my technical approach to photography. I essentially was breaking away from my architectural training, which was a lot harder than I thought it would be.

By the time I got to SVA I had changed my process and had a better focus on what my interests were which allowed me to then solely concentrate on producing art and applying what I had learned during my Post-Baccalaureate studies. Additionally, I found NY to be an ideal city that houses the types of sites I tend to photograph.

J: Are there any new projects that you are working on, or processes you are exploring?

G: I am currently working on a project called "30 Baseball Stadiums" (a take on Ed Reucha's book "Twenty-six Gasoline Stations") where I am documenting all 30 MLB stadiums across the country. I started this project back in 2015 and so far I've covered 14 baseball stadiums. Stadiums offer the "on and off" aspect that I focus on in a vivid way. There's an anticipation that a fan feels before the game, a crowded-intense energy during the game and finally a dramatic end when the game is over. The "end of the game" feeling is intensified even more during the off-season when the sites are low lit and exudes a feeling of loneliness (especially the ones that are located in the city outskirts). As a baseball fan, it's fascinating to experience the space beyond its allotted game time. In a way I am cataloging these sites and hoping that I can create something with the different and/or similar qualities that may emerge when all are presented together.

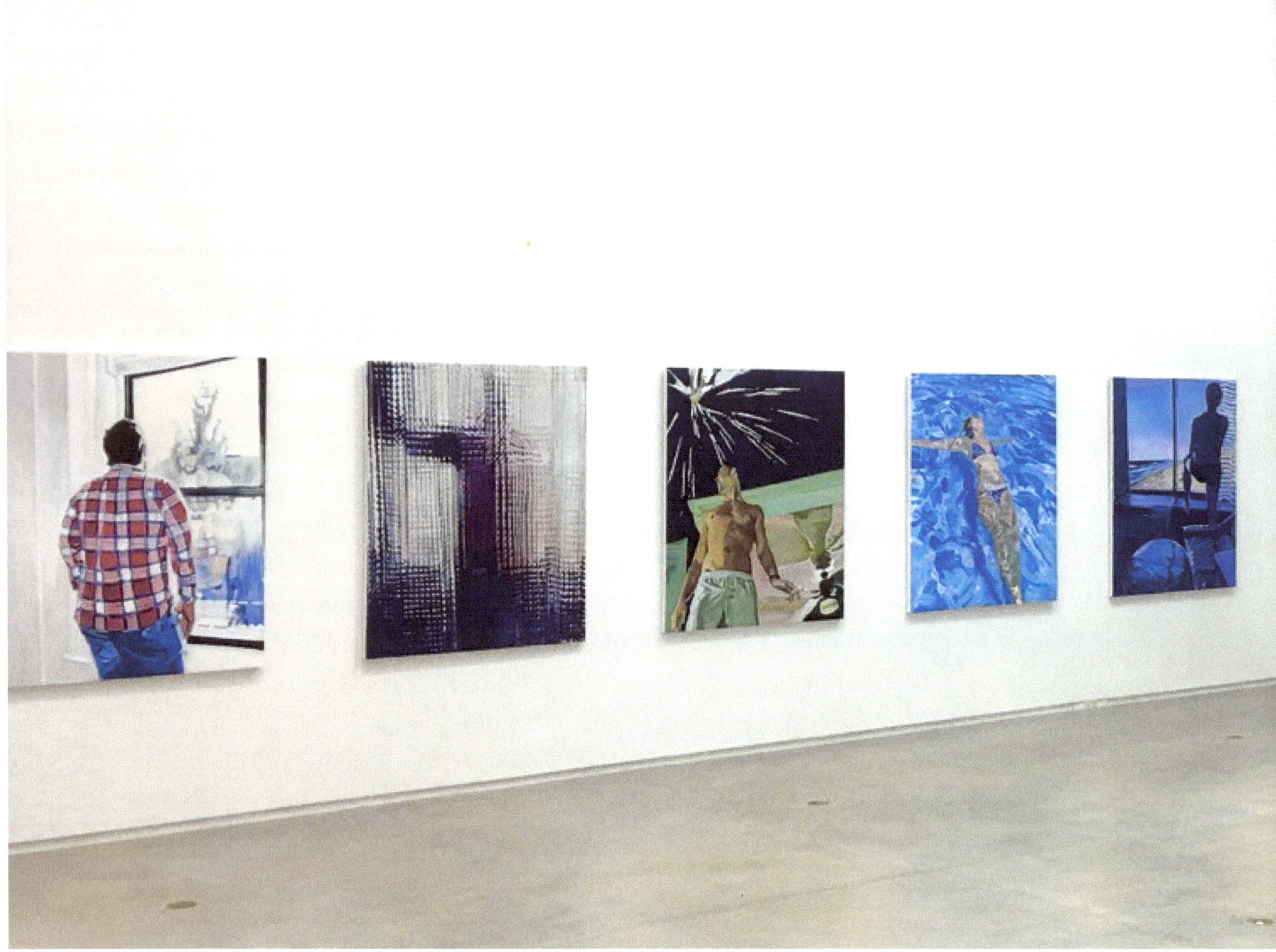

Interview with Rajab Sayed

Parallels to Experience

Works by Rajab Sayed

Interview by Dannie Liebergot

D: You mentioned that you spent your childhood navigating two cultural identities. What role does the portrayal of white male figures play in your work?

R: In a greater context, I think my body of figurative work represents my personal relationships with different people who belong to different ethnicities and cultural backgrounds. I don't think I consciously paint "white male figures", but the male figure who oftentimes repeats in my paintings is my partner, Laramie, who happens to be white. I think as people we often think about why we end up with the person we end up with, and I read a beautiful book by Celeste Ng called *Everything I Never Told You* not too long ago which explores the nuances of interracial relationships. Of course, I'm a painter, and I do my best thinking when I paint. So, painting my partner, or my exes, or anyone I share a close intimate

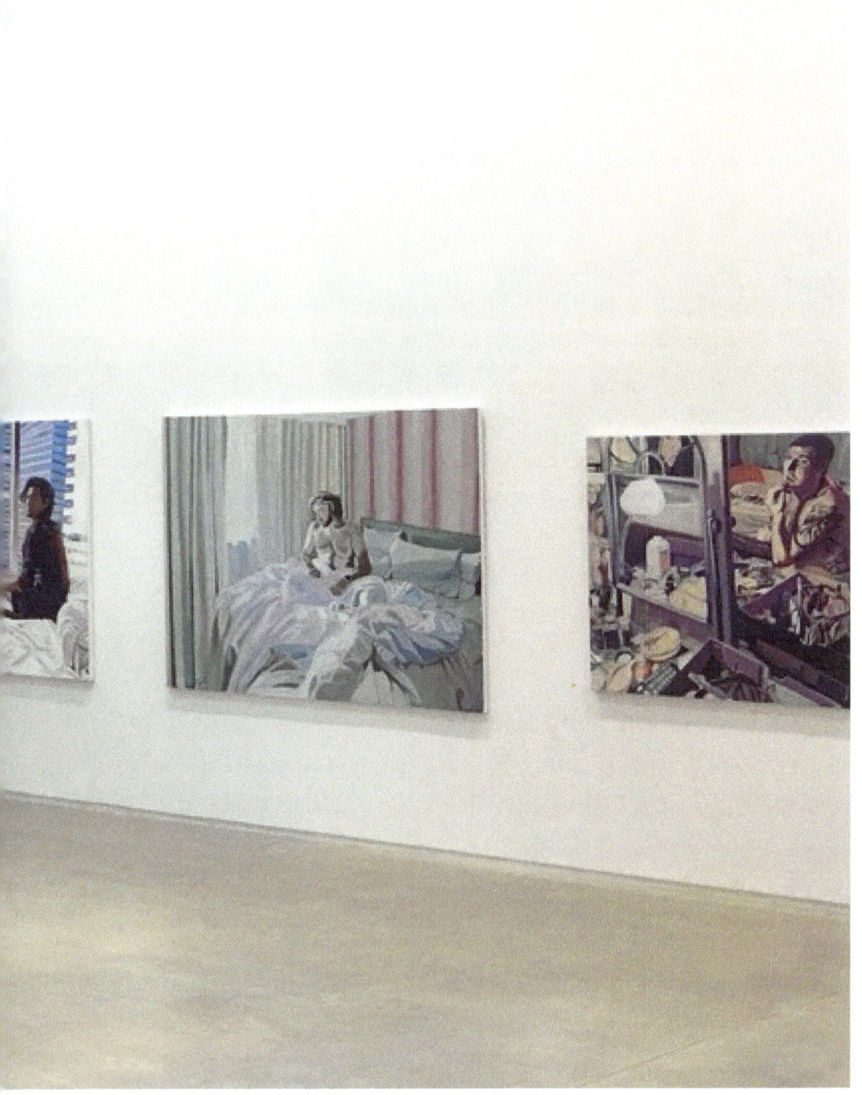

at Vermont Studio Center. There is an expectation when someone is staring right at you, and I find that turning them around solves that problem. I've also always been in love with German Romantic painters, who I see as underdogs in the greater context of art history. They often have figures with their backs to the viewers looking out into a sublime landscape, and to some extent my paintings do that too, but in a contemporary setting. Lastly, some of the people in those paintings literally turned their backs on me, so I guess that is where the sense of loneliness and apathy comes from.

D: Do you paint in a studio or plein air?

R:I have always preferred painting in a studio. There are less variables to deal with. The last time I painted plein air was probably in undergrad. I am not opposed to it, but I always like to say that I paint from life. I paint people and places from my immediate reality - friends, lovers and spaces that I spend a lot of time in. I am 27 years old, and I think painting from life has a different connotation in the times that I live in. So, painting plein air wouldn't be appropriate for what I'm trying to achieve as far as attempting to capture organic, transient moments.

D: When I interned at the Holly Johnson Gallery in Dallas, we installed a Gael Stack show that completely shifted my mindset towards painting. The depth within the blues and fragmented narratives shook me. How was studying under Gael at UH and do you find your paintings as a form of a diary?

R: Do I have a story about Gael Stack! If you reach out to her she will corroborate this! We actually did not get along very well during our first meeting, on my first day of my first year of grad school at UH. I think up to the point that I had entered the program, there was a tradition at the school of bringing work from your undergrad into your grad studio, which a lot of my cohorts did. I had just recently moved to Texas with my family not too long before I started at UH and most of my undergrad work had sold prior to me moving to Houston. Anyway, I met Gael in my

relationship with helps me understand them better, and in turn, helps me understand myself and what I'm attracted to.

D: There is a strong sense of loneliness and apathy within the compositions and figures with their backs turned away from the viewer. Were you trying to display those emotional aspects within the context of cultural identities?

R: The figures with their backs turned to the viewer is a visual device that works for me on so many levels. They are portraits at the end of the day, but I've always found painting people straight-on too confrontational and a little unnerving. I shared this sentiment with Gideon Bok, who I had a studio visit with while I was an artist-in residence empty studio where I attempted to show her my photo references on my computer. She refused to see the images and let me have it! She went so far as to question my place in the program, reminding me that I got into the program as painter, and that too on a fellowship. This obviously did not go very well with me. I was very passionate about what I wanted to do! Voices were raised on both sides. Fast forward three years later to my MFA Thesis defense and Gael Stack says, and I quote, "I'm proud of you", also adding, "You're the only one who's ever stamped their foot down at me, and turned it around." I committed those words to my memory while simultaneously holding back tears. So yeah, I love Gale. I think we both share a fondness for the color blue and also fractured narratives. I have also co-opted her use of the word "tinies" from her last show at Moody Gallery to refer to my small-scale paintings. I do think my work is diaristic in that I paint retrospectively. A reading of my work chronologically will reveal parallels to my lived experience.

D: Where do you get your imagery from?

R: My imagery comes from my iPhone! It's perfect. It's an unobtrusive social device, which has integrated into all of our social functions. Whereas most people use their cellphones to capture candid moments to post on social media, I use mine to make paintings. Sometimes I paint using multiple references from different moments, syphoning them into one canvas to construct a psychological space. Increasingly I've been painting from memory too. But I take pride in creating and composing my own imagery, it's very important to me that I do that.

D: Do you ever struggle with artist insecurity in addition to the hardship of identity politics? If so, how do you overcome this using painting?

R: I don't think my artist insecurity stems from my work, which deals with identity politics. The identity politics part fuels my work. I have a huge stake in wanting to represent personal mythologies and ideas about representation within the history of painting.

I think the insecurity part comes from the fact that I am a not a Sunday painter, I'm a full-time artist. And that means sometimes work sells, or teaching positions open up, or I get a fellowship or grant based off of my work. A lot of times that is not the case. Judy Ledgerwood, who runs the Critical Art and Theory MFA program at Northwestern University once told me that the art world is 95% rejection. Aaron Parazette often says that life after grad school is a vast empty wasteland. It's hard for me not to feel a little sideswiped when I get a rejection letter, or a painting is returned to my gallery because it is "too gay". The only thing that makes make me feel better is to make more paintings, because I think that is my contribution. However, I also feel like I don't have a choice in the matter, because I would be terribly unhappy doing anything else.

D: What do you hope for your viewers to take away from your work?

R: I would like my viewers to see my work and discover something new every time. There are physical and metaphysical layers to my work. I'm always consuming information, all the time and all at once. Whether it's something I'm reading, listening to, watching, observing, or experiencing, it always comes back into the canvas, and thickened with paint. My titles try their best to act as the "key" to my paintings, and if the viewer uses that key and gets an emotional response out of my work, I think I've succeeded.

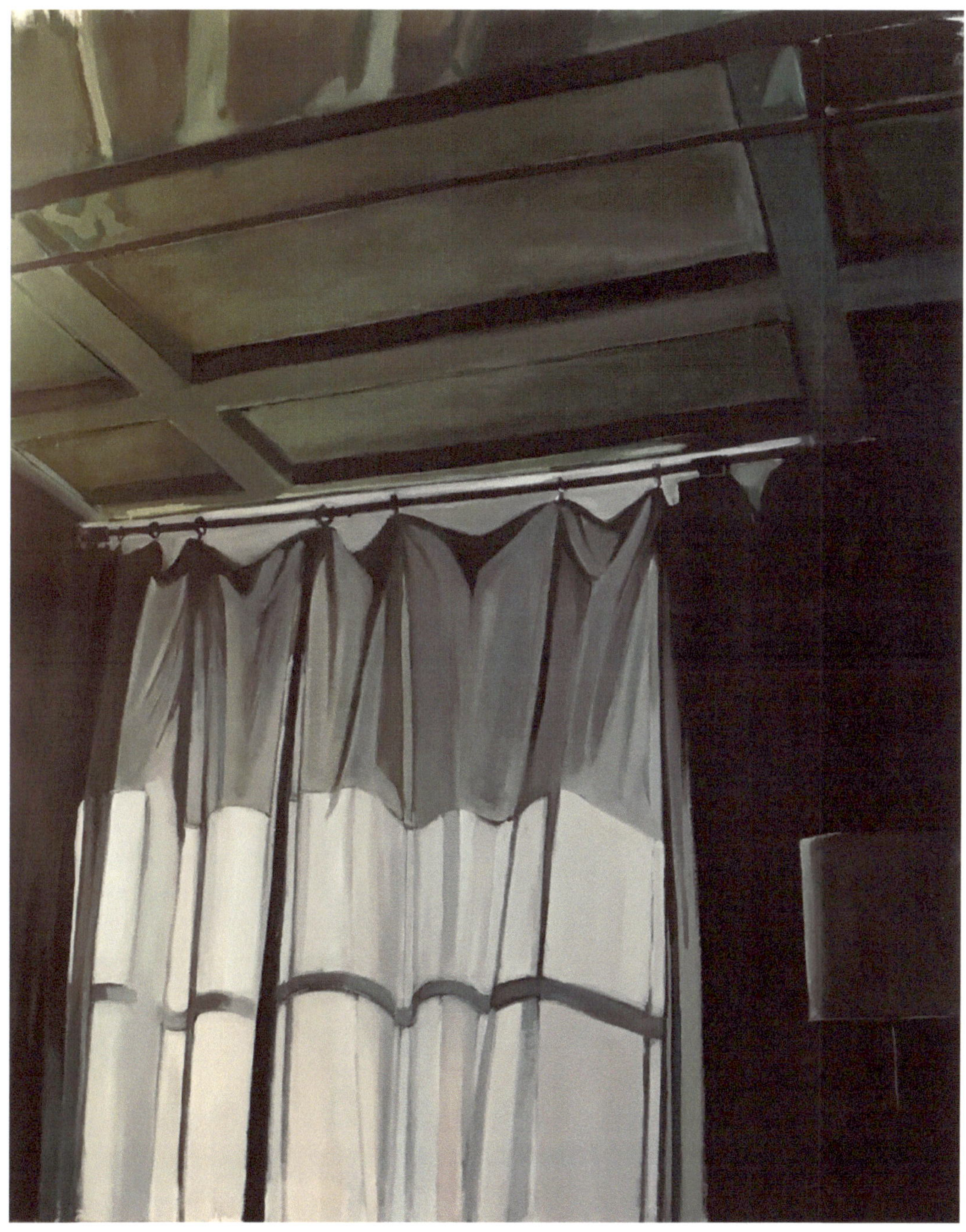

Rajab Sayed
Night so long, 2017
Oil on canvas
55 x 44in.

Gabrielle Jones

Sydney, Australia

gabriellejones.com.au

Painting for me is process based – I like to consider the painterliness of the artwork; the formal qualities and manipulation of abstract and physical properties of paint to convey or capture the effect of what I am seeing, thinking about, experiencing. Whilst going at the canvas with as much energy as I can muster and trying not to think too much, I conversely end up with musings on life, art, history, contemporary culture etc. Many times, the paintings seem to paint themselves and are a record or externalization of my thoughts, decisions, and social interactions -a culmination of internet, creative and natural images mediated and processed through the act of painting.

This body of work is the result of extensive travels in Italy over the last year. It reflects the "busy"ness of contemporary life and travel; as well, I hope, as the lushness and beauty of the surfaces, colours, textures, subjects and spiritual elements of Western painting traditions that I was seeing daily. As an abstract painter, I was connecting the abstract entities such as gods with the "otherness" or effect of experiences I seek to convey when painting.

In particular, I began to reflect on the importance and prevalence of deities in Canonical art of different cultures, the role of veneration, education and inspiration that such subjects played in the past; and how this contrasted with subjects in contemporary art and a culture where the "self" (or "selfie") is paramount.

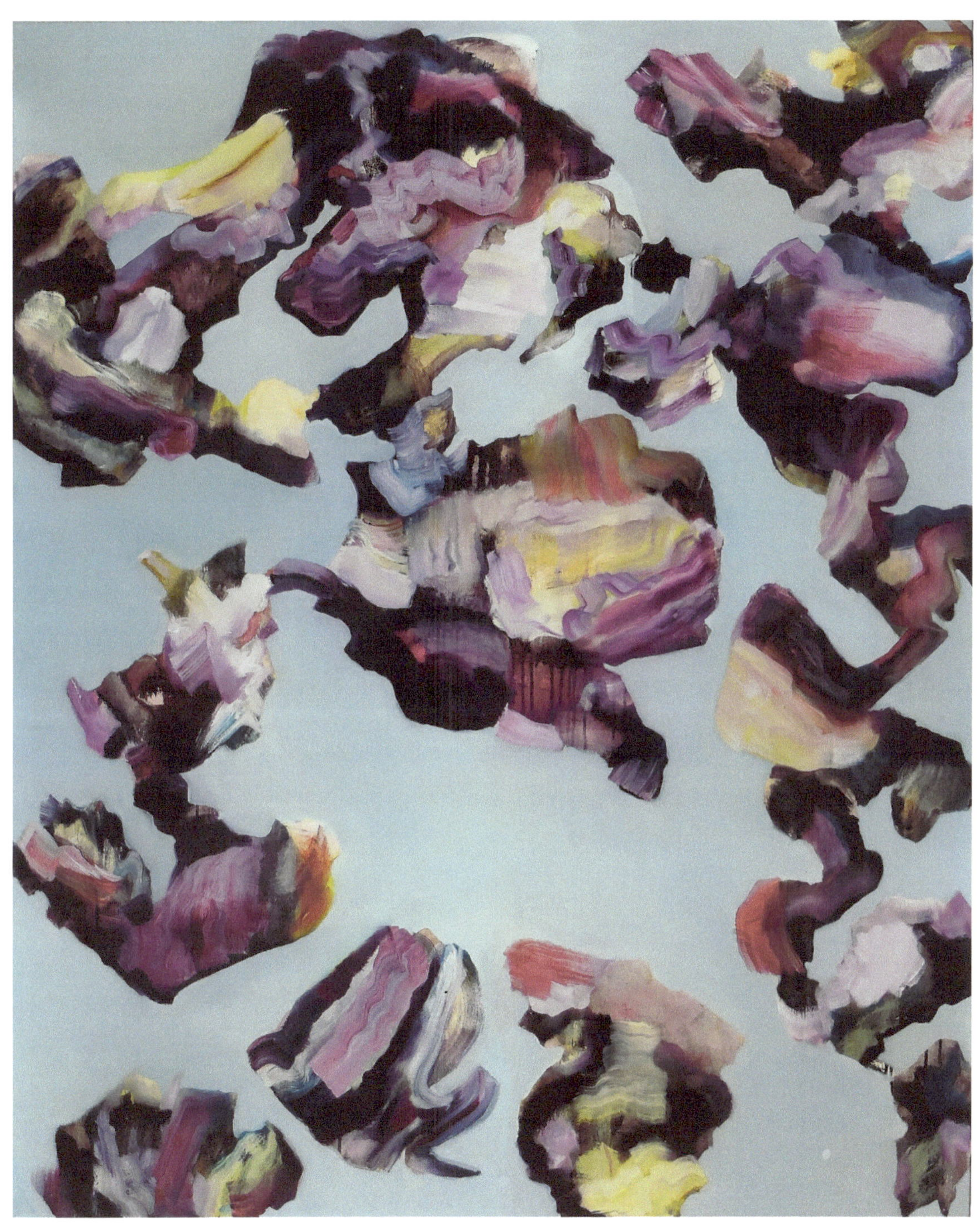

Gabrielle Jones
Celestials, 2017
Oil and acrylic on canvas
60 x 48in.

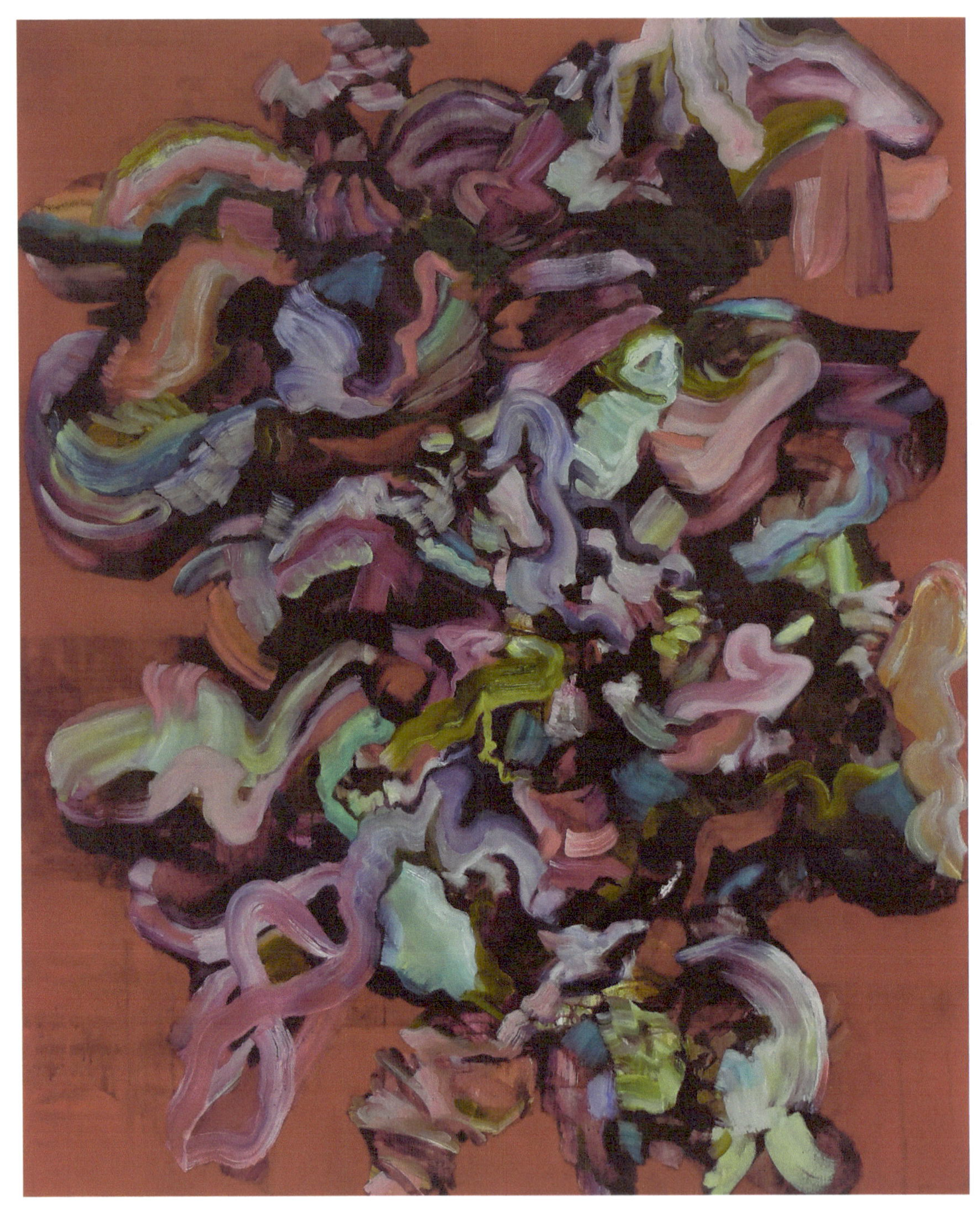

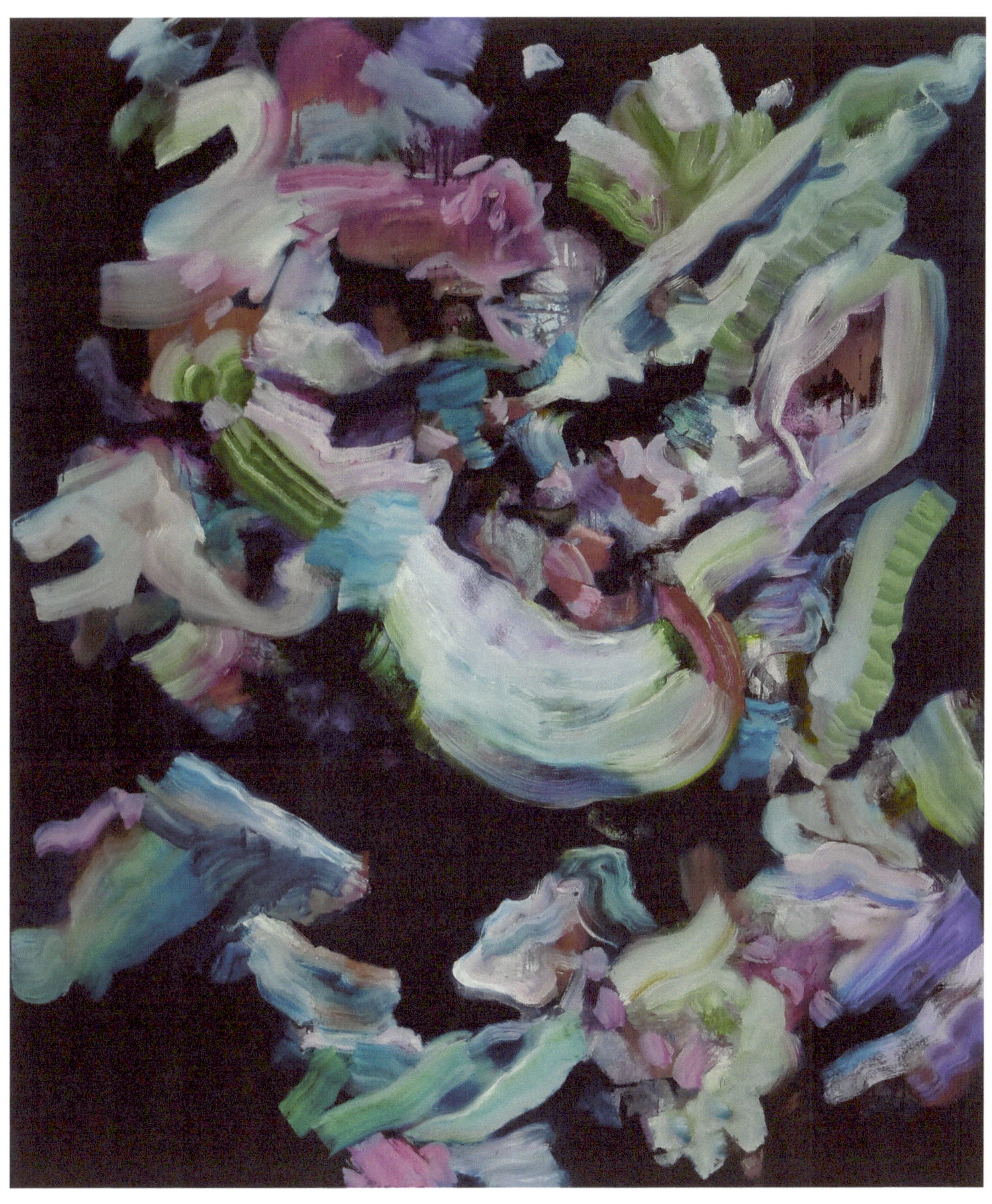

Gabrielle Jones
Durga's Victory, 2017
Oil and acrylic on canvas
60 x 48in.

Mya Kerner

Seattle, Washington   myakerner.com

I think about the individual in the context of the mountains and their immensity. As we have continued our supposed domination over Nature, removing ourselves and regarding Nature as resource rather than Source, we have forgotten these concepts are constructs, built through the deconstruction of mythology. The mountains remain, while our perception shifts, like atmospheric effects, obscuring, then revealing, in erratic flow. In my work, I attempt to depict a tragic joy, a recalling of the Sublime.

My studies in permaculture influence my art practice. I regard the mountains as stoic icons reflected by mortality, records of the movements of the earth and the torrents of the sky. They represent a collision or maybe a collaboration of the elements and the forces of life. Though continuously rising or falling, the mountains stand, silent, weighing on the shifting fragments of the earth, moving at an incomprehensible rate.

I depict geological disruptions, carved moments and parts within the landscape. Records of denudation captivate me, as these notes present a segmented image of the whole. The mountaintops stand crisp against a stark white, reaching for an infinite sky. Descending are scratched lines, which break through the slopes, while flecks of white dapple on eroded surfaces, recalling cooler seasons. Light moves across planes, marking time with stretched and shortened shadows.

Recording these moments by drawing and writing, I return to the studio to paint in attempt to capture this vulnerability. Often, my finished pieces CONTINUED ON PAGE 130 →

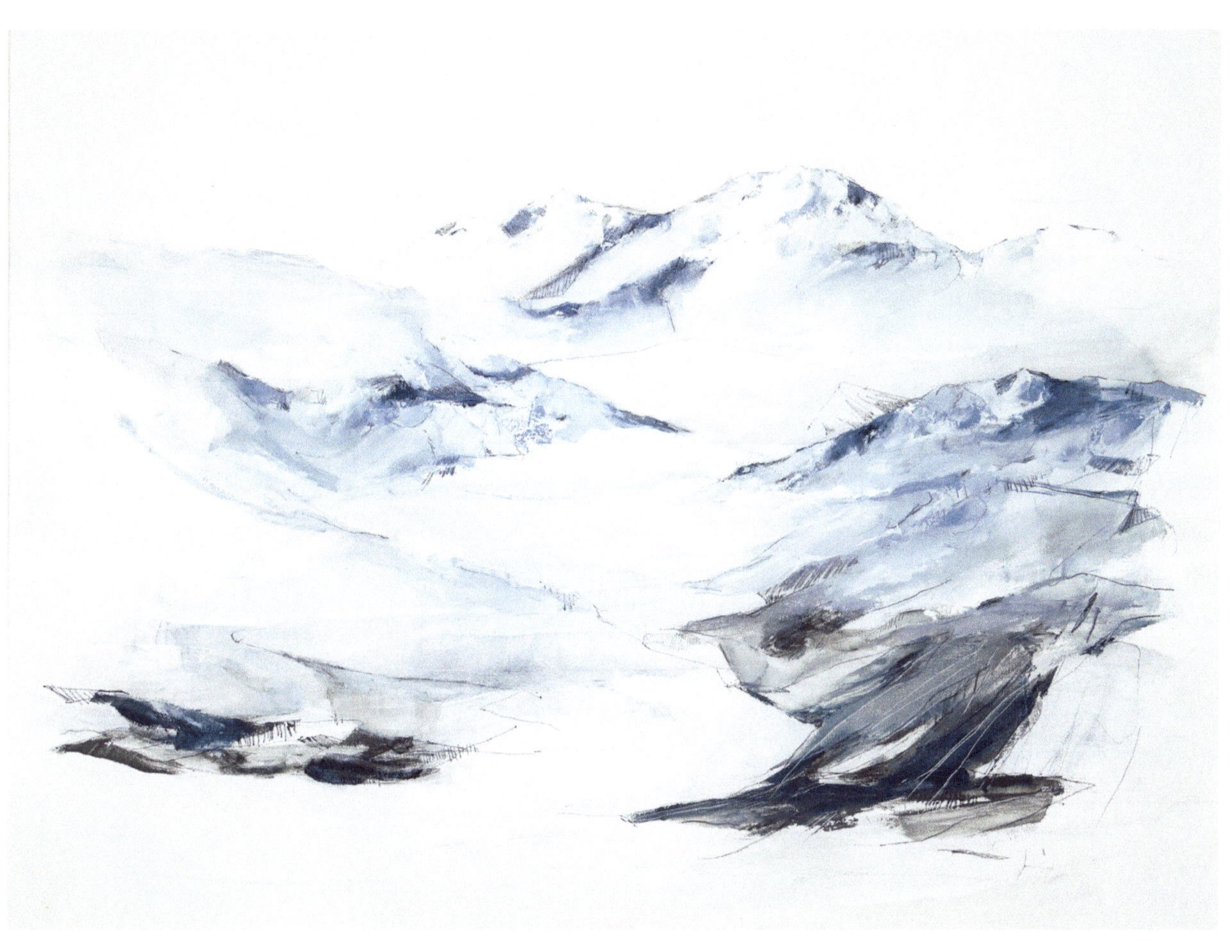

Mya Kerner
Compiled Memories (A Landscape without Reference)
Mix media on canvas
36 x 48in.

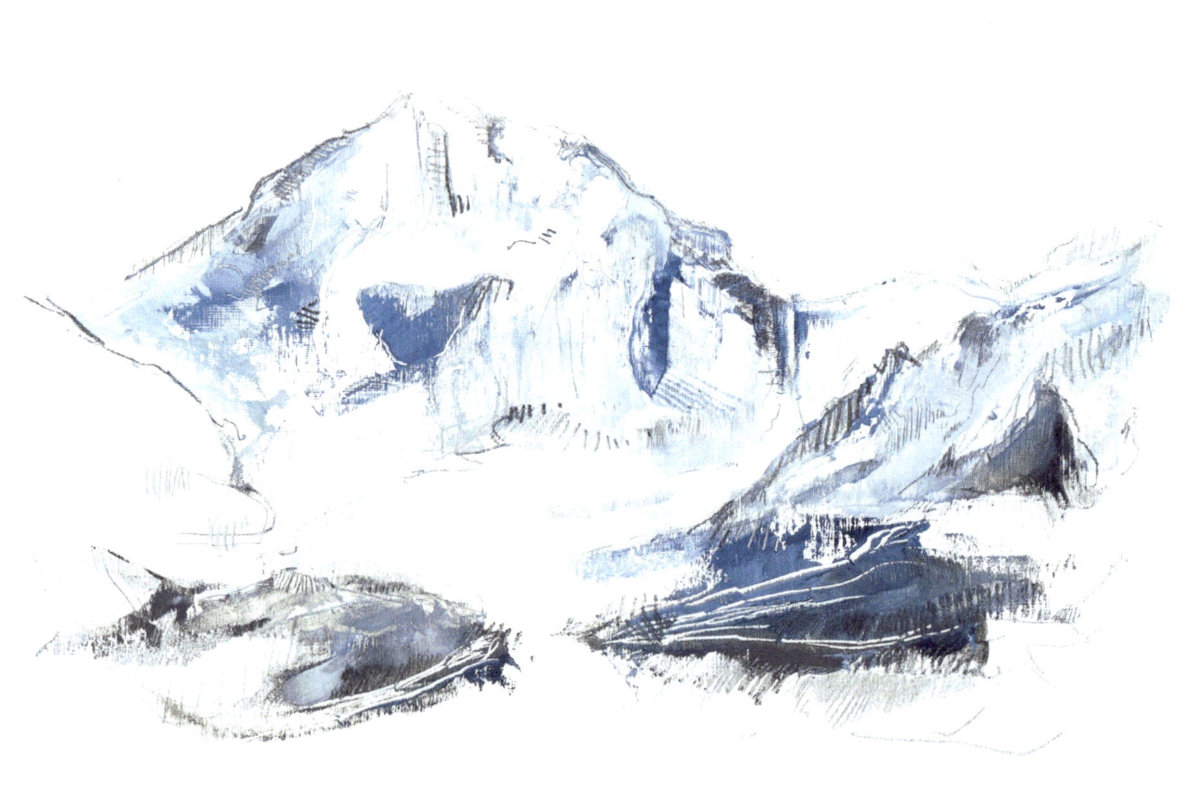

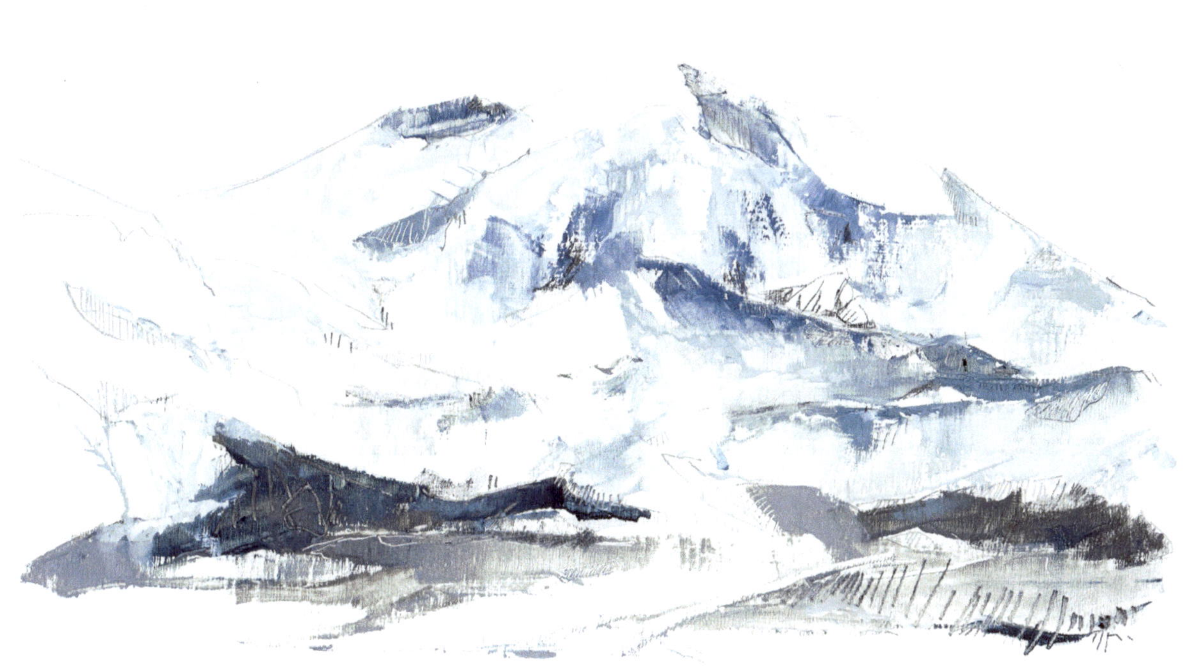

Mya Kerner
on sloping sites we settled, 2017
Oil and graphite on birch panel
9 x 12in.

Gemma Lopez

Brooklyn, New York kgemma-lopez.com

I am interested in the dynamics of the urban environment and how its many transformations over time reflect the activities, movement and people that create an event- the occurrence, the experience of space and the way these qualities animate an architectural setting.

Through photography I analyze, deconstruct, and reinterpret urban and architectural settings in order to portray the multi-layered experience of occupied space.

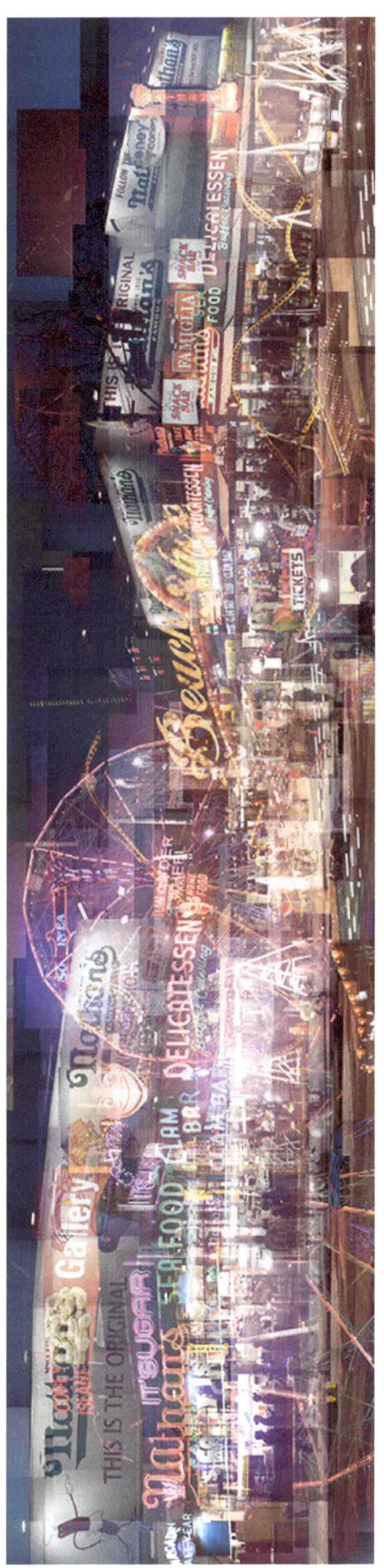

Gemma Lopez
Untitled Fall, 2017
Ink Jet Print
12 x 40in.

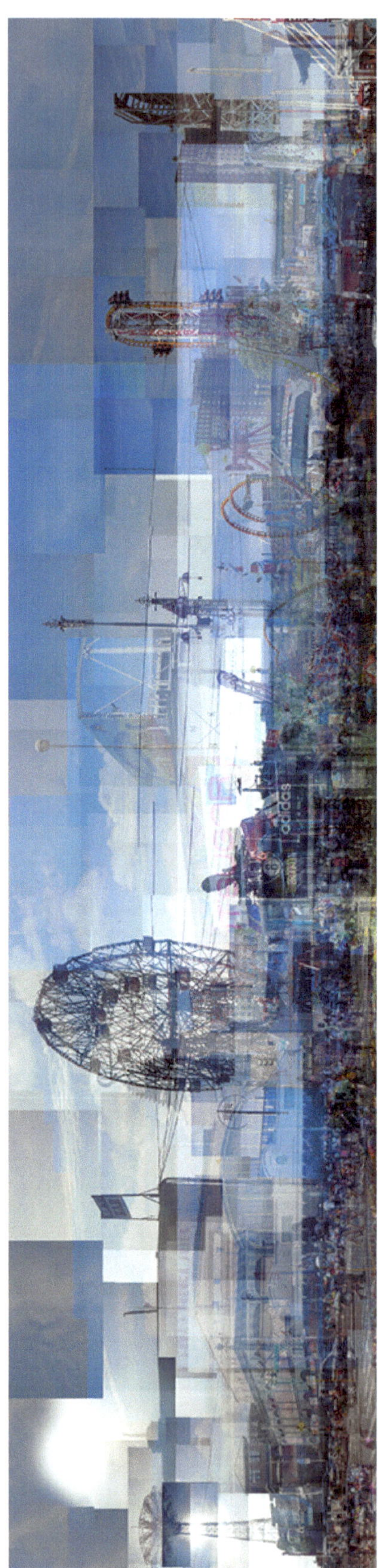

Gemma Lopez
Untitled Summer, 2017
Ink jet Print
12 x 40in.

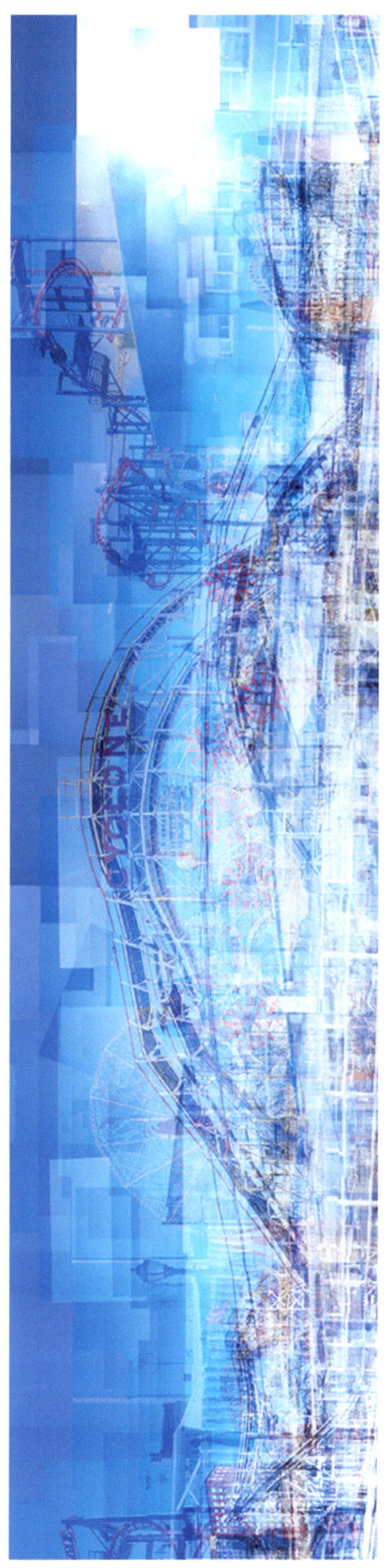

Gemma Lopez
Untitled Winter, 2017
Ink Jet Print
12 x 40in.

Ken Wood

St. Louis, Missouri kenwoodstudio.com

In these prints I explore the relationship of line to line and color to color using big, simple gestures. I used a set number of plates and printed them in different combinations and orientations (and with different colors and levels of opacity), trying to play up contrasts of saturation, color, and gesture while creating structure and space on the page. Each plate consists of a single gesture painted on with large brush-tools that I make myself.   These marks are applied using a thick mixture of carborundum and acrylic medium, thus maximizing their texture. The large scale of the line and the detail of the texture invite scrutiny; I'm trying to get people to stop and pay attention to what two or three simple, distilled lines can convey.convey when painting.

In particular, I began to reflect on the importance and prevalence of deities in Canonical art of different cultures, the role of veneration, education and inspiration that such subjects played in the past; and how this contrasted with subjects in contemporary art and a culture where the "self" (or "selfie") is paramount.

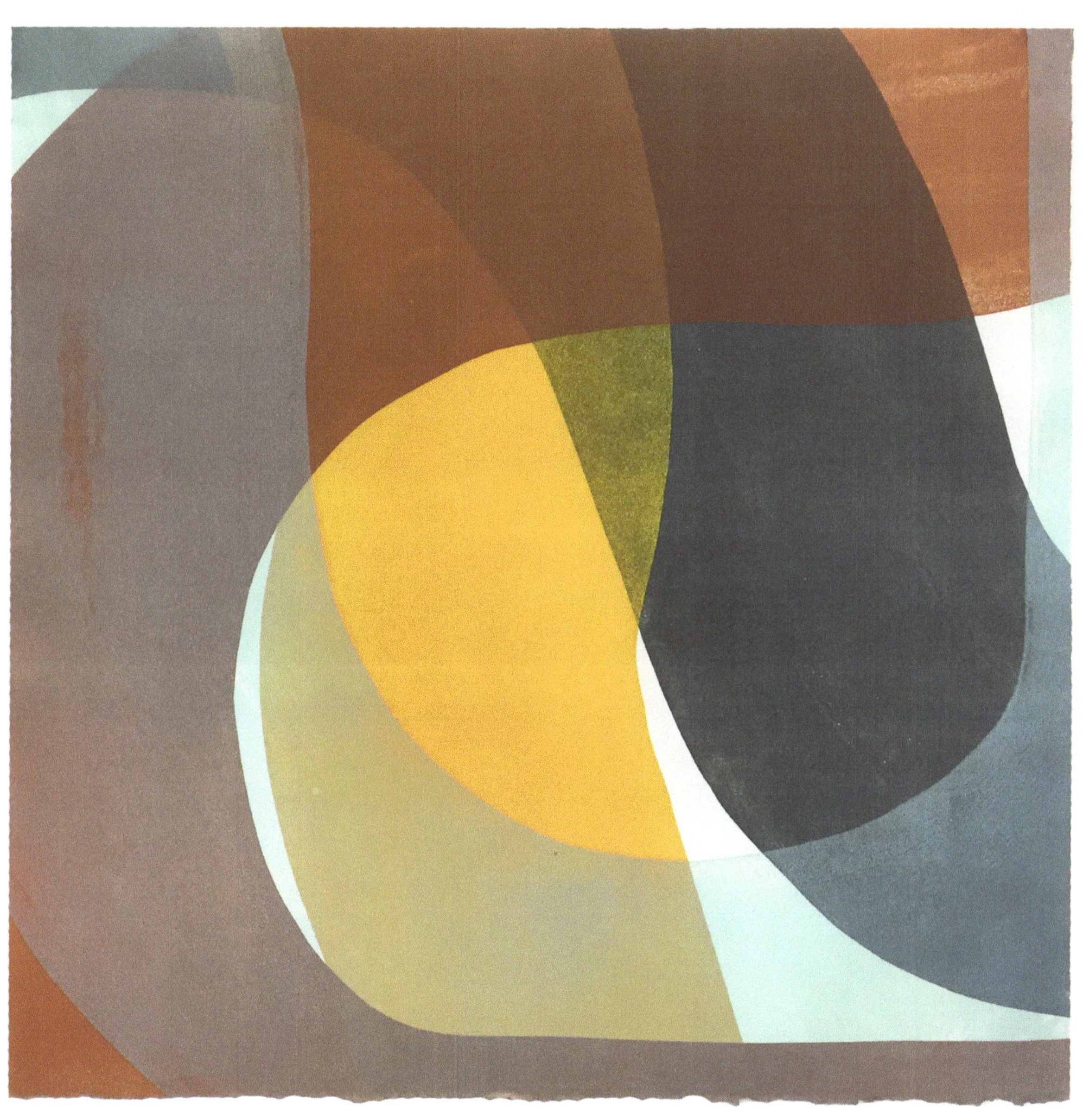

Ken Wood
PBX Foxtrot2 (314), 2016
Relief Print
28 x 28in.

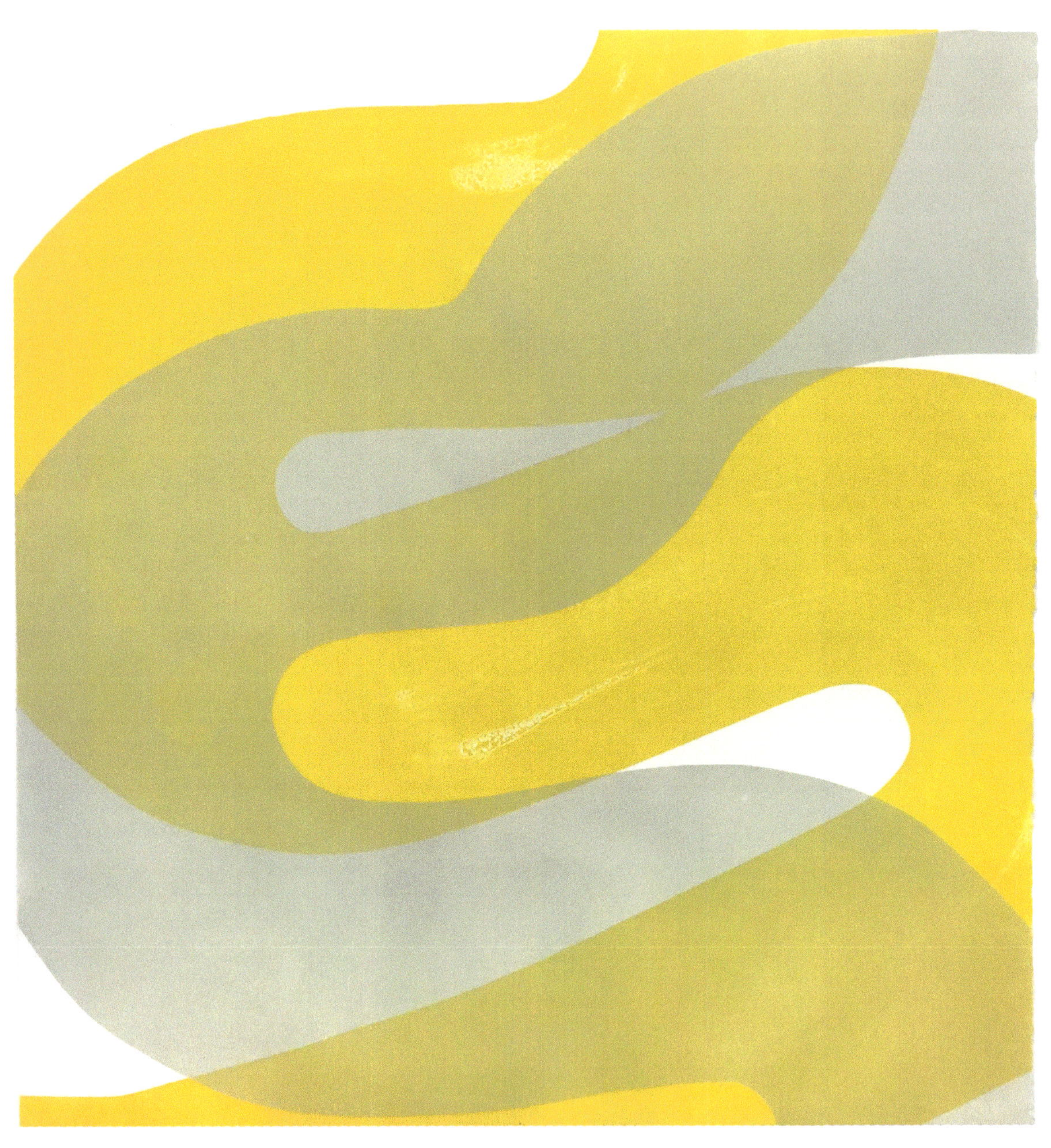

Ken Wood
Writ Large I, 2016
Relief Print
40 x 40in.

Friend of The Artist

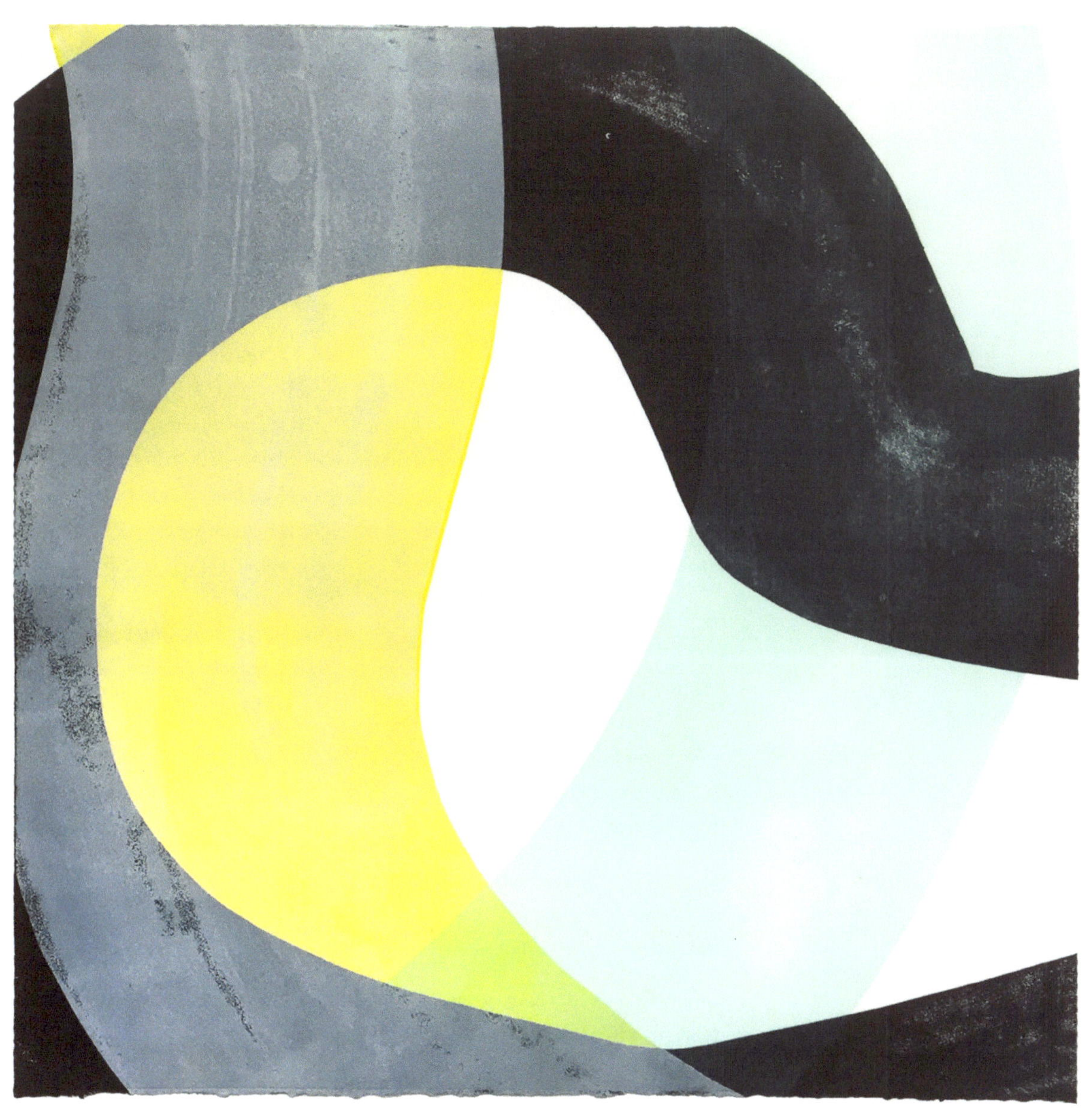

Ken Wood
PBX Echo1 (2565), 2016
Relief Print
28 x 28in.

Artist Statements Continued

Dara Engler this character, I prevent myself from becoming her.

The paintings play with flatness, pattern and line juxtaposed with the rendered form. It is unclear whether the figure is outside or whether the background is a backdrop in an invented space. The work teeters between real and imagined worlds, between fact and fiction.

Juan Granados this material, it lead me further and further into an exploration of clay as a means of expressing my experiences, observations and associations within my environment.

As an artist, I have grown to accept my past and to rely on memories to help me in the present. I cannot deny, ignore, or forget who I am or where I have come from. My work is a mirror of a past that I constantly reconstruct for visions of the future.

Evan Sheldon photograph towards me, each viewer may bring their own personal assoiations to these non-objective images.

Once I've chosen the parts of the chemigram that I want to keep, I then delete the rest with commonly utilized photo-editing tools such as the magic wand and lasso. I allow Photoshop to reinterpret the negative space using Content-Aware Fill. The space is filled in by the application, wondrously appearing as if by magic. I repeat this filling process until the compositions reach a point of balance; this happens either between the organic forms left from the original chemigram and the re-interpreted generation of data by the computer or the relationship of more minimal versus maximal elements.

After a point of balance is achieved, I apply some final polishing actions to the canvas such as sharpening, spot-healing, dodging, and burning. I make no action to the canvas that I wouldn't make to a traditionally captured photograph from a camera.

The final results are compositions that allow the viewer's eye to explore the contrast of computer-generated pattern/approximate-pattern and the automated marks left by my hand, chemistry, and light. Is this still photography, or is it more like a painting? Is it something more honest than the current state of photographic representation, or is it sending photography even deeper into a state of dishonesty?

Mya Kerner linger on the threshold of completion, for what memory is complete upon its conception? Form denotes the flow of water through rocky slopes, and the image often disintegrates as it nears the base of the painting, referencing the deposition of mountain and mythos.

Material exploration is an important part of my practice. My foundation in sculpture has heavily influenced the way I approach oil paint as a material; I manipulate in a way more like sculpting than brushing. By combining paint and graphite on birch panel, which accepts both forceful and gentle application without distortion, I explore a language of texture in a satisfying range of marks.

In these work, I wonder what memories

the mountains hold, and what
indefinable futures are foretold on
our deaf ears. We have redefined the
individual as the ultimate; however,
the threats of a changing climate
are reawakening our terror of the
Sublime. In this loss of control we fear
the loss of cities, of homes - human
constructs within the false façade of
permanence. We are now reminded
that, to Nature, the individual is
irrelevant, lost to the vastness and
susceptible to the ephemerality of
being.

My concern for humanity's precarious
relationship with nature drives my
romantic exploration of the intricacies
of terrain. I seek the potential for
understanding and balance through
material studies and, eventually,
the reformation of a contemporary
mythology.

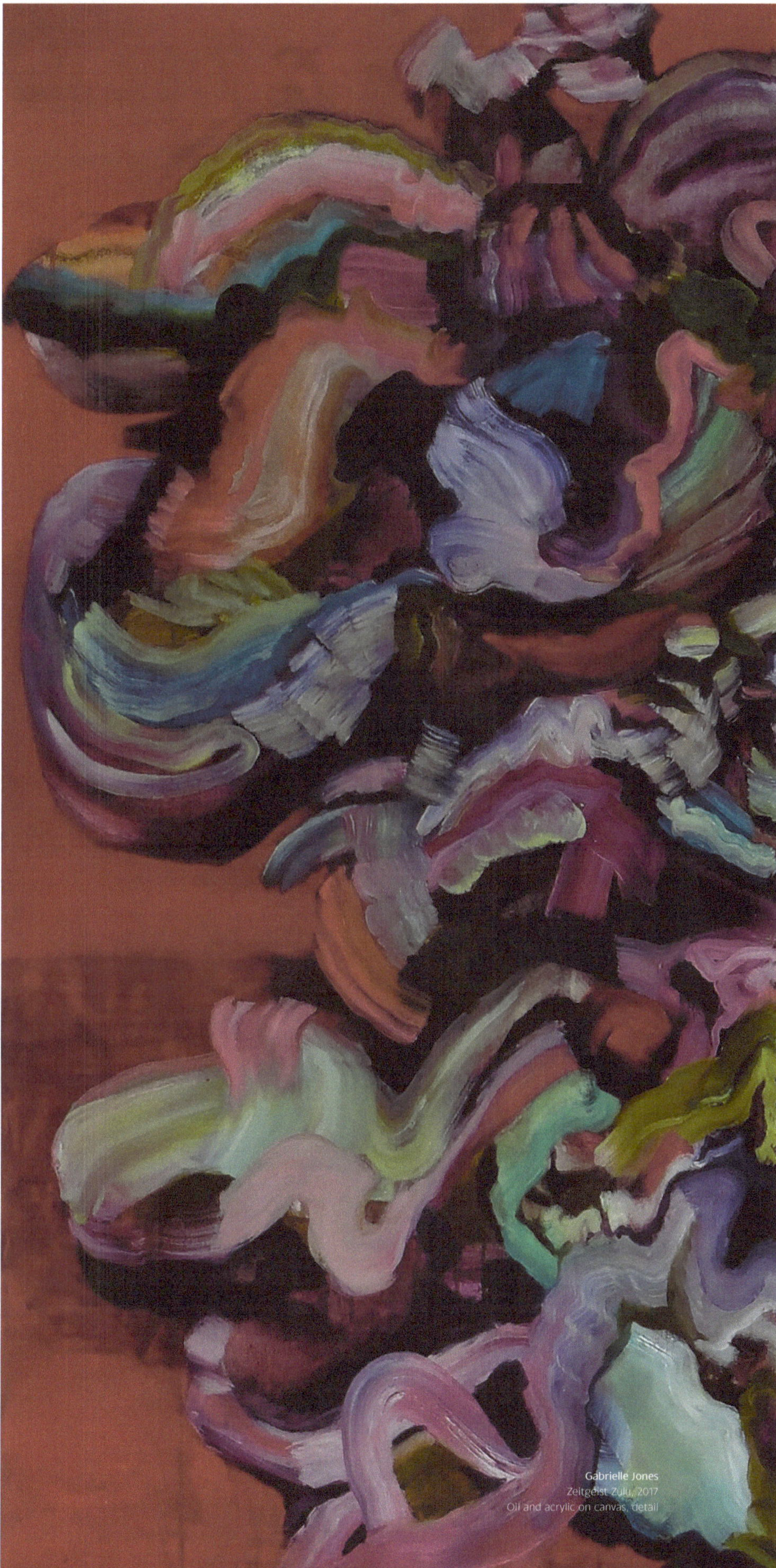

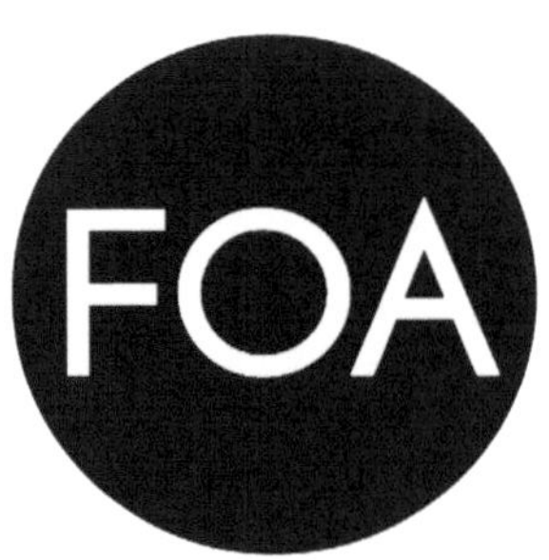

Friend of the Artist
Fall 2017

Thanks for reading. We want your feedback. Send us an email at
contact@friendoftheartist.com

Learn more and see other FOA publications by visiting
friendoftheartist.com

www.ingramcontent.com/pod-product-compliance
Lightning Source LLC
Chambersburg PA
CBHW042200030726
47599CB00004B/808